Plessy v. Ferguson

LANDMARK LAW CASES

&

AMERICAN SOCIETY

Peter Charles Hoffer

N. E. H. Hull

Series Editors

For a complete list of titles in the series go to www.kansaspress.ku.edu

WILLIAMJAMES HULL HOFFER

Plessy v. Ferguson

Race and Inequality in Jim Crow America

UNIVERSITY PRESS OF KANSAS

Published by the University Press of Kansas (Lawrence, Kansas 66045),
which was organized by the Kansas Board of Regents and is operated
and funded by Emporia State University, Fort Hays State University,
Kansas State University, Pittsburg State University, the University of Kansas,
and Wichita State University

Library of Congress Cataloging-in-Publication Data
Hoffer, Williamjames.
Plessy v. Ferguson : race and inequality in Jim Crow America /
Williamjames Hull Hoffer.
p.   cm.
Includes bibliographical references and index.
ISBN 978-0-7006-1846-0 (cloth : alk. paper) —
ISBN 978-0-7006-1847-7 (pbk. : alk. paper)
1. Plessy, Homer Adolph—Trials, litigation, etc. 2. Segregation in transportation—
Law and legislation—Louisiana—History 3. Louisiana—Race relations—History.
4. Segregation—Law and legislation—United States—History. 5. United States—
Race relations—History. I. Title. II. Title: Plessy versus Ferguson.
KF223.P56H64   2012
342.7308'73—dc23
2011047230

British Library Cataloguing-in-Publication Data is available.

Printed in the United States of America

10 9 8 7 6 5 4 3 2 1

TABLE OF CONTENTS

The author of *Plessy v. Ferguson* has confided to the editors that researching and writing the book was an emotionally draining experience. He came to dread each return to Plessy's world of dashed hopes for racial justice and forgotten promises of equality. Over and over in the years of preparation and writing that went into the work, he fantasized about what would have happened if the High Court had decided this landmark case differently; if the justices had followed John Marshall Harlan's lead in declaring the Constitution color-blind and striking down state-mandated segregation. Would a different outcome of the case have so undermined Jim Crow that it could not survive? Would the "Redeemers" of the South instead have mounted massive resistance to the decision, as segregationists had in the years immediately following *Brown v. Board of Education* (1954)?

But the author set aside fantasy to write this compelling, often compassionate account of the bold men and women of color and the courageous lawyers who spoke for them in the challenge to the Louisiana Separate Car Act and the racially divided nation for which it stood. By 1896, the case law had already narrowed the promise of the Reconstruction Amendments to a knife edge. The culture of casual racism following the Civil War, reinforced by pseudoscience and social science, had blunted the idealism of abolitionism and reform. A realism indifferent to the reality of racial oppression undergirded Northern thinking. The determination of a wide segment of whites in the South to harass black fellow citizens made the legal campaign unlikely to change attitudes. But a victory in the courts might begin the long process of disassembling Jim Crow. It was worth a try.

Hoffer's *Plessy v. Ferguson* brings to life New Orleans before the Civil War, in Reconstruction, and in the Gilded Age. His account of the passage of the Separate Car Act is a model of clarity, poignant and yet infuriating to the modern reader. Against a turbulent background of sinister conspiracy and openly orchestrated violence, a group of *gens de couleur* also known as Afro-Creoles gathered its resources to find a plaintiff willing to challenge the new segregation law. Hoffer explores the legal strategies that counsel for Homer Plessy developed for the struggle. Some of these strategies were years ahead of their time, while others conceded—tragically—the very categories of race that the state's law embodied. The author then takes us through the state litigation, exploring new ground in Louisiana's defense of segregation. It too reminds the reader of the defense Southern governors and attorneys general made of segregation fifty years later.

Two chapters open the doors to the U.S. Supreme Court's chambers, introducing us to the Fuller Court's members, tracing the oral arguments of counsel, and brilliantly analyzing Henry Brown's opinion for the Court and Harlan's dissent. Again, it is hard to read Brown's words, but Hoffer renders them and the ideas behind them with a clarity that almost—almost—enables one to overcome one's revulsion. Harlan's dissent, now a classic of American literature as well as constitutional jurisprudence, concludes these chapters.

A final chapter and an epilogue follow *Plessy* into the world of movies, novels, and education. Hoffer brings together succinct accounts of the precedents upholding segregation and those that later began to undo it. Brown stands near one end of that story, but the final chapters are still being written. As the author reminds us, the long shadow of *Plessy* still falls over our national conscience. This is must reading.

ACKNOWLEDGMENTS

The author is indebted to the following individuals for their assistance with the research and writing of this book: my copyeditor and indexer; Mike Briggs, editor in chief at the press; my two anonymous readers; my mother, N. E. H. Hull, who helped with the research and legal conundrums involved in the case; the scholars of H-Law who answered my queries; and my father, Peter Charles Hoffer, who without complaint listened to me talk about the book, gave me excellent feedback, went above and beyond the call of duty in editing the manuscript, and championed the cause in my many dark moments. I owe everyone a debt greater than I can repay. All the errors, infelicitous phrasings, and other mistakes are mine and mine alone.

Plessy v. Ferguson

Introduction

A Test Case

On May 18, 1896, the United States Supreme Court issued opinions in the case of *Plessy v. Ferguson*. Justice Henry Billings Brown's opinion for seven of the eight justices participating in the case upheld Louisiana's Separate Car Act. He rejected the argument of Homer A. Plessy's attorneys that the law violated sections of the Thirteenth and Fourteenth Amendments, most notably Plessy's right to "equal protection of the laws" under the Fourteenth Amendment. Though the Louisiana law segregated passengers on railroads on the basis of whether they were white or colored—in other words, on the basis of race—Brown found that the law's requirement that the accommodations be "equal, but separate" met the constitutional standard. In a dissent that has become a classic of constitutional jurisprudence, Justice John Marshall Harlan declared that the Constitution was "color-blind." States could not make distinctions that were based on perceptions of race, no matter how race was categorized. The impact of the *Plessy* case was clear to all: states and their agencies were free to use racial categorization to segregate public places, as they had been doing and would continue to do.

Though largely ignored at the time it was issued, *Plessy* would become the standard-bearer for a long line of "separate, but equal" decisions upholding what was colloquially called the Jim Crow system of pervasive, invidious racial distinctions. These were not just a matter of law; they reflected the discriminatory attitudes of a power structure. Ironically in light of the racialist connotation of categories of color, one can only describe this mind-set as white, so widely held was it among Americans of European ancestry. It was a set of prejudices shared in North and South, though only in the South did local authorities carry Jim Crow to such a wide extent, with separate colored and white water fountains, restrooms, railroad station benches, and a whole host of other areas of public life. The colored facilities were usually vastly inferior, despite the injunction of the *Plessy* case that they be equal. Jim Crow stereotypes of superior whites and inferior blacks were staples of film, radio, popular literature, and advertising. The long, hard-fought, and wrenching battle to dismantle the Jim Crow system in law may be over, but its consequences still echo in American education, business, and politics. Not surprisingly, then, the story of the *Plessy* case is neither simple nor easy to tell.

For scholars and jurists, the controversies over the meaning of the *Plessy* case continue. If the majority of Americans in 1896 believed that separation of the races (or perceived racial traits) was good for everyone, was segregation a legitimate democratic policy? Was the formula "equal, but separate," or its later incarnation, "separate but equal," an appropriate gloss on the equal protection doctrine of the Fourteenth Amendment? Can courts, in particular the U.S. Supreme Court, uphold state legislation, in effect following the election results when the very people stigmatized and harmed by the formula are denied their right to vote, as people of color were in the Redeemer South? These questions are not just legal ones. They reveal that Plessy's story also involves much of U.S. political history in the post–Civil War period. What was the impact of Reconstruction— that massive reworking of law and society—on American life? Why did it end as it did, in one noted historian's view, as an "unfinished revolution"? Ultimately, why would a case ratifying racism in the South elicit so little response from the rest of the nation?

Plessy's own story should not be neglected. Crucial aspects of it remain obscure. Homer A. Plessy was no random passenger in a whites-only railroad car that a conductor spotted. In fact, it is unlikely that the conductor would have confronted him, reported him, and had him arrested without prompting. Homer A. Plessy appeared to be just as white as anybody else in the train car. His great-grandfather was a recognizable African American, although the word used at the time was Negro, a term that owed its origins to the Spanish word for "black," a reference to the hue of someone's skin. However, even according to court documents, Plessy was not recognizably black. How could he have been arrested for sitting in the wrong car of the train?

2

The answer lies in a deal among Plessy, a group of like-minded, similarly situated individuals in New Orleans known as Afro-Creoles, and the train company itself. They arranged to have Plessy arrested for violating Louisiana's Separate Car Act so he would be able to challenge that law in court. They wanted a test case, and they had to have a real case or controversy to bring that case to court. Test cases were nothing new because courts are averse to issuing declaratory judgments. Therefore, the defendant and the occasion had to be carefully chosen to fulfill the requirements of constitutional litigation.

To win a constitutional challenge to a legislative enactment, one also needs persuasive arguments. These must derive from the text of the Constitution, from relevant precedent (earlier appeals court cases that are on point), and from evidence of the intent of the legislators (though not every judge agrees that legislative intent should be considered when the text of the law is clear). Counsel may also introduce historical, moral, and economic considerations, though these policy arguments are not accorded the same weight as the purely legal ones.

Plessy's counselors were not hired guns. They were committed to the cause of racial justice (if not to the end of racial thinking), and they carried on long after Plessy had retired from the battle. They gained the ear of the highest court in the land, and their written and oral presentations were able and thorough. But they lost, and in another of the ironies surrounding this case, the result was the opposite of what they desired. A case brought to chip away at Jim Crow instead added concrete foundation to it.

But the Plessy team had no choice but to turn to the federal courts. The U.S. Congress, along with much of the nation, had tired of Reconstruction, and the state courts in the South were hostile to a challenge to segregation. Louisiana's government by that time was dominated by white supremacist Democrats who wanted a system of racially discriminatory laws. The Louisiana courts heard the challenge to the law and denied it. In fact, the very language of the State Supreme Court's decision found its way into Justice Brown's opinion. Federal courts may decide to "defer" to legislatures when counsel for the state can show a rational relation between the legislation and a legitimate purpose for it. Plessy's counsel argued for a higher standard of judicial review of the Louisiana law. The High Court had already shown its willingness to apply a stricter standard to review the constitutionality of state laws regulating employment contracts and working conditions. Brown, however, did not apply that stricter standard in the *Plessy* case.

It is clear that one cannot fully appreciate the *Plessy* story without thinking about the role of lawyering, the nature of appellate litigation, and the intricacies of the Louisiana and the U.S. Supreme Court's approach to deciding cases during the Gilded Age and afterward. The means by which the litigants in *Plessy* and their opponents addressed the procedural issues involved had a great influence on the outcome. These attorneys, as much as their clients, made the decisions that shaped this litigation. It is often said that a good attorney can make a case and a bad one can undo it. The written arguments that they presented to the courts reveal their larger strategic decisions as well as the often critical tactical ones.

One must unpack the arguments looking for nuances and methodological reference points so vital to appellate litigation. Sometimes this necessary rereading of the arguments (above and beyond simply presenting them) appears a species of Monday-morning quarterbacking. Certainly hindsight can see where the counsel could have made different or additional arguments, avoided pitfalls, or gone beyond precedent. Counsel arguing later civil rights cases had the benefit of these insights, but they may appear inappropriate in a history. After all, the counsel were men of their own time and place, subject to and immersed in the values (and the prejudices) of that time and place.

At the same time, one of the purposes of good history is to see that other men of similar political views and experience did not share these values. If a man like the black abolitionist Frederick Douglass could argue, as he did, against all racial profiling in the same year that the counsel for Plessy conceded racialized categories, then surely they did not have to make such a concession. That they did might have been a bow to Louisiana's laws, or to earlier federal case law, or to the prejudices they may have anticipated from a Supreme Court bench that had already shown a complex approach to race and the law in the *Civil Rights Cases* (1883), but it also might indicate the limits of their own views of racism.

Of course, one does not want to impose the moral consensus of the twenty-first century on men who lived and died a hundred years earlier. Much has changed in American life, and in moral values, in those years, and perhaps nothing more than in the relations of people of European and African ancestry. Moral condemnation is almost too easy when it comes to Jim Crow. But again, one of the great strengths of history is to lead its readers to see moral injustice and condemn it. If history did not do this, it would have no claim to contemporary relevance. It would be mere antiquarianism.

The judges in Louisiana courts and the justices on the U.S. Supreme Court in Washington, D.C., also had an impact on the case. Their backgrounds, jurisprudential approaches, and use of precedents—the decisions of past courts that form the basis for future case law—all played a role in seven justices declaring that "separate but equal" was constitutionally permissible. Many observers of the High Court have a kind of reverence for Supreme Court decision making. They argue that the justices' art of deciding cases is neutral, specialized, and apart from ordinary politics. Precedent, legal reasoning, and the desire to gain the respect of the legal community supposedly influence the justices more than their politics or their prejudices. Others are more critical and find that judges are very much political figures whose judicial robes both literally and figuratively hide their partisanship from public view. Racism is one of these deep-seated prejudices. Was the Court in *Plessy*, and Henry Billings Brown in particular, racist? Or was his opinion just his recognition of the social, cultural, and political realities in late nineteenth-century America? Did Harlan share these prejudices? What then influenced Harlan to write as he did in *Plessy v. Ferguson*?

Looking beyond the case, one must ask what *Plessy* actually accomplished. Some students of our laws believe the case did nothing except recognize a phenomenon already in place. No court can change such well-entrenched social mores as the Jim Crow system the High Court encountered in 1896. Others maintain that the case gave the go-ahead for a new wave of segregation to sweep the South and spread to other parts of the Union. In the same vein, was segregation a predictable result of the rise of mass transit, industrialization, and urbanization, throwing the races more and more closely together? What role did gender play in this story? While the litigants in this case were all male, nationally, this was not the case. African American women were very much affected and were at the forefront of challenges to Jim Crow. The Louisiana Separate Car Act made an exception for African American nurses attending white children. If nothing else indicates the gendered nature of segregation, this certainly does. African American women tending to a white child were no threat to racists, but African American men were.

Regardless of the answers one supplies to these questions, Jim Crow law in America was sanctioned by *Plessy*. Some scholars have gone so far as to label segregated America the world of *Plessy*. If the case did not create this environment, it certainly became an emblem of it.

But again, this is not the whole story. A close reading of the case law, the litigation, and the meaning of *Plessy* itself raises some serious questions about this common understanding. There is a great deal of debate as to whether *Brown v. Board of Education* (1954) actually overturned *Plessy* or even seriously undermined the basis for deciding it. Though John Marshall Harlan's ideal of the color-blind Constitution is seldom cited without praise, it is not the law of the land—not yet. Americans are still living in *Plessy*'s world, a world in which segregation is alive and well, and sanctioned by law.

For the Landmark Law Cases and American Society series, the story of *Plessy* cannot end with legal doctrine, for the case opens a window onto a world that we have lost. We can look through that window to revisit one of the most remarkable of Gilded Age American cities. One cannot tell the story of the *Plessy* case—indeed, there would have been no *Plessy* case—without New Orleans. The unique nature of this city's ethnically mixed population; its Creole culture and politics; its ability to find joy in the midst of tragedy; and its vital economic role as the port and depot connecting the Mississippi River to the Gulf of Mexico make it special. From its earliest history at the confluence of the Spanish and French American empires, through its acquisition by treaty, and its central role in the slave trade, to its part in the Civil War, up to the more recent tragedies of Hurricane Katrina and the Deep Water Horizon oil well spill; New Orleans is always on America's mind. The Big Easy, Tremé, the Crescent City—it is an essential part of the story of the *Plessy* case.

As well, a fresh examination of *Plessy* affords an opportunity to learn about an extraordinary time in American history. Reconstruction of the defeated states of the Confederacy gave way to the harsh and sometimes bloody embrace of the Redeemers. Industrialization, urbanization, professionalization, and immigration reshaped the country, raising new and often unexpected problems. The American people confronted contradictory pulls on their conceptions of who they were and where they were going, and ever-increasing involvement with the rest of the world. Their universe became smaller as they learned how large it truly was. Americans confronted issues of identity, religion, and humanity's place in this challenging world. It was a contested time. It was a time that produced a remarkable case.

One final note: As the reader of the passages above will have noticed, I have used words like *white*, *black*, *colored*, and *Negro*, all depicting racial differences that many modern scholars have found based solely on culture rather than biology. Much as I would wish to dispense with any language connecting race, itself a cultural construction, to color, itself a matter of perception, I find I cannot. This is, I believe, another evidence of the grip that the history of race still has on the present.

The Crescent City

The city of New Orleans existed long before its citizens initiated one of the most important civil rights cases in the post–Civil War period. The French deposited the first settlers on the high ground above the bayous in 1718. The settlement was relatively safe from the flooding of the Mississippi, and the trade conducted with the Native Americans of the interior soon brought a level of prosperity to that isolated outpost. From the first, however, New Orleans could never be safe from the insecurities of early modern capitalism. Its founding was part of a larger plan by a Scottish adventurer named John Law to float a land development scheme in connivance with the French government.

Burdened by debts from the wars of the recently deceased Louis XIV, the French hoped Law's financial legerdemain would ease their financial burdens. Law's bubble collapsed when the pestilential truth of his venture (New Orleans was plagued by malaria, yellow fever, and other semitropical diseases) reached Paris, but the settlement named for the underage Louis XV's regent, the duc d'Orleans, remained. Joined by other French settlements in Biloxi (in what is now Mississippi) and upriver in St. Louis, New Orleans became a substantial port with a large mixing of the peoples of the Caribbean and the larger Atlantic world.

The Crescent City—so called for the bends of the Mississippi— thus began its life at a crossroads of cultures, commerce, and imperial aspiration. The city was never peaceful. It lay on the borders of the French and Spanish empires in the Americas and was eyed by the British. Though France would lose New Orleans to Spain as part of the larger Louisiana territory in the Seven Years' War, French language, French culture, and French architecture left a permanent mark on the multiple cultures of the city.

After the conclusion of the Seven Years' War in 1763, a layer of Spanish culture added to the diversity of the city's population. France gained possession once again through political chicanery in 1800, but when Napoleon's plans for restoring France's empire in the Americas failed, he offered it to the United States as part of the Louisiana Territory. President Thomas Jefferson jumped at the chance to add millions of acres of fertile land to the nation.

Both France and Spain had brought slaves to New Orleans. It became a major center of the slave trade. French and Spanish law allowed for relatively easy manumission if the master desired, and a class of mixed-race freemen and freewomen soon plied crafts and trades in the city. When the city changed hands in 1803, the Americans, French, and Spanish descendants were living alongside not only a large African American population, but also the hard-to-define group of mixed heritage and ancestry that some have called Afro-Creoles. Partly descended from slaves imported to work the docks and the plantations of sugarcane and later cotton, they lived both among and apart from their fellow residents.

As a result of a shortage of European women, many French colonial men took slaves as their partners. At the so-called quadroon balls (a quadroon was a person of one-quarter African American ancestry), freemen could form liaisons without condemnation. The offspring of these unions sometimes became free and inherited property. French- and Spanish-ruled New Orleans adopted a congeries of racial distinctions to classify this population, some of which were enshrined in law and some of which remained custom.

These concepts of racial divisions divided New Orleans, like the rest of the Louisiana Territory, into a caste system. Free persons of either sub-Saharan African descent—or, more likely, mixed ancestry—could and did own property, businesses, and sometimes slaves. They constituted an elite in and of themselves, self-conscious and proud. Their music and literature expressed a distinct New Orleans culture. Within the framework of culture, custom, and law, Louisiana's free people of color, known in French as the *gens de couleur libres* or Afro-Creoles, formed their communities explicitly sneering at the ruder ways of the plantation slaves, the snobbery of the master class, and the rough culture of the riverboat men just a few days' journey upriver. Many had received educations as far away as France or Spain.

They spoke French fluently and were proud of their heritage. They often sued in the courts to make sure they were not classified as Negro. Their identity separated them and made great difficulties for anyone attempting to apply hard-and-fast categories to the ethnically diverse population of New Orleans.

When New Orleans passed into American hands with the Louisiana Purchase in 1803, a new set of legal relationships caused complications for every property owner, including the United States. (The federal government claimed a portion of the *batture*, the elevated levee around the city.) The city and the state retained aspects of French and Spanish law in its civil code, but the city's commerce tied it to a nation that followed the English common law and the U.S. Constitution. Both of these were far harsher when it came to slavery than the French and Spanish traditions—indeed, during the French Revolution, the estates general had ended slavery in the French colonies, something that would not happen in New Orleans until the Thirteenth Amendment in 1865.

The economic importance of the city was obvious to its American rulers. Driving that boom in trade, finance, and general movement of people and goods was the expansion of the Cotton Kingdom made possible by Eli Whitney's cotton gin. The Connecticut Yankee's invention could process even the sticky, embedded seeds of the short-staple cotton. Thus, cotton production, and the slavery that went hand in hand with it, could spread to the uplands of the slave South, eventually reaching the Black Belt—the region of the Deep South with the fertile, black earth so essential to sustaining the ravenous cotton plants. The heavy bales of cotton could then be carried down the Mississippi by steamboat, offloaded at New Orleans, and then loaded on to ships bound for Britain and New England's textile mills. This trade, along with the sugar trade of the bayou plantations, made the city one of the richest in the world.

Slaves performed the heavy lifting that made the system go. New Orleans under American rule once again became a major slave trading site. When the overseas trade in slaves ended in 1808, slavers continued to sneak bondmen and bondwomen into the city from the Caribbean and Africa. As with the rest of the slaveholding states, color was the badge of slavery: the darker the skin, the greater the presumption that a man, woman, or child was chattel, personal property. Slaves in New Orleans had greater freedom of movement than slaves upriver or on the bayou sugar plantations, but slaves in the city were still someone else's property and could be sold, purchased, inherited, leased, punished, and sent away from family and friends at the whim of their masters. Again, these classifications of human beings as a form of chattel—that is, movable property—were inextricably linked with concepts of race. Part justification, part explanation, race classifications allowed one group of people to control the hopes, aspirations, fears, and futures of another people. Even when slaves had lived in America for three generations, they remained less human (in the eyes of the law) than newcomers.

In areas like southern Louisiana, where African American slaves greatly outnumbered free persons, the master class feared slave revolts. By the early nineteenth century, slave states had refined their "slave codes" to prevent such uprisings. Slaves were not to bear arms, prepare or administer medicines, go about at night, gather in groups of more than three, or offer offense to any white person. Extensive law enforcement mechanisms policed this suspect population. Patrols formed out of the state militias policed the slave quarters. Governments had special powers to deal with slave conspiracies, and special provisions of law allowed for torture and summary whippings of those deemed suspect. Hostile even to those of color who were not slaves, these societies existed in a permanent armed state. Indeed, the Second Amendment guarantee of the right to own and bear arms reflected the felt needs of a white population surrounded by the enslaved.

These measures did not prevent slave uprisings. One of the largest took place on a Mississippi River sugar plantation just north of New Orleans. In January 1811, four slaves named Kook, Uamana, Henry Kenner, and Charles Deslonde (names that demonstrated how diverse the slave population was) led hundreds of slaves in a march down the riverside toward the city. A hastily assembled force of militia, local whites, and other slaves met and defeated the rebels in pitched battle. Although that event was never duplicated, the whites of southern Louisiana lived in fear of its repetition. That fear echoed in their laws and their attitudes long after slavery itself was gone.

Alongside the laws defining slavery lay social conventions of racism. These carried the seeds of prejudice far beyond the Deep South. The minstrel shows wherein white performers blackened their faces, allowing them to tell crude stories and sing lewd lyrics, included stock negative stereotypes. The Sambo, whose stupidity was matched by his desire to avoid work; the Mammy, a bossy dispenser of bad advice and large helpings of unhealthy food; the Pickaninny, whose silliness and lack of common sense constantly created trouble for herself and those around her—these stereotypical figures delighted minstrelgoers both in the North and the South, and hid the tragedy of slavery. Last but not least at the minstrel show was Jim Crow. The character was introduced by the noted minstrel performer Thomas "Daddy" Rice, whose awkward, rhythmic dances and ribald songs evoked a crippled, elderly slave. Though the performers created these stereotypes to match their audiences' expectations, these tropes also reinforced and perpetuated these social constructions. Hardly a person throughout the United States would not have encountered these ideas, not only about the existence of race, but the inveterate characteristics of the disparaged population.

Another feature of the American takeover of New Orleans was segregation based on color. Public accommodations like restaurants and hotels simply would not offer service to those they perceived as colored. The arrival of streetcars in the 1830s gave the impetus for state-mandated segregation in 1835. What schools there were already were segregated, but the "star cars"—set aside for Negroes and indicated with large, white stars on their sides—became for the Creoles of color the symbol for their oppression.

Despite the arrival of a far less tolerant regime, the free Creole population did not disappear or give up its values, identity, and concept of how they should be treated in the new New Orleans even as the lighter skinned among them served in the slave patrols, passed for white, and took part in the newly divided society. They continued to teach their children pride in their culture, run their businesses according to their customs, and participate in public life in such celebrations as Mardi Gras. Visiting the city, Northern traveler Frederick Law Olmsted found that the Creoles held themselves to be better men than the mean-faced Irish and the narrow-minded German immigrants just off the boat. Racist ideas were not confined to white folks in New Orleans. Immigrants, particularly German "redemptioners," were pouring into the city, adding one more layer to its culture.

While the opening of the Erie Canal led New York City to surpass New Orleans as a financial and commercial center, the people of the Bayou State formed an exceptional polity within the diverse region that was the antebellum South. Their extraordinarily complex population divided on issues of race but still managed to form a functioning society—until the Civil War.

———

Early in the war, a combined naval and land force took the city, and for the rest of the war, New Orleans was occupied by Union troops. It was one of the first areas to deal with the vital questions surrounding what was to be done with the rebelling areas after the conflict. Confederates, particularly those of the upper classes, greatly resented the occupation. The commanding general of the occupying forces in 1862, Benjamin Butler, responded to their provocative and insulting behavior with strong measures (gaining the nickname "Beast"). But Butler had strong views about slavery and the master class. In the first days of the war, he had allowed runaway slaves safe haven in Union lines, a policy preceding President Abraham Lincoln's on emancipation and to some extent forcing Lincoln's hand.

New Orleans' Afro-Creole or *gens de couleur libres* population complicated the issue even more. They took up arms in the Louisiana Native Guards and become the first people of color to serve in the U.S. armed forces. What was more, the Guards took part in the extraordinarily bloody campaigns to extend Union control upriver, taking a great many casualties in the process. This population saw itself both as the natural leadership of a free Louisiana and as a people apart. But we cannot view what was happening locally in isolation. Insofar as national politics greatly affected what happened in New Orleans, our gaze must shift to the debates in Washington, D.C., in particular presidential and party politics.

———

Initially, President Abraham Lincoln took a cautious approach on how to deal with the territory federal forces occupied. This policy, which eventually became the basis of Presidential Reconstruction, owed its mild treatment of regions in rebellion as well as its noncommittal position on what to do with slaves to several factors. As later presidents and presidents before him dealing with a major political crisis, Lincoln had one eye on military necessity and the other on coalitional governance. Lincoln's Republican Party was now predominant in both houses of Congress as a result of the departure of the Confederate states' delegations, but the Republicans were far from a unified group. These fissures ranged from overall ideology to the specifics of how to treat the Confederate areas, and they would survive the war only to grow in significance.

The traditional way to break down the Republican Party's factions is into three parts: the conservatives, the moderates, and the radicals, based not by accident on their attitudes toward slavery. In some ways this reflected the Grand Old Party's origins as a conglomeration of conscience Whigs, Free Soilers, and American Party or Know-Nothing adherents. What united this diverse group of men from throughout the free states of the North and West was their opposition to the expansion of slavery. According to one noted historian, the political organization that formed in Michigan in 1854 cobbled together an ideological appeal to the free state white men based on the concepts of "free labor, free men."

Both a harkening back to the Jeffersonian ideal of the yeomanry and the political program of Alexander Hamilton, the Republicans defined themselves as a truer reflection of the real nation. They adopted the protective tariff, internal improvements program, and sound money stand of the Whigs, and stood in opposition to the Democrats' marriage of labor in the North to the slaveholding societies of the South. As a result, ideologues like Senator Charles Sumner of Massachusetts sat side by side politically with more practically minded men like William Seward of New York and Lyman Trumbull of Illinois, and fiscal conservatives like William Pitt Fessenden of Maine. Though moderates in the party might sympathize with the plight of African Americans, they were not inclined to risk their own political fortunes at home for them. Conservatives had no interest in African Americans except as the vital labor force of the South, which produced the cotton for Northern mills and provided a market for Northern manufacturers, farmers, and financial services. In order to lead this diverse group, Lincoln had to tread carefully, lest his legislative agenda be derailed along with his ability to wage the war. Military necessity was also a considerable factor in Lincoln's treatment of occupied areas and populations like New Orleans. The border states—Missouri, Kentucky, and Maryland—were all slave states. They provided not just manpower, resources, and strategically important staging areas for the Union cause; they also lent a legitimacy to the effort it would not have otherwise had. Their presence, albeit in the case of Maryland at the very least reluctant, as slave states let the nation and the world know that this was a rebellion or civil war, rather than a war of Northern aggression or a war between the states, or, worse, the war for Southern independence—all labels that people used or would use to describe the conflict.

What should also not be ignored is the considerable influence that the perception of Southern unionism had on Lincoln and others. Looking at the way the conventions adopted the articles of secession, Lincoln and a considerable number of people outside of the rebelling areas concluded there was a large, possibly predominant in some places, sentiment against the "fire-eaters" who were driving the secession movement. The Radicals' call for liberating the slaves, much less their desire for granting them full rights and land, would alienate this supposedly sympathetic group. Therefore, at Lincoln's insistence, potentially revolutionary measures like the first Confiscation Act of 1862, which possibly could have resulted in widespread land redistribution, were critically weakened or laxly enforced. No permanent forfeitures of land were to result from a landholder's commission of treason by joining the rebellion. As a Southerner himself in origin, if not in politics, Lincoln believed moving too quickly on slavery would damage the cause, and winning the war was the paramount goal.

One might adduce an additional factor in Lincoln's "go slow and be merciful" approach to the former Confederacy: presidential politics. As early as 1862, Lincoln was thinking about reelection, and thus he was constantly looking at the Electoral College that elected presidents. While radicals might be able to command majorities in New England and the Upper Midwest, the key to national victories lay in more moderate, Southern-leading regions like the mid-Atlantic states of New York and Pennsylvania, which were rich in electoral votes. Although they made great human and economic commitments to winning the war, they suffered from it. Seeking electoral votes in these states, Lincoln could not ignore the racism among otherwise staunch Republicans. After all, a party built on free states' populations' hostility to the migration of African Americans out of the South as slaves could not be relied on to enthusiastically endorse a policy of liberation that might well lead to free black migration to Northern states.

The legal problems associated with runaway slaves also confronted Lincoln with a host of issues. Given that the legal and political institutions of the rebelling areas were no longer compliant with the Constitution or the Union, how should the military forces of the United States treat the populations of these areas? It was a well-recognized principle of Anglo-American law that military forces could not treat citizens or their possessions summarily, at least under ordinary circumstances. There were legal procedures to follow, strictures governing everything from use of goods and lands to the processing of alleged criminals. However, all of these items were court-based actions, and those courts, both federal and state, were no longer functioning. To a greater extent in the United States than in Great Britain, law depended on the consensus in the community. Now that those communities were in open rebellion, law could not function.

Upon even the rumor of an approaching Union army, slaves ran for the Union lines. Union commanders, without general instructions from the White House, much less a comprehensive policy in law, treated these runaways in various ways. Some of these officers were lifelong Democrats, racist, and committed only to waging the war. Those runaways whom they could not use, they returned to their masters. Other commanders took pity on these desperate people or became converted to their cause as a matter of experience with their would-be masters on the battlefield. A much smaller number of Union officers were committed abolitionists and took advantage of the situation to liberate these slaves. All referred to the doctrine of contraband to justify their actions. Under this military concept, the slaves were resources being denied to the enemy, thereby limiting the Confederacy's ability to wage war.

{ *Chapter 1* }

What, then, were Union forces to do with the slaves and Afro-Creoles of New Orleans when, on April 29, 1862, Flag Officer David G. Farragut and his men captured the Confederacy's main port? At this time, New Orleans was the South's largest city, and arguably its most important one. It was home to much of the region's commerce and banking. Reflecting its international role as a depot for cotton and finance, it had a diverse population of 144,000, including some 11,000 free persons of color. Its majority had voted for the Constitution–Union ticket of John Bell of Tennessee in 1860. Of its predominantly white population, almost half were foreign born. Its surrounding parishes were considerably less diverse and cosmopolitan, largely made up of cotton and sugar plantations mostly Unionist in sentiment. New Orleans became, for a time, the focus and test site of Reconstruction. From 1862 until 1882, New Orleans was the capital of Louisiana, and with few exceptions, it was the center of the continuing war over African American civil rights.

In part, the early problems of Reconstruction stemmed from Butler's more radical notions of what needed to be done, given the combustible situation in the Delta. Unionist sentiment had been fairly strong before hostilities erupted, and it only grew more manifest by the time of federal occupation. Butler needed to pacify the region quickly so he could move his troops upriver. Dealing with a hostile population would consume manpower he simply could not spare. Despite his misgivings about enforcing slavery on African American runaways, he accommodated planters who swore oaths of loyalty, and he enforced labor agreements on those persons who refused their labor. He also refused the Afro-Creoles' call for an end to segregation.

However, other aspects of his regime clashed with Lincoln's desire to reach a settlement with Unionist Louisiana. Butler allowed the Afro-Creoles to form militias and participate in local government. They in turn pressed for full rights and equal treatment. The colored troops assisted heroically in the siege of Fort Hudson in the Vicksburg, Mississippi, campaign. Butler, a Massachusetts Republican politician, could see that these freeborn troops more than demonstrated their worth; they also might be potentially loyal as voters in the Reconstruction government.

Butler pursued other policies that shortened his tenure in New Orleans. When Confederate women harassed his troops, going so far in several cases as spitting on them as they passed, he issued General Order Number 28, known later as the Woman Order, declaring, "When any female shall, by word, gesture, or movement, insult or show contempt for any officer or soldier of the United States, she shall be . . . held liable to be treated as a woman of the town plying her vocation." Although there is some doubt whether ordering well-born white women to be treated as prostitutes caused a swift end to the infractions, it definitely ratcheted up the level of animosity against the occupying forces and scandalized the foreign consuls. British and French diplomats also objected to Butler's methods. Their protests coincided with an independent report of corruption on Butler's staff by Maryland senator Reverdy Johnson, and Lincoln had to choose between his inflammatory general and his delicate foreign diplomacy. British and French recognition of the Confederacy would be their equivalent of the rebelling United States' alliance with France in 1778, a critical loss for the Union cause.

Because of these issues and his more radical views on African American equality, Butler lost his command in Louisiana in December 1862 to General Nathaniel P. Banks, former governor of Massachusetts, whose views more closely resembled the commander in chief's. At the same time that he committed himself to ending slavery in Louisiana, Banks also seemed to be more interested in reconciling whites to Unionism. He issued orders to the occupying army virtually reestablishing slavery. Every African American had to carry a pass. Only passes issued by army officials or by their employers could allow them to move about freely. Otherwise, they were considered vagrants subject to removal and relocation to a plantation. Federal troops enforced the pass law much as slave patrols had enforced the pass system before the war. Whites who had sworn oaths of loyalty received pardons from the president and could resume life as masters of their vast holdings. The promise of a radical reconstruction had evaporated.

Oddly enough, Lincoln was undergoing an evolutionary transformation on the African American question in the opposite direction from that of Banks. It simply did not seem fitting that the same slave owners who had advocated secession should retain the rights and status slavery gave its master class. Military necessity also gave impetus to a policy of emancipation. Depriving the Confederates of their slaves weakened them militarily and on the home front. Finally, it was good foreign policy to associate the Union cause with one of liberation. Britain and France were less likely to favor a war for slavery than one for Southern independence.

In September 1862, after the marginal Union victory at Antietam, Lincoln announced that on the first day of the New Year, he would issue an Emancipation Proclamation liberating all slaves in territories then in rebellion. On January 1, 1863, he followed through on his promise. On the battlefront, the sacrifice of African American regiments like the Massachusetts 54th and 55th convinced even a reluctant Lincoln that free African Americans could serve in capacities other than burial duty, digging fortifications, and serving whites. Based on his war powers as commander in chief, the proclamation transformed a war for the Union into a war for human liberty. It has been hailed as a landmark decision. At the conclusion of formal hostilities, Congress proposed, and the requisite number of states ratified, the Thirteenth Amendment, ending slavery as a matter of constitutional law. Southern states returning from secession had to ratify to be readmitted to the Union.

———

Looking forward to what promised to be a hotly contested presidential election in 1864, Abraham Lincoln dumped the more radical antislavery Hannibal Hamlin of Maine from the bottom half of the ticket in favor of Tennessee's Andrew Johnson. Johnson had stayed in the Senate when Tennessee's secession convention favored removal. As a reward for being the only member of Congress from a Confederate state to do this, Lincoln appointed him the Volunteer State's military governor when the Army of the Cumberland arrived. Acting with a vigor that belied his Democratic Party credentials as a congressman, governor, and senator, he gained the reputation of being a staunchly loyal Unionist. After Lincoln was shot on April 14, 1865, and died the following morning, Andrew Johnson became president and moved ahead with his version of Reconstruction—an even more lenient one than Lincoln had contemplated.

Johnson's plan, readmitting the Southern states that ratified the Thirteenth Amendment after one-tenth of the male population swore allegiance to the Union, may have been expedient. After all, who could then arrest and hold all of the Confederates who had waged war against their country? Who would try them for their crimes? What juries of the vicinage would convict them? The alternative of military tribunals (in peacetime, with the regular courts in sessions) was an issue that had already brought much criticism. The Republicans were unlikely to reopen it. On the home front and the battlefront, the Union was exhausted. With peace, the South could provide the raw cotton for Northern mills and the consumer markets for Northern products. Northerners were already eyeing moving their businesses south to rebuild wrecked infrastructure and build railroads and factories. With this local desire for peace at any price came the concomitant desire to eliminate the wartime taxation policies, government borrowing, and other exigency measures installed during the war. In short, economic and political positions came together with traditional notions of limited government to form a perfect storm opposed to any radical notions of reconstructing the South, much less a second revolution in American government, society, and ideology toward African Americans.

President Johnson understood this sentiment all too well. After all, he was not far removed from his humble beginnings in North Carolina. Largely illiterate until his wife taught him enough so he could pursue his political career, he was a firm believer in the limited government, states' rights, and strict construction of the Constitution views of the Democratic Party. He also knew his future did not lie with the Republicans. He was a Democrat in a Republican administration. Moving cautiously at first, then more boldly as he gained his footing, he began the rehabilitation of former Confederates largely while Congress was away on its long summer and fall break with his announcement in May of his version of Reconstruction.

His first targets were those adherents to the Confederacy not yet rehabilitated under Lincoln. With blanket amnesty provided to all those whose wealth did not exceed $20,000, provided they made personal appeals to him or, better yet, traveled to the White House to pay their respects, Johnson was prepared to make full use of the pardon power for even the most prominent leaders of the rebellion. Second, he countermanded General O. O. Howard's and Grant's field orders for the Bureau of Refugees, Freedmen, and Abandoned Lands to treat the newly freed slaves as persons entitled to benevolent treatment. Even more than they already had, Freedmen's Bureau agents were ordered to cease and desist any activities that might upset the labor relations Banks had pioneered in Louisiana, virtually reestablishing plantation slavery through unfair labor contracts.

Johnson's appointees to the provisional governorships had one instruction: resume as before, though without slavery. He disparaged any attempt to treat the freedmen and freedwomen as citizens and equals. Again, Louisiana was a model of Presidential Reconstruction for the rest of the South, along with Johnson's home state of Tennessee. Dominated by former Confederates who shared the South's Democratic Party's great fear of Negro domination, Louisiana's state government recognized the end of slavery, then proceeded to recreate it under another name. What became known in the Northern press as Black Codes merely took General Banks's system to its natural conclusion. All those African Americans who could not demonstrate employment by a white were classified as vagrants. Vagrants could then be sentenced to terms at hard labor. A rigid system of classification divided the population into either white or Negro. Mixing between members of these two groups was forbidden in all aspects of life. Penalties under the criminal law for African Americans were harsh in the extreme, including whippings, beatings, and executions for even minor offenses. Any civil rights, much less the franchise, were permanently denied on the basis of previous condition of servitude.

The Afro-Creoles of New Orleans were appalled by these new restrictions that did not recognize their historically free status, their cultural attainments, or their military service. They complained to the U.S. army officers in occupation of New Orleans, to no avail. Louisiana, like the rest of the former Confederacy, was now under the control of white supremacists. These former Confederates feared that Louisiana's African American majority would combine with the whites in the nascent Republican Party to form a permanent ruling class without regard to race. All that the freedmen and the free people of color had to back their rights was the force of U.S. army bayonets and the funding they gave to Unionist and Republican newspapers. For a time, this was enough, but without hope of overthrowing the Republican regime through democratic, peaceful means, the white supremacists and the Democratic Party began a period of sustained paramilitary violence that would last into the twentieth century. Lincoln's and Johnson's failure to prosecute the perpetrators of the rebellion condemned the Southern part of the nation to decades of an inner civil war.

———

However, Johnson's steps, and their impact on freedmen and freedwomen, did not go unnoticed. Republicans in Congress were appalled at Presidential Reconstruction's consequences. The reports from the remaining Republican newspapers in the South were reverberating with their fellow journalists' headlines throughout the North. The headlines alone were enough to spur conspiracy theories: Black Codes, the reinstitution of slavery through race laws, beatings, murders, vigilante groups with strange names like the Ku Klux Klan and the Knights of the White Camellia for Louisiana. Most alarming of all was the return of former Confederates, including officers who led the armies, to political dominance in their state governments and congressional delegations. It was this last galling point that caused a considerable ruckus when the Republicans returned for the fall session.

Noting their authority under the Constitution to determine the qualifications of their members, the Republicans refused to certify former Confederates returned to Congress by Southern voters. Whole swaths of seats from the former Confederacy were left vacant. At issue was more than just control of the Congress (the Southern congressmen were Democrats), but the nature of the nation's recent victory in the Civil War. Johnson and Democrats from both North and South wanted a return to the antebellum status quo when white males controlled the destiny of the country. Now that emancipation under the Thirteenth Amendment had eliminated the reduction in the male population count of the three-fifths clause, the South's representation would increase. When this increase, combined with the single-party dictatorship the Democrats were establishing under the banner of white supremacy in the South, they could overcome the Republicans' dwindling appeal in the North and West. The expansion of slavery and winning the war were gone as issues. All that was left of the

Republicans' raison d'être were high tariffs, internal improvements, sound money, and temperance—not the most exciting platform on which to base the party's future.

Seeking to learn more about conditions in the former Confederacy than their own admittedly partisan press's warnings, the Congress sent a fact-finding commission of generals and aid workers to examine actual circumstances on the ground. The commission's report portrayed an even worse situation for the freedmen than the newspapers' stories. Poverty, destruction, violence, and lawlessness were rampant. The region was on the verge of humanitarian crisis of mammoth proportions. The conclusion was clear to the Republicans: Congress needed to provide a commitment to order, relief, and genuine reconstruction.

The Republican majority's first act was to recharter the primary clearinghouse for aid, the Freedmen's Bureau, and this time to provide funding for its operations. The second act was to pass a landmark civil rights bill authored by the influential chair of the Senate's Judiciary Committee, Lyman Trumbull. The Civil Rights Act of 1866 allowed private rights of action—lawsuits—against public authorities for violations of civil rights, the section 1983 litigation that is still the foundation for these kinds of suits. No longer would law enforcement merely be in the hands of local public prosecutors. Litigants could take state and local officials to court and get treble damages. With local juries unsympathetic to their cause, they could seek a bench trial in federal court. This could be a game-changing aspect of civil rights litigation, considering federal judges were lifetime appointees by the president and affirmed by the U.S. Senate, not elected or appointed by the governor like state and local judges. Events would prove, however, that even these substantial federal government interventions were insufficient to protect the freedmen of the South.

President Johnson vetoed the legislation. Though unable to save the Freedmen's Bureau, Congress did override Johnson's veto and pass the Civil Rights Act, overriding a presidential veto for the first time in U.S. history. The battle lines had been drawn. The upcoming congressional elections of 1866 would be a referendum on whether the nation should continue with Presidential Reconstruction or take further steps toward Congressional Reconstruction. Johnson decided he would campaign in person on behalf of Democratic candidates and put his presidency on the line in the process. In retrospect, it seems an odd move for an unelected president with no political organization to speak of to campaign on behalf of a party to which he no longer belonged and did not represent. It might also have given him pause if he had considered the trend in U.S. elections that presidents tended to lose seats from their party when they themselves were not on the ballot. Voters in localities usually dislike interference from Washington in matters of local concern. In addition, Republicans were initiating a strategy for victory in the postwar nation: "waving the bloody shirt."

Democrats invented the term to deride Republican campaigning based on Unionist sentiment after Butler had waved a bloody shirt at a campaign rally. But the bloody shirt campaigns were highly effective, given the large numbers of Union veterans in the North as well as their surviving relations. Although the tactic may have been partisan, it spurred Union army veterans' genuine outrage at the postwar Confederates' campaigns of terror. They remembered their sacrifice and those of their neighbors. They remembered who had caused the war, and why. Republican majorities came from those veterans who formed the nation's first and possibly greatest lobbying organization, the Grand Army of the Republic, those who had no intention of being reconciled to the former Confederates—not just yet. Johnson's own occasionally rambling, seemingly intoxicated performance—he later claimed the baleful influence of cold medicine—on the campaign trail did not aid his cause.

————

If voters needed any further proof that Presidential Reconstruction had failed to protect freedmen and freedwomen, they received it in the form of the Memphis and New Orleans race riots in early May and late July 1866. Neither was actually a riot. White supremacist mobs, joined by police and Democratic Party irregulars, engaged in wholesale assaults on African American neighborhoods. In Memphis, the violence began with a traffic accident between an African American and a white that escalated into three days of violence, leaving forty-eight people dead (all but two of them African American), five black women raped, and hundreds of African American homes and churches burned to the ground.

The New Orleans events were more purposeful: a white supremacist mob of Democrats assaulted a group of Republicans, some of whom were African Americans, at a convention to lobby for a reform of the 1864 Louisiana constitution. This day of violence stemmed from Governor Wells's call for a new constitution. Former Confederates had rigged the city of New Orleans elections by threatening all Republican voters with death. It would have been an easy threat to fulfill, for voting was not secret. By the time federal troops arrived in sufficient numbers to quiet the crowds in the capital, thirty-four blacks and three white Republicans were dead, and over a hundred people were injured. Cyrus Hamlin, a veteran and the son of the former vice president, reported that "the wholesale slaughter and the little regard paid to human life I witnessed here" was worse than anything he had seen in the war. Judge Advocate General Joseph Holt concluded that Presidential Reconstruction had led to "the barbarism of the rebellion in its renaissance."

Between these two disturbances, Congress proposed a new amendment to the Constitution. The proposed amendment sought to repeal the Black Codes, undo *Dred Scott v. Sanford* (1857), which denied that African Americans could ever be citizens, and provide for a new constitutional order to govern the nation. It was the product of a joint reconstruction committee. Ratified in 1868, the Fourteenth Amendment's first section had three major provisions, all of which applied to the states: the privileges or immunities clause, the equal protection clause, and the due process clause. No state could deny to any person the fundamental right to the privileges or immunities of citizens of the United States and the state wherein they resided, "nor shall any State deprive any person of life, liberty, or property without due process of law; nor deny to any person within its jurisdiction the equal protection of the laws." Although the final draft did not include a right to vote, it did provide for the reduction of a state's delegation to Congress if it did deny the vote to any "male inhabitants" otherwise classified as citizens. Its elevated but imprecise formula provided little protection to black voters against the more subtle disfranchising measures like literacy tests, but it was a start.

The negative construction of the amendment's language reflected its narrow scope. Its authors had to make it narrow in order to gain approval outside of the South. Some Northern state legislatures were just as discriminatory in their enactments as Southern states. Outside of New England, segregation and the denial of equal rights to African Americans were commonplace. Even congressionally controlled Washington, D.C., was segregated during this Congress—a fact that would add to the arsenal of those arguing that the Fourteenth Amendment did not prohibit segregation by race.

Additional evidence that the amendment was not intended as a radical shift in constitutional priorities comes from the remarks of its supporters in the Northern states. For example, Governor Reuben E. Fenton of New York recommended the amendment to his legislature by arguing that it would provide the basis for laws to "educate, improve, enlighten, and Christianize the negro; to make him an independent man; to teach him to think and to reason; to improve that principle which the great Author of all has implanted in every human breast, which is susceptible of the highest cultivation, and destined to go on enlarging and expanding through the endless ages of eternity." This view of African Americans presupposed special treatment based on inherent inequality. The extremely high illiteracy and innumeracy rates among the vast majority of the white population in the South went unnoticed. It was region, not race, that correlated with the need to "educate, improve, and enlighten" Americans.

———

Victories in the election of 1866 gave the Republicans their veto-proof majorities in Congress, but only so long as the Southern delegations were kept from taking their seats. Thus the basis for Congressional Reconstruction was as much partisan as idealistic. Though most history textbooks repeat contemporary observations that this was a "radical" program, better-informed scholarship treats this program as fairly moderate in its origins, support, and aims. Despite the outcome of the 1866 elections, Republican radicals like Charles Sumner, Benjamin Franklin Wade of Ohio in the Senate, and Thaddeus Stevens from Pennsylvania in the House were still an unpopular minority within their party.

While President Johnson was urging the Southern states not to ratify the Fourteenth Amendment, Congress passed the first Reconstruction Act in March 1867 and overrode Johnson's veto. The act suspended all the state governments of the former Confederacy save Tennessee's, and divided the rest into five military districts. The act renewed the Freedmen's Bureau. In addition to modifying their state constitutions to provide all their male residents civil and political rights, including the franchise, the states under military occupation needed to approve the Fourteenth Amendment. This reflected the Republicans' lack of faith that Democratic-leaning states like Kentucky, Maryland, and New Jersey would ratify the new amendment. While these measures provided some relief in the upper South, the Deep South—especially South Carolina, Mississippi, and Louisiana, states with the highest percentages of African Americans—proved highly resistant to genuinely democratic elections and equal treatment for all.

Johnson's executive authority, which gave him the ability to make or remove officials in the executive branch, including the army, continued to wreak havoc with congressional legislation and the policy it represented. For example, when General Philip Sheridan presided over a negotiated settlement between the African Americans of New Orleans, who were campaigning against the segregated star cars, and the railways, resulting in integration of the cars, Johnson dismissed Sheridan from his post.

Congress responded with the Tenure of Office Act in March 1867. This law prevented Johnson from removing Lincoln's appointments without a Senate-approved successor during the rest of what would have been Lincoln's second term. Believing on good authority that this was an impermissible, unconstitutional interference with his executive authority, in February 1868, Johnson dismissed Edwin Stanton, the secretary of war, a Lincoln holdover working with congressional Republicans. This action triggered impeachment proceedings against the president that spring. Ably defended by some of the finest attorneys in the country, many of whom objected to what they saw as high-handed action by the Congress, Johnson managed to escape conviction by one vote. Six Republicans had crossed the aisle and voted not guilty.

In the meantime, in Louisiana and across the reconstructed South's legislative groups, the white supremacists derisively called the "black and tans" were writing some of the most progressive state constitutions in the nation. These documents were the first of their kind in America in providing for a truly race-blind society. With the Afro-Creoles playing an important, if not critical, role in the process, Louisiana's was the most progressive of these egalitarian documents. It not only provided for universal male suffrage, but made commitments to a nonracist and integrated society. Thus, Article Thirteen of the Bill of Rights of Louisiana stated: "All persons shall enjoy equal rights and privilege upon any conveyance of a public character; and all places of business, or of public resort, or for which a license is required by either State, parish or municipal authority, shall be deemed places of a public character, and shall be opened to the accommodation and patronage of all persons, without distinction or discrimination on account of race or color." Schools, streetcars, public establishments, and appointments to office were all to be nondiscriminatory. This stemmed from the Afro-Creoles' dedication to the concept of public rights, or those rights present in what many theorists today refer to as the public sphere—that is, public spaces like shops, restaurants, parks, streets, and theaters.

This constitutional enshrinement of public rights did not go uncontested. A judge, former slaveholder, conservative Republican, and constitutional convention delegate, William H. Cooley, denounced the provisions as so much blather, "because, I never heard the term 'public rights' mentioned as a private one, and because I cannot understand the idea of a private individual exercising public rights." English and American common law did not recognize such a concept; however, there was no reason why Louisiana could not innovate. A majority of the voting public agreed, and the constitution of 1868 became law.

Congressional Reconstruction had made the Louisiana constitutional revision possible. With former Confederates lacking the franchise and federal troops securing the fairness of the election, Louisiana elected its first truly democratic and representative government (with the notable exception of equal rights for women). Their first Reconstruction legislature had thirty-one African Americans out of 105 in the house. The Senate had seven African Americans out of thirty-six members, most from New Orleans. And, like other states under Congressional Reconstruction, it sent African Americans to the U.S. Congress for the first time in the nation's history, let alone that of the South's.

Louisiana's African Americans were to vote for the first time in a national election, the presidential race of 1868. Republicans nominated the war hero and army general Ulysses S. Grant. Grant had recently resigned as the overall commander over his disagreement with Johnson over the course of Reconstruction. At least in part, Johnson's dismissal of Grant's longtime comrade in arms, General Philip S. Sheridan, from his post as military governor of the fifth district, headquartered in New Orleans, had played a significant role in Grant's decision to run for president.

Grant's Democratic opponent was the former governor of New York, Horatio Seymour. Seymour's popularity in that electorally rich state meant Grant had to win significant votes in the former Confederacy in order to prevail. The Democrats' vice presidential candidate, Francis P. Blair Jr. of Missouri, made the cost of a Republican loss plain when he described Congressional Reconstruction as having placed a "semi-barbarous race" in charge of the South whose purpose was to "subject the white women to their unbridled lust."

The Democrats were a party of states' rights, white supremacy, and reconciliation with the former Confederacy. It is a testament to the passions of the time that Blair, a man who had been instrumental in keeping Missouri in the Union by force, a founding member of the Free Soil Party, and a successful general commanding a corps for Sherman during the March to the Sea, had turned so vehemently against Reconstruction. With race rather than Union his concern, his stance was typical of Northern democracy.

The election, though highly contested and in some areas bloody, came out in Grant and the Republicans' favor. Besides the violence in Louisiana and elsewhere, there was disturbing news in the final result. If the Democrats had retained their traditional Southern base instead of losing Texas, Mississippi, and Virginia to Reconstruction, as well as Arkansas, Tennessee, Alabama, Florida, and the Carolinas to a fair vote that included African Americans, they would have prevailed. White supremacist intimidation succeeded in delivering Louisiana and Georgia to Seymour. It pointed the way to domination of the Union they had but three years before been trying to tear asunder.

Seeing this threat to their national fortunes and hearing the plaintive pleas from their brethren in the South, Republicans in Congress proposed the Fifteenth Amendment in February 1869. Ratified in 1870, it did what the Fourteenth Amendment had specifically declined to do: it provided protection against any state seeking to deny to any citizen the right to vote based on "race, color, or previous condition of servitude." It also, like the Fourteenth Amendment, included a clause allowing Congress to pass legislation to enforce its provisions. Congress made full use of the enforcement clauses in passing the Enforcement Acts, which provided for criminal penalties for those violating the Reconstruction enactments. The last of these acts became known as the Ku Klux Klan Act because it specifically targeted that organization and others like it that sought to interfere with elections through violence, intimidation, and terrorism. It created a national electoral law and the mechanisms in federal courts for enforcement of that law.

———

But law could not overcome the white South's determination to restore white supremacy. Louisiana was once again a battleground in this campaign. Emblematic of the South's travails, the so-called redemption of Louisiana is a sad tale, but because of the large, well-educated, and prominent African American community in New Orleans, Louisiana's brief experiment with equality might have turned out differently. It was no accident that the city originated a court-based challenge to segregation in the 1890s. What went wrong in New Orleans, and in Louisiana in general, thus says much about the inherent weakness of a revolution based solely on law.

The challenges these governments faced went far beyond even the mammoth task of constructing a biracial society, something never before attempted in the Americas or Europe. The region had been devastated by the war. Property damage, the destruction of the rail network, and the sheer loss of life—one in five white men died fighting for the Confederacy—left the South bereft enough, but the instantaneous and complete financial evaporation that came from emancipation of the slave owners' key capital asset, the failed investment in Confederate war bonds, and the conversion of all currency into worthless Confederate money meant that the South was completely prostrate. The dislocation of the entire society gave the new governments little fiscal surplus to work with, and no substantial aid from the national government was forthcoming.

That these Reconstruction governments managed to achieve minor miracles in education, infrastructure repair, and public health improvement is a testament to the boldness of the largely Republican coalitions that attempted these tremendous tasks. No doubt New Orleans' Afro-Creoles gave the state a step up in this process, but they had help from immigrants from the North as well as those from overseas seeking opportunity in the New World, much as others had done in the centuries before. Union Leagues organized potential voters. Aid workers staffed the freedmen's schools as well as the South's first public school systems. Investments poured in from out of state to revive banking, commerce, sugar, and cotton production. The state governments issued bonds to pay for civic improvements, including the all-important levees that kept out the floodwaters and the seas from New Orleans streets and neighborhoods. They did all these things despite the unending tide of violence from the White League, which had sprung up to replace the now-defunct Knights of the White Camellia.

Unfortunately, for many throughout the country and for generations thereafter, the white supremacists of the Democratic Party were able to label these governments as corrupt. For less than incorrupt motives of their own, the Democrats charged their Republican adversaries with financial malfeasance, electoral irregularities, and abuse of office. Although there was some evidence of this, such self-dealing was a regrettable feature of American politics before the war and continued in local, state, and national politics after hostilities ended. For the Democrats, particularly former Confederate officers and soldiers engaged in widespread lawlessness of their own, to decry the misconduct of the Republicans may hint of hypocrisy exceeding even that characteristic of partisan politics, but the accusations stuck. This was because the Democrats had not forgotten a fundamental lesson about politics in the antebellum South. The race card trumped the public interest. The message that ran all through the Democratic campaign was the fear that the Republicans were elevating the black man to the same level as the white man.

The damage Republicans did to themselves through infighting and sheer incompetence in Louisiana did not help their cause. The battle for valuable appointments, combined with the need to establish political machines from scratch, created a witch's brew of rival factions. The often unbalanced behavior of their governors like Henry Warmoth and his sometime ally, P. B. S. Pinchback, America's first African American governor, did not help either.

Thus the Democratic story of greedy carpetbaggers, venal scalawags, and their easily mislead compatriots of lustful Negroes found a ready audience in some Republican circles in the North. The distrust for "government by bayonet" combined with the Credit Mobilier scandal (the nineteenth-century equivalent of the Keating Five savings and loan scandal) to propel the so-called Liberal Republicans like Lyman Trumbull and E. L. Godkin, editor of the influential magazine *The Nation*, to bolt the Republican Party and endorse newspaper editor Horace Greeley for president instead of Grant in 1872. When the Democrats nominated Greeley, a fully national coalition was now calling for all Americans to, in Greeley's words, "clasp hands across the bloody chasm," reconcile, and end Reconstruction. Though Democrats' distrust of Greeley led to a poor turnout against Grant, the damage had been done. The election signaled the Republicans' weakening resolve.

In Louisiana, the Republicans were still at war with themselves. Seeking to clear up the horrific health hazard that was the slaughterhouse industry in New Orleans and neighboring Jefferson City, the Republican majority in the legislature passed a law creating a central slaughterhouse with a monopoly of the business in the state. This allowed for a regulated downriver space for the unwholesome activity. The newly fashioned monopoly had kicked back some of its anticipated profits to members of the legislature. The flood of litigation from butchers who did not want to be absorbed into the state-mandated monopoly became a vehicle for those who opposed the Reconstruction government to challenge it in court. Former Supreme Court justice John Archibald Campbell played a key role in this complicated affair, using it to obstruct Reconstruction. In a case that many have misunderstood, the United States Supreme Court did not oblige them in 1873 in the case known as the *Slaughterhouse Cases*.

{ *Chapter 1* }

In an opinion by Justice Samuel Miller, the Court ruled 5 to 4 that Louisiana's creation of a slaughterhouse monopoly was a reasonable exercise of its police power, namely to secure the health of the people of New Orleans. Miller rejected the plaintiffs' Fourteenth Amendment claims under the privileges or immunities clause that the amendment was meant for Negroes and the white butchers of New Orleans. Furthermore, he restricted the privileges or immunities clause of citizens of the United States and the states wherein they resided by differentiating between the rights of citizens of the United States and the rights of citizens in a state. National privileges or immunities included travel on interstate waterways and the high seas, but nothing else of significance, such as political rights, voting, or basic civil rights, which were for the states to decide. Although likely intended to support Reconstruction governments, the restrictive reading of the Fourteenth Amendment's privileges or immunities clause came to be a highly limiting precedent for civil rights lawsuits.

In other realms, though federal prosecutions under the Grant administration were effective in suppressing vigilante groups like the Klan in South Carolina, especially after the creation of the Department of Justice in 1870, violence continued to plague states like Georgia, Mississippi, and Louisiana. Given the routine call on federal troops to quiet civil disturbances, one must ask why state criminal laws were so lax—or, at least, so infrequently applied. The answer was a widespread conspiracy against the laws. The White League in Louisiana was conducting a criminal campaign against the state government, a paramilitary effort that led to the deaths of hundreds of Louisianans, and the destruction of a considerable amount of property. Why were there no prosecutions, let alone more stringent law? Why were the Reconstruction governments in Louisiana and elsewhere so ineffective at using their own militias? Why in Colfax, Louisiana, the site of the worst race riot in U.S. history, with the slaughter of over fifty African Americans by white supremacists, were the Democratic mobs armed not only with rifles and revolvers, but a cannon?

Part of the answer lies with a dilemma African Americans faced during Reconstruction. In order to prove themselves capable of being granted full rights and opportunities for political office, they needed to present a better than clean, more than civilized appearance. Because whites supposedly feared that freed slaves would wreak a terrible vengeance on their former masters, as they had in Haiti in the late eighteenth century, African Americans made sure to pursue policies of mercy, forgiveness, and civility. African Americans had to avoid any sign of anger, brutality, or radicalism. Trapped in a policy straitjacket, they and their fellow Republicans could not take the actions that might have deterred, or at least endangered, white terrorist groups' violence.

Instead of engaging in their own guerilla war for rights promised them by federal law, African Americans attempted to integrate public accommodations and schools during the 1870s. But even after the passage of the Civil Rights Act of 1875, guaranteeing these rights, white racists found ways around the law. They would adulterate African American meals in restaurants, adding pepper and salt and other disincentives better not described. Litigation foundered for lack of plaintiffs (deterred from coming forward by threats and assaults) and an increasingly irate white vigilantism.

In the election of 1874, the violence against blacks and Republicans escalated. The White Leaguers struck in Red River Parish in Louisiana in August in what became known as the Coushatta Massacre. Killing Republicans who had signed a pledge to leave the state and then African American witnesses, some twenty murders in all, the White Leaguers fled after Grant sent troops to restore order. Although twenty-five men were charged with the crime, the prosecution never proceeded for lack of evidence. As usual, no one was brave enough, or sympathetic enough to the cause of justice, to speak up. When Marshall H. Twitchell, whose three brothers-in-law were among those killed, returned to the parish he had helped found and organize after the war, he became the white supremacists' next target. The Vermonter had served with distinction in the eastern theater of the war, but that patriotism worked against him in Louisiana. Two years later, he was ambushed and shot once in each of his four limbs. Miraculously, he survived, though he lost both arms. Like many former immigrants with noble intentions to settle in the postwar South, he left the region in 1878, and died after a distinguished career as an American consul in Canada.

By 1875, toward the end of Grant's second term, the writing on the wall in Louisiana was plain for all to see. Buffeted by nearly routine violence, the Republican Party and the rights for African Americans that went with it were sunk. Grant asked Sheridan to Louisiana to report on the situation. The letter Sheridan wrote in response makes for grim reading. He offered the following statistics: over 3,500 killed by white supremacists since 1865, with 1,880 in 1868 alone killed or wounded; and over 1,200 killed since 1868, with not a single successful criminal prosecution. This would include the perpetrators of the Colfax Massacre, in Grant Parish, no less, whose convictions the U.S. Supreme Court vacated in *U.S. v. Cruikshank* the year after Sheridan wrote his letter.

Though the developments in Mississippi mirrored rather than inspired what happened in Louisiana, the Mississippi Plan gave its name to the successful strategy white supremacist Democrats used to brutally end Reconstruction in Louisiana. Enacted first in Vicksburg, the scene of Grant's great victory, the Democrats' militia, among whom the Red Shirts were the most notorious, initiated a military campaign of murder and destruction that only ended when Grant dispatched troops to the area. (The red shirt was a prized possession because it signified that its wearer had killed an African American, rather like gang colors in modern America.) The Republican sheriff, who had to flee the area, returned, only to be shot in the head by his white deputy. "Rifle clubs" then turned to disrupting Republican gatherings by shooting into the crowd. With their better military organization and superior training—they were, after all, largely made up of the Confederate veterans who had spent four years in campaigns against much larger federal forces—these paramilitary organizations were able to suppress the African American and white Republican vote so well that districts with several thousand Republican voters reported single-digit outcomes a year later.

With these methods repeated throughout the South, the end of Reconstruction came not with a whimper, but with a great deal of violence during the election of 1876. Democrats engaged in a domestic terror campaign to dampen Republican turnout in the South. Although the corruption of the Grant administration had created difficulties for the Republican Party, they were unified behind Rutherford B. Hayes, but they were not as effective at turning out their vote. Samuel Tilden's majority of the popular vote reflected the effectiveness of organized political violence by 1876. Now only the electoral votes of Florida, South Carolina, and Louisiana stood between the Democrats and white supremacy and the "redemption" of the white South.

Signs of Republican weariness in continuing to stand up for the rights of all Americans were everywhere. When Governor Adelbert Ames of Mississippi asked for federal troops to quell the violence in his state, Grant hesitated. Senator Roscoe Conkling from New York advised caution. Conklin had already pressed Grant to name conservatives on civil rights to the High Court and to administrative posts. Among the latter was Edwards Pierrepont, a former Democrat skeptical of Reconstruction, to the post of attorney general. Pierrepont's views were in noted contrast to his predecessor, Amos Ackerman, whose vigorous campaign against the Klan virtually eliminated the organization by 1873. Pierrepont advised Grant against interfering in the violence.

Still, Grant was ready to send troops to Mississippi, but a delegation of Ohio Republicans had begged him not to do so until after the elections in Ohio had been decided on October 13. Ohio's majority had been opposed to granting African Americans rights. They did not want African Americans to come into the state. Southern Ohio in particular was Southern leaning. Any Republican move to help African Americans in Mississippi would adversely affect the state Republicans in Ohio. This appeal, combined with Pierrepont's pressure, led to Grant writing to Ames, "The whole public are tired out with these annual, autumnal outbreaks in the South."

After the disputed electoral count of 1876–1877, the special congressional committee set up to determine the outcome of the presidential race with respect to the disputed votes in Louisiana, Florida, and South Carolina voted along party lines to give Hayes the presidency. In exchange, Hayes had let it be known that he would be withdrawing federal troops from those states, signaling the end of the nation's commitment to free and fair elections in the South and to Reconstruction in general.

———

Democrats wasted no time in New Orleans. A swift coup d'etat at the statehouse awarded the disputed gubernatorial election to Democrat and former Confederate general Francis R. T. Nicholls. In effect, the Democrats were on the way to winning the civil war after the Civil War. There remained some hope among the African American community that the laws still on the books could provide a means for equal treatment, if not fair treatment. It is to that effort that we shall turn in the next chapter.

CHAPTER 2

An Odious Law

When the Louisiana legislature met in May and June 1890 to consider House Bill No. 42—what would become the Separate Car Act—they were fiercely divided on more than party lines separating Democrats from Republicans. The Gilded Age had brought prosperity, industry, increasing urbanization, and a massive railroad infrastructure to the nation, but it had also brought severe strains on state and local government. These strains were part of the redemption of the state government by white supremacists after the 1876 electoral debacle.

Beginning in 1877, Democrats controlled the Louisiana legislature and the governorship, as well as the U.S. House of Representatives. They consolidated this authority using a sophisticated legal strategy. Because the Fifteenth and, to a lesser extent, the Fourteenth Amendment as well as the Civil Rights Acts only applied to a specific category of discrimination, state-mandated denial of the vote, the Democrats decided to impose a series of qualifications for voting that were widespread in the North and use them to discriminate against African Americans. By imposing a poll tax and a literacy test prerequisite to voting, not facially as discriminatory as the third device to deny former slaves the vote (the grandfather clauses—the requirement that, if your grandfather had voted, you were exempt from the literacy requirement), Southern states could effectively disenfranchise black voters.

But the Southern state voter registrars needed help, and it came from the U.S. Supreme Court, albeit possibly inadvertently. The Court signaled its willingness to go along with these state laws in the case of *Reese v. U.S.* (1875), decided on the same day and with much the same effect as *Cruikshank*. In *Reese*, Hiram Reese, a Kentucky poll worker, had refused to let an otherwise qualified African American vote despite his paying the poll tax and presenting a receipt proving it. Reese's refusal to accept such proof makes little sense except when one takes into account the fact that Reese's job was a party appointment and Reese, as a loyal Democrat, was performing an important political function for the party. Seemingly a clear violation of the Enforcement Acts and the Fifteenth Amendment's explicit guarantees in these matters, Reese was prosecuted for this offense.

In an opinion by Chief Justice Morrison Waite, the Court held that, as in *Cruikshank*, because the action was not officially commanded by the state, the Fifteenth Amendment did not apply. Reese was not following orders (though in fact he was, because the Democratic Party ran the state). The way was now clear for untold numbers of unofficial actions by officers of the state to deny African Americans basic rights. Considering that no African American would conceivably vote Democrat in this time period, the virtual elimination of the Republican Party from the states of the former Confederacy was the death knell of African American voting. Though at least one present-day scholar has questioned whether the Court intended this result, the practical effects reverberated all the way to Louisiana.

Louisiana's Redeemer governor, Francis R. T. Nichols, signaled the nature of the new regime when a group of African American Creoles led by Aristide Marie came to him to protest the continuing segregation in New Orleans' public schools. He told them "the courts are open, and there lies your redress." Taking him at his word, if not his probable intent to dissuade them from any action, they brought a lawsuit. Although whites thwarted the attempts at integration of some schools by placing their children into private schools and attacked African Americans seeking entry into others, Paul Trevigne, an editor of an African American paper, sued the state, alleging a violation of the Fourteenth Amendment's guarantees of equality.

In *Bertonneau v. Board of Directors of City Schools et al.* (1878), a decision by federal circuit judge William B. Woods, a future Supreme Court justice, declared that separate schools were not inherently unequal. "Equality of right does not necessarily imply identity of rights." Woods was a carpetbagger, a Northerner who went South after the war. He was an Ohioan who opposed the war in 1861, but political pressure and reputation led him to resign as Speaker of the Ohio House and join the Union army. He fought with distinction under fellow Ohioan William T. Sherman, eventually participating in Sherman's March to the Sea, and mustered out as a brevet general. As a Republican settler in Alabama, he raised cotton until Grant appointed him to the federal bench. Hayes nominated him to the Supreme Court in 1880, where he served seven undistinguished years as a conservative member of many majorities.

His opinion in *Bertonneau* cited a case from Ohio upholding school segregation there. It was more than just a reminder that mass segregation by law began and was still prevalent in the free states of the North. Indeed, it reflected one of the anomalies of Congressional Reconstruction. With the exception of the New Englanders, the congressmen who voted for the Reconstruction amendments and legislation had no intention of breaching their own states' segregation laws. The decision in the school case did not deter Marie and Trevigne from playing key roles in the litigation that would become *Plessy*.

Two years after the case, in December 1879, Louisiana officially ratified its newest constitution. On its face, it banned discrimination on the basis of color or race in voting, but it allowed for the creation of poll taxes to limit African Americans' actual participation in the political process. The new constitution also provided for the relocation of the state capital back to Baton Rouge, the pre-Reconstruction capital. It was a powerful, symbolic signal of departure from the cosmopolitan, diverse, and Afro-Creole populated city downriver. The new constitution also gave the appointed justices of the Louisiana Supreme Court twelve-year terms instead of ten.

The Redeemers in Louisiana, now known as Bourbons after the restoration of that royal family in France, went about establishing a peaceful Louisiana, white supremacist style. With their dreams of landownership, civil rights, and the franchise under siege, Louisiana's upcountry African Americans had two stark choices. They could sharecrop, in which they borrowed money, supplies, and necessities at high interest rates from local merchants in exchange for a share of their forthcoming crop, or they could migrate. Alarmed by this second prospect, which would dilute their labor force, Southern whites accommodated their black neighbors by promising some degree of schooling and public services.

In recognition of this situation throughout the South, African Americans like Booker T. Washington accepted practical inequality, if not legalized subordination, on the grounds that African Americans had to earn equality through their labor. Because of his later prominence at the time of the *Plessy* case, it is worth noting his earlier experiences at this time. By the time of his widely publicized speech at the Cotton States and International Exposition in Atlanta on September 18, 1895, known later as the Atlanta Compromise Speech, he had lived the supposed lessons of Reconstruction. At the Hampton Institute, a Freedmen's Bureau normal school, he received instruction in farming, the mechanic arts, and the value of hard work. Former Union general Samuel Chapman Armstrong headed the school and fended off criticism by preaching the importance of low expectations for his charges. Washington imbibed this form of uplift racism and brought it to Tuskegee, Alabama, where he established another institute to perform a similar function to Armstrong's Hampton: prepare African Americans for low-skilled jobs and to accept their place in a racialized South.

In the same period in which the Afro-Creoles were waging their legal battles against segregation, Washington excelled at his less confrontational approach. He took the run-down facilities at Tuskegee and turned them into a model educational enterprise. With deference to whites, who reciprocated with donations and political support, preaching his lessons of thrift, enterprise, and (diminished) hopes for his African American students, he became a paragon of virtue to many whites and blacks. In letters and speeches, he let the world know that segregation by race protected both, was accepted by both, and came naturally. His speech in Atlanta rang with the harmonious tones of acquiescence. "To those of my race who depend on bettering their condition in a foreign land or who underestimate the importance of cultivating friendly relations with the Southern white man, who is their next-door neighbor, I would say: 'Cast down your bucket where you are'—cast it down in making friends in every manly way of the people of all races by whom we are surrounded." Gone were the tales of terror and violence. Now, Washington reassured his audience with African Americans' humility. "No race can prosper till it learns that there is as much dignity in tilling a field as in writing a poem. It is at the bottom of life we must begin, and not at the top."

For Washington, equality in law and fact were goals for the future. All who were affected by white supremacy, however, did not share his view. Men like Paul Trevigne and Aristide Mary of the Afro-Creole community in New Orleans looked at the growing chasm between those seeing themselves as white and those who did not, and they found it a profound disappointment. It is important to note that Jim Crow racism did not arrive all at once with the redemption of the South. It was concurrent with—some argue caused by—the urbanization, industrialization, and transformation of the South from a cash-crop economy into a more diversified, commercial one. Though not nearly as industrial and urbanized as the Northeast or Midwest, the South's transition was no less striking.

As *Atlanta Constitution* editor Henry Grady and others trumpeted in the New South campaign of the 1880s, some entrepreneurs in the redeemed South saw virtue in economic Reconstruction. A non-slave-based economy of free labor and capital freely invested in commerce could rebuild the South. The antebellum South had had railroads and canals, to be sure, but they were paltry compared to the network of rails that crisscrossed the region after the war. Though Grady and his fellow Democrats attributed this great work to the post-Reconstruction polities, the foundation was laid under with Republican governors and legislatures. The Redeemers boasted of what Grady, in an 1886 speech to the New England Club in New York, called the end of the feudalism of the Old South: "Thus was gathered in the hands of a splendid and chivalric oligarchy the substance that should have been diffused among the people, as the rich blood, under certain artificial conditions, is gathered at the heart, filling that with affluent rapture but leaving the body chill and colorless."

In that same speech, Grady noted the contribution of African Americans to this New South, as well as the New South's reciprocal commitment to African Americans: "No section shows a more prosperous laboring population than the negroes of the South, none in fuller sympathy with the employing and land-owning class. He shares our school fund, has the fullest protection of our laws and the friendship of our people. Self-interest, as well as honor, demand that he should have this. Our future, our very existence depends upon our working out this problem in full and exact justice." African Americans supported the South's development, not only by their (cheap) labor, but also in the unequal burdens in taxation, services received, and lack of privileges they suffered. Because they paid their fair share of sales and property taxes, but did not receive their fair share of the service their taxes helped provide, African Americans were subsidizing the rest of the population—not as much as under slavery, certainly, but for a considerably more precarious existence for industrial laborers at least.

In certain enclaves like New Orleans, beset populations had the opportunity to make a better life for themselves than was possible for the mass of freedmen and freedwomen in the rural South and the unpaved alleys of other Southern cities. These came in many forms. New Orleans blacks benefited from the arrival of a substantial inter- and intrastate railroad system, department stores, a growing tourist industry, and all the benefits of becoming part of an increasingly national and international marketplace. Armour & Swift, along with their compatriots, shipped cuts of meat in refrigerated cars as far as the rails would take them. Produce from points west, east, north, and south, and consumer durables including clothing, furniture, fixtures, dry goods, and packaged foodstuffs arrived in New Orleans. Although New Orleans was a far cry from being the center of a regional economy, it was one of the hubs of a growing network of connections in business, trade, and finance. To the distaste of some of its African American citizens, it was also a destination for immigrants.

In some ways, the disruption of the Civil War was the only low point in immigration into New Orleans. It was one of the ways the Crescent City was exceptional. Although most immigrants avoided the South in the nineteenth century, New Orleans still had its share of those seeking a better life. The steady stream of immigrants became a torrent during the Gilded Age. Though some of the well-to-do and middle classes established settlement houses like Jane Adams's Hull House in Chicago to teach "the great unwashed" how to be Americans, others sought to circumscribe the newcomers in much the same way African Americans were treated in the South. The nation's first major immigration restrictions were against the "yellow horde" from China in the form of the Chinese Exclusion Act of 1882, which stated its rationale as "in the opinion of the Government of the United States the coming of Chinese laborers to this country endangers the good order of certain localities within the territory thereof." While other groups avoided such draconian restrictions, Italian Americans, among others, received the same treatment as the Irish had, and still did to some extent, in the 1840s and 1850s with the rise of outwardly anti-immigrant groups like the American or Know-Nothing party, so called because, when asked whether they were a member of a group that originated as a secret society, they would reply, "I know nothing." White supremacy was thus a danger to many groups besides African Americans so long as they did not gain acceptance as white.

Another strike, as it were, against the harmonious tale Grady told of the New South was the arrival of labor unrest along with industrialization. While the Great Railroad Strike of 1877, the Haymarket Affair in 1886, and the Homestead Strike of 1892, along with other incidents, gained headlines, the nation's second worst strike in terms of casualties came in the cane fields of Thibodaux, Louisiana, from November 1 to 4, 1887, in what would come to be known as the Thibodaux Massacre. The problems began when a Knights of Labor lodge decided to organize for better wages for 10,000 workers, of whom 1,000 were white. The Knights of Labor were an early labor organization based on a lodge system like the Masons and the Kiwanis. Under the leadership of their grand master, Terence Powderly, their maximum strength of several hundred thousand members during the 1880s made them one of the most influential organizations in the country.

The plantation owners were well connected to the governor, who ordered the state militia into the fields. They were joined by several white supremacist paramilitary groups. By the time the troops suppressed the strike, thirty to thirty-five African Americans were dead, and so was the cause of organized labor in Louisiana. Suffering from similar setbacks around the country, the Knights of Labor largely disappeared by 1890. More conservative organizations, like Samuel Gompers's American Federation of Labor, which concentrated on organizing skilled labor and maintaining industrial peace, replaced them. More radical organizations made their presence felt, but their influence was small and sporadic at best.

New Orleans' people and prospects were thus divided along many fault lines. Political agenda, immigration status, class status (as working and middle class), and race were the most visible of these. Out of its total population of over 220,000 people, African Americans were just under 27 percent—approximately 64,000. There were over 13,000 Irish, just under 14,000 Germans, and just under 2,000 Italian immigrants in 1880, with steep declines as a result of anti-immigrant violence and economic downturns. Religion also divided the city's population, with the Catholic population the majority of the city's 95,716 church members, with 67,176 in 1890. Declining African American adherence to the Roman Catholic faith led to the creation of the archdiocese's first all–African American church, St. Katherine's, in 1895. Segregation was on the march even in the previously integrated areas before God.

Though segregation by law in the post-Reconstruction South would not take its most iniquitous and ubiquitous form until the early twentieth century, in Louisiana and elsewhere, there was a trend in this direction as early as the 1880s. The leading sector of public accommodation segregation was not the schools. It was public transportation, when states began to pass laws separating passengers on railroads and their urban equivalent, streetcars. It seems an odd place for racism to make its greatest impact, given the more intimate and provocative nature of schooling young children, but the rails were a greater source of tension for white supremacists because of the closeness of the quarters on public cars. Although schools were built in neighborhoods that were segregated by custom, the daily commute, the jaunt to amusement sites, and the regular business of navigating travel in this period necessitated a mixing of peoples.

In addition, segregation by sex—the presence of "lady cars" occurred alongside the arrival of the star cars for African Americans—presented white supremacists with the unpalatable prospect of white women unaccompanied by male escorts (nonladies, in other words) being forced into integrated male cars. The concern of the white supremacists was that African American men would interact in any way with white women as equals. Victorian attitudes toward women combined with racism to create a combustible reaction to such thoughts.

Although segregated in theaters and excluded from restaurants and hotels, African Americans rode railroad, trolley, and trolley-bus cars. This forced an intimacy between the races. The response of whites to mixed seating and service was a series of planned and unplanned attacks on black riders. Some of these attacks led to litigation. The violence the white supremacists and would-be segregators accused black men of committing in these settings was almost always in fact instigated by whites against African Americans, as in the case of so-called race riots. In effect, in demanding the segregation of public transportation, segregationists were engaging in the heckler's veto, wherein free speech is curbed because hecklers make it impossible for the speaker to continue. Legislation mandating separation based on these incidents conceded either that white aggression toward blacks could not be contained or that law enforcement agencies could not be trusted to distinguish instigators from victims. Perhaps it was a combination of both.

Although race played its part in the violence on the streetcars, Gilded Age American cities were violent places. New Orleans streets were an example. The 1880s saw several gun battles on the streets of the Crescent City, often involving members of the municipal constabulary on both sides. The most notable of these involved the future police superintendent, David Hennessy, whose own colorful murder would lead to the roundup of several hundred Italian immigrants, and, upon some of their acquittals at trial, the largest lynching in American history in 1891 and anti-Italian immigrant riots.

Arson was as common as mayhem, and the volunteer firefighters had their hands full with the literally combustible city. Odd though it may seem for a city next to the Mississippi, they often could not get the water pressure they needed to suppress the flames. Adding to their difficulty were the iron shutters on almost all windows, locked from the inside to prevent break-ins. Crowbars and axes were of no use in getting access to a burning building. The firemen had to wait for the fire to collapse the roof in order to douse it from neighboring rooftops.

Politics in the city offered its own version of rough and tumble. The paralysis in the city's politics caused by the suppression of the Republican Party led to the Democratic organization's monopoly on power, locally known as the Ring. Like political machines in other large U.S. cities, the Ring doled out contracts and positions in government to their supporters in exchange for their rounding up votes. Sometimes a reform ticket would prevail, only to run out of steam when it came up against natural disasters, downturns in the economy, or simply the limits of trying to run a major metropolis with little to no help from the state or professional city workers.

Although Redemption had ended the Republican majority in Louisiana, New Orleans still sent African Americans to the legislature, the Republicans were still a force to be reckoned with, and Louisiana still gave, albeit begrudgingly, civil rights to its African American population. These Republicans retained their commitments to using state government to foster industry, commerce, and economic development throughout the state, as well as their ebbing commitment to civil rights. In 1890, this took the form of favoring the rechartering of the Louisiana Lottery Company, though not all Republicans saw the merits of the scheme. Oddly enough, it was this issue that possibly led to the passage of the separate car bill as part of yet one more complicated maneuver of partisan politics.

———

The Lottery Company began its life in Reconstruction Louisiana as a way to raise money for the continuously money-starved state. Under its twenty-five-year charter, the company kicked back money to the state, and allegedly some amount to its sponsors, by running a lottery out of the state that gained a nationwide market. However, the Lottery Company's activities provided perfect tinder for the Democrats to once more promote themselves as the party of "good government."

They found allies in Louisiana's more fervent religious sects. Religious groups in Louisiana were undergoing their own revival of fervor, and the sin of gambling was high on their list of proscribed activities. Although this was not the height of religious revivals that swept the nation in the 1870s, fundamentalist Christianity was in the midst of forming its powerful critique of the modern, industrial, technologically sophisticated world. This crusade against the moral bankruptcy of this scientific age would eventually lead to bans on the teaching of evolution, alcohol in the form of the wider prohibition movement, and Sunday closing laws, among other pieces of legislation. They had already given their support to Anthony Comstock's crusade against "obscene" literature. The successful federal law that resulted from this effort, the eponymous Comstock Act of 1873, with Comstock's considerable machinations, managed to not only ban literature like *Lady Chatterly's Lover*, but also all medical literature relating to sexual matters, including contraception. The Lottery Company incurred similar objections as a source of sin and iniquity.

As a result of a federal lawsuit, *Louisiana State Lottery v. John Fitzpatrick et al.*, in 1879, the lottery had managed to avoid its abolition on the grounds that such abolition would have been an unconstitutional impairment of its contract with the state. However, the state constitution of that year abolished the company's monopoly and set its charter to expire in 1895. Thanks in part to a spate of good publicity from the company's donation of hundreds of thousands of dollars that year to help repair levees along the Mississippi in a particularly bad flood year, one of the lottery company's major supporters, John A. Morris, thought it possible to gain renewal of the company's charter through a constitutional referendum. Morris was from Jersey City, New Jersey, and had moved to Louisiana after he married a local heiress. Better known for building the nation's first loop track for horses in Westchester, New York, Morris was a summa cum laude graduate of Harvard and a shrewd businessman. But on this occasion he had badly miscalculated.

His proposal set off a firestorm of controversy. The legislature divided into pro- and antilottery factions, with the pro side commanding substantial majorities amid charges of payoffs and deal making on both sides. The prolottery forces argued that the legislation was democratic because it gave voters the choice of whether to renew the company's charter. The antilottery forces aligned with Governor Nicholls's message at the beginning of the session that the lottery was a degrading influence on the state. Though the vote had to be delayed several times because one or another member came down sick, the house, then senate passed the bill by the necessary two-thirds majorities. Reportedly, Republican and African American votes from New Orleans were critical components of these majorities.

Governor Nicholls, now serving his second nonconsecutive term as governor, seemingly had the last word when he vetoed the bill and the prolottery forces could not muster the same majorities to override. Nicholls was a Confederate war veteran and had lost limbs at the battles of Winchester and Chancellorsville. He did not lack courage when it came to political battles either. He declared that "at no time and under no circumstances will I permit one of my hands to aid in degrading what the other was lost in seeking to uphold . . . the honor of my native State." Bearing in mind that Southern gentlemen like Nicholls still clung to the prewar notion of honor, Nicholls's somewhat overheated language reflected his conception of himself as much as his desire to retain his office. He would not budge.

But the prolottery forces had one card still left to play. Arguing that a referendum on a constitutional amendment did not require the governor's signature, the lottery attorneys took the matter into Louisiana courts, suing the state secretary of state, L. F. Mason. In the case of *State ex rel John A. Morris v. L. F. Maxon, Secretary of State*, the Louisiana Supreme Court agreed with Morris. The referendum would go to the voters in 1892. Voters defeated the referendum, and the company lost its charter.

At the same time the lottery legislation was making its way through the Louisiana legislature, another proposal was also making the rounds. Representative Joseph Saint Amant of Ascension Parish, just outside of Baton Rouge, introduced a separate car bill. There is considerable debate over the genesis of this proposal; Amant and the bill's supporters left few clues in the official record of the debates or in the newspapers about their intention. When the bill passed on the last day of the session in June, only its detractors made considerable noise about its requirement that black passengers sit in separate cars, no matter the ticket they purchased.

———

Why did Amant introduce this popular measure at that time? What were his reasons? One group of historians sees its genesis and ultimate passage as revenge against the prolottery Republicans, among whom African Americans, mostly from New Orleans, still voted. Their votes on the lottery were decisive, but they were outnumbered when it came to the question of race. These historians point to the fact that the separate car bill got stuck in the senate without the required supermajority to pass until the prolottery forces engineered their constitutional referendum. This otherwise attractive thesis neglects to explain the large majorities in both the senate and lower house that favored it, as well as the fact that Amant introduced it long before the lottery debate began in earnest.

Another group of historians point to ever-increasing railroad travel and urbanization that went hand in hand with the New South's integration into the national economy. Segregation was already custom. Now, in bits and pieces, state by state, lawmakers sought to make the custom into law. While some historians emphasized the growth of Jim Crow segregation after *Plessy*, there can be no denying that Tennessee in 1881, Florida in 1887, Mississippi in 1888, and Texas in 1890 had all passed separate car laws before the Louisiana legislature's action, and Alabama, South Carolina, Georgia, North Carolina, Virginia, and Oklahoma would soon follow with their own.

Although these enactments were often ineffective and irregularly enforced, they showed a growing purpose among Southern states to segregate, despite (or perhaps in reaction to) legal challenges from African American plaintiffs like Ida B. Wells and others in Tennessee. These lawsuits relied on the common-law doctrine of common carriers. Operators of conveyances for hire had special obligations of care for their passengers, based on laws and legal precedents going back to England in the eighteenth century. The American lawsuits were for damages, and unlike suits under the Civil Rights Act of 1875, which limited damages to $500, suits at common law could yield extensive compensatory judgments. Unfortunately for African American litigants, judges and witnesses (who referred to them as "darkeys" and "niggers" in the legal record) were not likely to award them any kind of damages, even for the frequent and sometimes horrific injuries they suffered at the hands of conductors who were either required or had decided to enforce segregation laws and customs.

In one of the many ironies that would surround the *Plessy* case, it is possible the Tennessee law of 1881 was an attempt to do right by African Americans who had purchased first-class tickets but who were being shunted into second-class or smoking cars by conductors or other passengers. Because the smoking cars were foul, unpleasant places where crude and abusive behavior was commonplace, it is understandable why the Tennessee legislature would have felt they were enhancing black ridership rather than demeaning it. In any case, the law provided that "all railroad companies located and operated in this State shall furnish separate cars, or portions of cars cut off by partition walls, in which all colored passengers who pay first class passenger rates of far, may have the privilege to enter and occupy." Further, it commanded that "such apartments shall be kept in good repair, and with the same conveniences, and subject to the same rules governing other first class cars, preventing smoking and obscene language."

It is also possible that the Tennessee lawmakers had less benevolent motives. The state had repealed its common law of carriers provisions in retaliation for the passage of the Civil Rights Act of 1875. The Tennessee supreme court upheld the separate car law and rejected Ida B. Wells's lawsuit under the guise of the "equal accommodations" in *Chesapeake, Ohio, and Southwestern Railroad Co. v. Wells* in 1887.

Attempts to fight this national trend led to the formation of one of the nation's first African American rights groups in Washington, D.C. In February 1890, the American Citizens' Equal Rights Association (ACERA), with P. B. S. Pinchback as its first president, was born. Like the Southern Leadership Conference in the mid-twentieth century, ACERA also had strong religious ties, personified in this case by Joseph C. Price, a Methodist minister, founder of Livingstone College and leader of the Afro-American League (AAL). Unfortunately competition between the two groups undermined their effectiveness. Both organizations were moribund by 1892.

While the civil rights groups met, racial segregation was spreading throughout the English-speaking world. Ubiquitous racist writings in the guise of science were widely read and respected in England and its African and Asian colonies. On June 7, 1893, a train conductor forcibly ejected a well-dressed attorney recently admitted to the bar in Britain from a train in Pietermaritzburg, South Africa, because a white passenger had complained about the dark-skinned attorney's presence in a first-class car. Mohandas K. Gandhi's first-class ticket did not protect him from being classified as a coolie and from receiving third-class treatment. After his luggage unceremoniously followed him onto the train platform, he reflected upon his condition as he shivered in the South African winter. In his memoir recounting the incident, the future leader of India's independence movement determined that his personal "hardship was superficial" and "only a symptom of the deep disease of colour prejudice." His inspired leadership for individual rights regardless of color or caste and ultimately successful fight for Indian independence was thus an example for the U.S. civil rights movement under Dr. Martin Luther King, among others, and gained international acclaim. Segregation was international in scope, and so was the spread of the fight against it.

But not at first, and not in the federal courts. For Louisiana was watching when the U.S. Supreme Court decided *Louisville, New Orleans, & Texas Railway Company v. Mississippi* (1890), upholding Mississippi's separate car law as a legitimate exercise of authority, even though it covered an interstate railway. Mississippi passed its law in 1888, and because Mississippi was a neighboring state, Louisiana's newspapers covered the passage of the law. The Mississippi law's first section contained the language soon to spread throughout the South. It was duplicated in Louisiana's version: "That all railroads carrying passengers in this State (other than street railroads) shall provide equal, but separate, accommodation for the white and colored races, by providing two or more passenger cars for each passenger train, or by dividing the passenger cars by a partition, so as to secure separate accommodations." "Equal, but separate" was the key phrase Mississippi used to meet constitutional challenges, though in this court case, Mississippi's law was being challenged by the railroad as a violation of the exclusive right of the national government to regulate interstate commerce.

If Louisiana legislators had not considered it before, they now had ample information not only on what Mississippi was doing, but that the U.S. Supreme Court was open to such laws' constitutionality. The Louisville Railroad case precedent differed from an earlier decision on this very issue, *Hall v. DeCuir.* This Louisiana case stemmed from a challenge under Louisiana law to a steamboat company that was discriminating against African American passengers. The U.S. Supreme Court declared the Louisiana nondiscrimination law for steamboat travel a violation of the exclusive right to regulate interstate commerce the U.S. Constitution assigned to the U.S. Congress. Now, in the Louisville case, the Court allowed a state to segregate on an interstate railroad. Why did the interstate commerce clause confer exclusive jurisdiction to Congress for steamboats, but not railroads?

Navigable waters were long considered federal highways, but so were rails that crossed state boundaries. The Court, in effect, had given the green light for such laws, at least with regards to interstate commerce challenges. Whether they were valid against Thirteenth and/or Fourteenth Amendment claims by an African American defendant had yet to be determined.

As a result, the Mississippi law in *Louisville* was an influential precedent, although it was not widely cited. Instead, it would be the Louisiana law that led to the foremost challenge to Jim Crow transportation laws. Given the spread of segregation throughout the nation by 1890, one may wonder why New Orleans became the source of so much antisegregation agitation, then mass action, then litigation. The answer lies in several important areas of consideration. First and foremost, as many an interested traveler reported, rigid race segregation did not occur uniformly and in all areas. According to former colonel Thomas Wentworth Higginson, a participant in John Brown's raid and leader of African American troops during the war, "a condition of outward peace prevailed" in the states of the Atlantic seaboard in 1878. A year later, Sir George Campbell, a member of the British parliament, reported much the same on the railroads he examined: "The humblest black rides with the proudest white on terms of perfect equality, and without the smallest symptom of malice or dislike on either side." As late as 1885, T. McCants Steward, an African American from South Carolina living in Boston, explored the region expecting the worst, but found to his pleasant surprise, "I think the whites of the South are really less afraid to [have] contact with colored people than the whites of the North." Though he had trouble getting service at times, he was able to eat and stay in the same places as whites.

These reports show the immense variety of the African American experience during this time. While some slept in fear of a lynch mob, others mingled with whites without concern. It should also be noted there were as many different African American experiences as there were regions of the South: rural and urban, Deep South and Upper South, commercial and agricultural, cosmopolitan and parochial—all had different conditions prevailing at any given time.

Recent scholarship has also complicated any attempt to generalize African American responses to segregation. Resistance did come from the middle class and the working class, from men and women. In New York City in the 1850s, for example, African Americans brought lawsuits and engaged in mass agitation against segregated streetcars. Although courts were occasionally favorable forums in which to bring civil suits for injuries sustained when conductors were violent, such as the Elizabeth Jennings case in New York City, large-scale progress did not occur until after the war had made racial segregation more odious. After the war, African Americans like Ida B. Wells fought, sometimes literally, to keep their seats, while others avoided what was an increasingly dangerous activity, fearful of the white mobs that could gather without any fear of prosecution. Though streetcars and railroads were common carriers subject to the higher common law of common carriers standard, they were often able to avoid liability for such conduct. Segregation by law was an entirely different matter.

———

New Orleans' participation in antiracist litigation had a unique quality in the richly diverse heritage of the city. Leadership came from the well-educated, relatively better-off Afro-Creoles, whose proud heritage still set them, in their own minds, apart from blacks. In response to the efforts of white supremacists to lump all African Americans together, these men and women strove for a color-blind society. They wanted to preserve their own identity, rather than be immersed in the alien one and seemingly artificial one of colored or Negro. Their contributions to the civil rights heritage of Louisiana cannot be understated. After all, they had contributed the public rights language to the Louisiana constitution of 1868. Most important of all, their syncretic heritage made them the embodiment of a society without distinctions based on race. However, the tide carrying the Separate Car Act would make no such distinctions.

When the separate car law proposal first appeared in May 1890, Pinchback encouraged the formation of a state branch of ACERA to fight it. This branch restricted its membership to African Americans; it gained immensely in popularity as it made its crusade against the proposal known. It did this through two newspapers that themselves represented a divide among those targeted by the would-be law. The

Southwestern Christian Advocate, under the leadership of its fiery editor, Methodist minister A. P. E. Albert, spoke for the non-Creole black Methodist community. The *Daily Crusader*, under the editorship of Louis Martinet, spoke for the Afro-Creoles.

Martinet was an exceptional person by any standard. He was the eldest of five children born to a Belgian and his Louisiana bride. With a law degree from Straight College, he was extraordinarily active in his community. Besides editing the *Crusader*, he was a notary public, an important official under Louisiana law, a member of the board of directors of Southern University, and an occasional lecturer on anatomy at the medical school. His wife, Lenora, was principal of a high school, and they had two children, though one would die in childhood. New Orleans was still a dangerous place for the young. From this position of leadership, Martinet would play a critical role in the opposition to segregation. For now, he left matters in other hands.

In a memorial entered into the *Official Journal of the House of Representatives of the State of Louisiana*, ACERA made a forceful argument against passage of the separate car bill. It declared: "That such legislation is unconstitutional, un-American, unjust, dangerous, and against sound public policy." The un-Christian law allowed an unfounded prejudice to make distinctions between citizens. "Citizenship is national and has no color," the memorial continued. Further, the separate car law was poor policy, more likely to incite bad behavior contrary to its stated aim of providing for "the comfort of passengers on railroad trains." The probable result was that it would give "a free license to the evilly-disposed that they might with impunity insult, humiliate and otherwise maltreat inoffensive persons, and especially women and children who should happen to have a dark skin." Paternalism was alive in every segment of the city, though the ACERA use of it here must be taken with a grain of salt, so dismissive were white supremacists of the feelings and welfare of black women.

ACERA described the separate car bill as both class and caste legislation. Both terms, in separate ways, correctly depicted the effect the law would have on the black community. Well-to-do blacks would have to ride with poor blacks. Color was the mark of caste—the only mark that mattered. The memorial stated that South Carolina and Texas had recently decided not to enact such laws. In this, the memorial erred. Those laws were en route. Despite this optimistic reading of the situation, ACERA concluded the petition hopefully: "We humbly trust that our protest may be heeded by the loyal hearts of our legislators, and that the chalice of political bitterness may be snatched from the grasp of intolerant persecution and made to melt into the sacred fires of patriotic mercy!" Their memorial was passionate, full of religious language, and appealed for a reliance on higher principles. Even if a more pragmatic course of action would have been more effective, they certainly did not lack for high hopes.

There were two speeches in the house against the law recorded in the legislative file papers. C. F. Brown cited the presence of "thousands of colored men in this State, who have labored hard, accumulated property, raised up a family of children, educated them, and they share equal the duties and responsibility in maintaining the government of this State." Either he was being defensive about the subjects of the bill, or he inadvertently admitted that they should only care about people if they were the best of citizens. He also conceded, "We are not appealing to you for social equality, but we are asking for equal rights before the laws of the land, which every other nationality enjoys who sees fit to tramp into this country, and are never questioned in regard to their standing before their advent." Hopes for a nondiscriminatory society that provided equal opportunity had faded since Reconstruction. Its pale substitute—equal treatment before the law—was the new goal.

Representative Victor Rochon took a more sophisticated line against the bill. He listed the main ways it violated the Louisiana constitution, predicting the Louisiana supreme court would void it. Then he cast aspersions on the intent of the white supremacists: "Can there be, Mr. Speaker, any legislation spread upon the statutes of Louisiana, that will cast the odium of pariahism upon the colored people of this State more than this bill?" He did not elaborate on why separating the two populations would be a wrong. Actually, he reinforced the idea there were two separate races when he mentioned the services "rendered by our people to the whites of Louisiana" back to the War of 1812. The most holistic and thus potent attack on the bill—its forcible classification of people into two different groups on completely fabricated grounds—did not appear in these two orations. Perhaps the two members of the house did not believe the argument would be persuasive, or perhaps they too had accepted the essentialism of race.

Justification for the law came from a *New Orleans Times Democrat* editorial denying that discrimination was harmful: "The Southern whites, in no spirit of hostility to the negroes, have insisted that the two races shall live separate and distinct from each other in all things," it stated. Then, contradicting himself, the editor pointed out, "They would rise to-morrow against the proposition to educate the white and black children together; and they resist any intercourse in theatre, hotel or elsewhere that will bring the race into anything like social intercourse." The law needed to separate the races because whites could not be trusted to act peacefully if it were otherwise. One of the key pillars of society in the South was that the government had to act badly, or mobs would act much worse. It came down to an inability, and behind it an unwillingness, to properly police its population.

The Louisiana senate did not debate the bill. Only senators Cage, Soniat, Henry, and Demas explained their votes. Soniat's was by far the most colorful. He objected to the bill because "it fails to exclude low white people of the worst possible stamp, and the Chinese, both more obnoxious than most colored persons." He also believed that "there is now no appreciable friction between the races, and it can serve no useful purpose to provoke it." Racism underlay both points, or at least the assumption that there were fundamental differences between people based on perceptions of race. Last, in contradiction to his earlier points, he argued it should not limit segregation to just railroads, but to all common carriers within the state.

The house, whose consideration of the bill took up just a few days in May and June, was more deliberate. Its members amended Amant's original proposal by adding an exception for black nurses of white children, making the criminal penalties specific instead of vague prohibitions, and rejected two proposals to include "Malays" and "mongolians" to the list of those to be separated from whites. With these minor changes, the bill passed on June 4, 1890, by a vote of 56 to 23, with 15 absentees. A representative named Harris voiced his disappointment that only colored people were separated out. He would have preferred the law exclude "Chinamen and Dagoes, which classes I consider not as desirable citizens as the colored people."

The senate provided a greater obstacle as it required a supermajority for approval. Initially, it failed by a vote of 15 to 13 on July 8. On July 9, thanks to the efforts of a Senator Hampton from Calcasieu, the senate voted on whether to reconsider the bill. Senator Demas registered his objections. "Twenty-five years ago this bill might have worked, but now, when you have erected colleges for the education of the Negroes, and educated them, for God's sake let these poor people alone." After all, he concluded, "There are some 50,000,000 of white people and 8,000,000 of Negroes in the United States, and you are bound to have white supremacy." These arguments failed, and the senate moved to reconsider by a vote of 17 to 9. The following day, the senate passed the bill 23 to 6. That vote came on July 10, after the lottery fracas had run its course. The bill quickly received Governor Nicholls's approval despite his promises of conciliation and respect for nondiscrimination, and became Act No. 111 in the general statutes of Louisiana.

Like the Mississippi legislators from whom they borrowed the language of the act, the Louisiana lawmakers had taken their cue from other pieces of segregation law that had been upheld in federal circuit courts. Those decisions all turned on the use of the word *equal.* As long as they used that keyword in laws discriminating between people on the basis of race, they could claim compliance with the Fourteenth Amendment's equal protection clause. If it had ever existed, the idea was now gone that any kind of discrimination based on a prohibited category, whether adverse or not, was prohibited.

The reliance on the single word, conceived in its legal form, diverted attention from the fact of discrimination, for in fact equal did not describe the separate cars. The shift from de facto conditions to de jure abstractions was a maneuver that the courts, upholding the act, would duplicate. In the *Plessy* case, the state courts and the U.S. Supreme Court would not consider the fact of equality so long as the state's counsel reported that the law contained the word *equal.* One might excuse the courts' willful disinterest in facts under the taught-law doctrine that appeals courts did not concern themselves with facts, but in historical fact, this rule of law was often disregarded. In case after case heard before Reconstruction and the Gilded Age state supreme appeals courts and the U.S. Supreme Court, facts mattered to the justices in economic regulation cases but not in civil rights cases. Some facts, one must conclude, were more judicially cognizable than others. When the fact implicated a question of private property, it mattered. When the fact related to a question of racial discrimination, it did not matter.

The relative absence of a record of legislative intent in the passage of the Separate Car Act also affected litigation against it. When those challenging a law had only the bare language of the law to go on, who could tell what the real purpose of the lawgiver might be? The transfer of attention away from the actual effect of discrimination on its victims to a mere de jure examination of whether the law provided for equality, denied opponents of the law critical evidence of how they suffered. It was a disadvantage to potential litigation that only massive fact gathering and a change in racial attitudes could, and nearly fifty years later would, overcome.

———

The editorial in the *Crusader* on July 19, 1890, nine days after the Separate Car Act became law, lamented the occurrence and theorized that the opposition movement had misplayed its hand: "It is now seen that the only safe course to have defeated the bill was the one pointed out by *The Crusader*—that the colored members refrained from voting on the Lottery proposition until the car bill was dead." They could have used their vital votes as bargaining chips to kill the separate car bill in exchange for voting to kill the lottery.

In pieces by R. L. Desdunes and Paul Trevigne in the same issue, the authors guessed that the Separate Car Act was revenge on the prolottery African American legislators and the population they represented. Trevigne stated unequivocally, "Its passage was due to a spirit of retaliation against the colored members of the Legislature, who had voted for the lottery bill." However, he was hopeful that the law would not stand. He cited initial objections to the first railroad in England: "Opposition to the laws of progress will always prove futile." The segregation law was bound to be repudiated. "The world will move and the locomotive too, even if the cow be on the track." Trevigne was a teacher, educated overseas at the Catholic School for

Indigent Orphans, also known as the Couvent School. The Couvent was a center for the Creole community. Homer A. Plessy, among others, received his education there.

Desdunes suggested a boycott of the railroads: "Let us learn at once that we should not feed the hand that smites us." Another law graduate of Southern University, Desdunes was on the metropolitan police force when White Leaguers attacked it and killed eleven of their number in 1874. A boycott would work in the 1950s when black riders used it to protest segregated bus seating in Montgomery, Alabama. But that was in the future. Whether it would have been effectual or not, the two legislators' advice was now irrelevant. The movement for genuinely equal treatment had suffered a defeat.

With the demise of ACERA after its failure to rally the legislature against the Separate Car Act, as Rodolphe L. Desdunes recalled years later in his *Our People and Our History*, he and his community knew they were fighting a lost cause in opposing segregation: "It was necessary to resist this state of affairs, even with no hope of success in sight." The major moving force behind this resistance movement was Aristide Mary, then seventy years old and a veteran of many failed crusades, including his own nomination for governor in 1872. After announcing their intentions on September 5, 1891, he and Desdunes organized a committee, whose name was French, reflecting the group's exclusivity: the Comité des Citoyens. In addition to Mary and the newspaper editor, Paul Trevigne, it included Arthur Esteves, president; C. Antoine, vice president; Firmin Christophe, secretary; G. G. Johnson, undersecretary; L. A. Martinet, the founder of the *Daily Crusader*; and R. L. Desdunes himself. Their formation and call for aid in a document they entitled "An Appeal," the self-titled "Citizens' Committee for the Annulment of Act No. 111 Commonly Known as the Separate Car Law" sought a national response. Their language suggests the urgency of the cause as well as their strident commitment to it: "No further time should be lost. We should make a definite effort to resist legally the operation of the Separate Car Act. This obnoxious measure is the concern of all our citizens who are opposed to caste legislation and its consequent injustices and crimes." From the organization's very start, they sought victory in the courts: "At all events, it is the imperative duty of oppressed citizens to seek redress before the judicial tribunals of the country. In our case, we find it is the only means left us. We must have recourse to it, or sink into a state of hopeless inferiority."

According to Desdunes's history, the committee was able to raise sufficient funds to support a lawsuit. Although it cannot be substantiated, Desdunes claimed friends in high places: "Among the eminent men who responded to our call, we may cite with pride the Honorable Albion W. Tourgée and John M. Harlan—one, an outspoken champion of black people; the other, one of the nine judges of the United States Supreme Court." Tourgée was a lawyer already committed to racial equality. But if Justice John Marshall Harlan (the only likely member of the Court to support the committee) had given some sign of his support other than his dissent in the *Civil Rights Cases*, he was skirting the fine line between being an impartial jurist and an interested party in the case. Harlan did not recuse himself, so it is possible his support (if Desdunes wrote the truth) was not sufficient to raise an ethical question.

Most of the Afro-Creoles, including those who resided in the Faubourg Tremé section of New Orleans, were much like Homer A. Plessy, skilled or semiskilled laborers trying to prosper as best they could. Plessy in many ways was typical. He was variously listed as a clerk, a warehouse worker, and an insurance collector in addition to his occupation at the time of the litigation: shoe repair and shoemaker. By 1902, he was counted merely as a laborer, evidence that he shared the fortune of many a skilled worker in industrializing America: deskilling.

Plessy was twenty-nine when the litigation began, and Desdunes confined Plessy to the status of one whom the committee had employed for the purpose of getting arrested, giving him the name Homere, though all the legal documents used Homer. There is some evidence confuting this lowly characterization as a pawn of his betters. Plessy was a Freemason and vice president of a benevolent society formed in 1887 called the New Amis Sincère (Sincere or Earnest or Loyal Friends or Companions) dedicated to educational causes. Plessy might well have been an activist in his own right even if the committee had not tapped him to ride the train.

The committee also depended on donations from the wider black community. By late October, most of the $1,400 they would raise came from skilled labor organizations like the Société des Artisans, the cigar makers' NCR Club, the Bricklayers' Union, and the Mechanics' Social Club. Civic organizations in New Orleans also gave money to support the cause, including the Le Silence Benevolent Association and the Creole of Color chapter of the Masons. Women and their organizations, some from outside New Orleans, also gave to the cause.

Although many of these organizations existed before the Civil War, many more demonstrated the organizational trend in American life in the postwar period. This flowering of professional groups, accrediting bodies, and labor societies played a substantial role in shaping America into the professionalized, bureaucratized society we know today. Many theorists call this conglomeration of private groups the civil society—a vital part of the public sphere, but noncoercive because they are not instruments of government.

———

Now that they had raised the money, the committee needed to select attorneys to conduct their test case. Again, the test case was a legal strategy that owed its origins to the intricacies of the common law. Oftentimes, the common law courts did not allow simple declaratory lawsuits. There had to be a contest over an issue for which there was redress in the courts. As a result, litigants often arranged a suit between themselves in order to have the court hear the case, but only so they could receive a ruling on the specific underlying issue that concerned them, like who owned what, whether there was legal title to an item, or even the status of one of the persons involved. Test cases had evolved from these fabricated suits into an accepted kind of lawsuit. One of the most important U.S. Supreme Court cases of its day, *Fletcher v. Peck* (1810), was such a semicollusive test case.

Test cases could involve the overturning of statutes. When courts adopted the doctrine of judicial review—that is, holding a statute up to the text of a constitution to determine whether it was constitutional—they set themselves up as the final arbiter of the meaning of the constitution. The case incontestably establishing judicial review in the federal courts under the U.S. Constitution was *Marbury v. Madison* (1803), although earlier state cases and *Hylton v. U.S.* (1796)

had broached the doctrine that courts had the final say on the meaning of fundamental law.

In the years after the Civil War, the U.S. Supreme Court exercised this authority with increasing regularity on both state and federal enactments concerning such diverse issues as civil rights, voting, criminal prosecutions, and the income tax. Some of these lawsuits were naturally occurring challenges to laws that affected the defendants or plaintiffs. Others were arrests arranged to establish a legal argument as law. Susan B. Anthony's trial in 1873 for casting her ballot in the 1872 election was a failed attempt at a test case to establish women's right to vote, but it did not go past the trial stage. Like the litigants in *Plessy*, the woman's suffrage movement did succeed in getting a test case, then proceeded to get an adverse decision from the U.S. Supreme Court in the case of *Minor v. Happersett* in 1874. There is no evidence particularly linking the Plessy litigation and the woman's rights litigation, but their parties' intent indicates they at least stemmed from a commonly understood tradition.

The committee determined that local attorney James Campbell Walker would handle the litigation in Louisiana. Walker was born on January 24, 1837, and fought in the Civil War on the Confederate side. After the war, he became a lawyer serving the Republicans, notably in the election dispute of 1876, before a falling out returned him to private practice. Known to all as Judge Walker from a spell on the bench, by the time of Plessy's trial, he was fifty-seven years old and married with seven children. He was the committee's second choice for local counsel. Their first choice, T. J. Semmes, had wanted $2,500 to do the case. Walker only wanted $1,000. The committee went with Walker.

The committee wanted a cocounsel of national stature and decided to ask Albion W. Tourgée. Albion Winegar Tourgée was born on May 2, 1838, in the New Englander–settled area of Ohio known as the Western Reserve—"a hotbed of abolitionism," according to Tourgée's most recent biography. When the Civil War broke out, he quit his studies at the University of Rochester and joined the 27th New York Infantry. He was shot in the spine at the First Battle of Bull Run and suffered from a temporary paralysis as a result, but he managed to recuperate sufficiently to rejoin the war as a first lieutenant in the 105th Ohio Volunteer Infantry. He ended his military service in December 1863 after participating in the battles of Chickamauga and Chattanooga. On his return to Ohio, he married Emma Doiska Kilbourne, a union that would produce their only child, a daughter.

At the conclusion of the war, Tourgée sought out opportunity consistent with his abolitionist commitment to a new nation based on equal rights by settling in Greensboro, North Carolina. He also hoped its milder climate would be better suited to recuperation from his lingering battlefield ailments. Finding himself in the midst of that war-torn state's internal civil war over race, postslavery adjustments, and the arrival of the Republican Party, he began a law practice. Tourgée's philosophy was one of radical individualism: a belief in the existence of races and racial differences, but a commitment to the idea that those differences did not matter. This stemmed from a deeply held Christian view that all men were God's creatures and entitled to pursue their lives free from prejudice or discrimination. Like the vast majority of abolitionists after the war, Tourgée believed it was his mission to arouse the public by moral suasion, rational arguments, and provocative language. His intemperate style resulted from this combustible mix of righteous certainty and urgency. He could not be dissuaded by compromise, political expediency, or hostile reactions.

In Greensboro, Tourgée's law practice income was supplemented by work for the Congressional Reconstruction's state government. He participated prominently in North Carolina's constitutional convention in 1868, served as a superior court judge from 1868 to 1874, and was a member of the constitutional convention of 1875. After an unsuccessful run for Congress in 1878, he published the work that made his name, *A Fool's Errand, by One of the Fools*, a fictionalized account of his experiences in North Carolina, in 1879. His tale of struggle against Klan violence, bigotry, and human folly made it a national best seller. When the Redemption government's toleration of hostility toward him and his family became apparent, and with his legal practice finished by bad investments, he moved back north to Mayville, New York, near the Chautauqua Institute.

There he continued to write about and advocate for what he labeled a "color-blind" law and society. It was in this vein that he came to the attention of the committee. In his regular column on race and the law, "A Bystander's Notes," for the *Daily Inter-Ocean*, a Republican paper in Chicago, he called for opposition to the Louisiana law segregating railroad cars. If this and his novels, writings, and organizing were not enough, Tourgée had been instrumental in the campaign against lynching, a practice that had spread to his native Ohio. The law against lynching he helped author demonstrated the effectiveness of such legal tactics, at least in Republican-leaning Ohio. Considering that Ohio had taken the lead in segregating before the Civil War and opposed the adoption of the Fourteenth Amendment, this was a considerable accomplishment.

But when the committee approached him, Tourgée was no longer practicing law. He had no appreciable experience in appellate litigation. He was an advocate for a cause, but largely for his conscience and public opinion's sake. Nevertheless, the committee sought his advice, then his services, which the dedicated crusader took on without charge.

It is plain from the correspondence between Louis A. Martinet and Tourgée that the latter was to be the senior member of the legal team. In a letter dated October 5, 1891, Martinet wrote to Tourgée at his home in New York, "You will be the leading counsel & select your own associate. We know we have a friend in you & we know your ability is beyond question." He added for good measure, "Local counsel too will have to conform to your views." In this same extensive communication, Martinet referred to the idea of having a person who could pass as white be the defendant as presenting a problem, because "there are the strangest white people you ever saw here." Though Tourgée and the committee were thinking along similar lines, Tourgée's experience in North Carolina could not have prepared him adequately for the situation in New Orleans, where making distinctions on the basis of color was as troublesome as maintaining the levees.

———

The committee needed to select their future defendant carefully to suit their purposes. Correspondence between Martinet and Tourgée shows that Martinet was reluctant to put himself forward and wary of Tourgée's suggestion that they use a woman. Whether from gallantry, genuine concern, or prejudice, they ultimately did not follow through with this intriguing possibility. A woman defendant would not have been subject to the "danger to white women" line of attack and might have been able to take advantage of the Victorian-era sensibilities of the male judiciary. Although the Victorian-era prejudices held women to be inferior to men in every professional and political capacity, the flip side of this sexism was a desire to protect women. Additionally, the tradition of segregation had begun with a designation for a ladies' car.

However, a female defendant would not necessarily have worked better even if the committee was not all male and as sexist as any of their era. Although white women were put on a pedestal, African American women received the double prejudice of a racist and sexist society. The case of Elizabeth Jennings's mistreatment by a train car conductor and Ida B. Wells's repeated experiences with segregation was the fact that white men frequently accosted African American women because of their supposedly looser morality. It was the female equivalent of the beastlike renderings of their male counterparts. The more like an animal you were, the more sexual your nature as a person closer to primitivism.

Tourgée and Martinet agreed that Tourgée's plan for a light-skinned man would be best. In language inherited from laws enacted before the Revolution, they determined an octoroon would be best—someone with a great-grandparent who was African American and likely could pass for white. They settled on Daniel Desdunes, the son of one of the committee members, whose ability to pass for white removed any doubt as to the arbitrariness of the law's iniquitous discrimination.

After a long search for a cooperative railroad, the Louisville and Nashville agreed to work with the committee. Their reason was not public-spiritedness, much less a belief in the equality of the races, but rather profit motive. Running entirely separate cars for the very few first-class colored passengers who were likely to board at any given time was a burden they could do without.

The committee decided to have Daniel Desdunes ride an interstate train. In this way, they could also level the charge that the law ran afoul of the interstate commerce power, as implicated in the Louisville Railroad case from Mississippi. On February 24, 1892, Daniel bought his first-class ticket for passage on the Louisville and Nashville Railroad to Mobile, Alabama. He boarded at Canal Street and sat in the whites-only car. By prearrangement, the committee employed two private detectives to aid the conductor in arresting Desdunes. Again, according to the plan, Desdunes identified himself as colored, refused politely to leave his seat, and did not resist his removal to the police station two miles from where he had boarded. Paul Bonseigneur, treasurer for the committee, was there to post his bond.

However, the Louisiana Supreme Court threw a wrench into the lawyers' well-oiled machinery when it decided the case of *State ex rel. Abbott v. Hicks* on May 25, 1892. Relying at least in part on the Louisville Railroad case decision in the U.S. Supreme Court, Louisiana's Supreme Court had thrown out the prosecution of a Texas and Pacific Railway conductor for allowing an African American passenger to sit in a whites-only car. One notes that the beneficiary of their decision was the white conductor. Their specific reasoning is difficult to discern from the case report, but its outcome was not: they preserved the Separate Car Act by declaring that it did not apply to interstate train travel. Fearing that this decision would render their chosen defendant's suit moot, the committee sought out another line of attack.

Thus, while Daniel Desdunes awaited his day in court, Homer Adolph Plessy made his contribution to the cause. His ride was on a railroad that ran wholly within the state, thus making it an entirely different challenge to the Separate Car Act. Once more, the committee set up the transaction carefully. On June 7, 1892, Plessy headed for the number eight train scheduled for a 4:15 P.M. departure to Covington, Louisiana, the end of the line. He boarded at the Press Depot, headquarters for the Eastern Louisiana Railroad, some two miles from his home in Faubourg Tremé. Before the train left the station, the committee's off-duty police detective, Christopher C. Cain, complied with the request of the train's conductor, J. J. Dowling, and arrested Plessy. He then escorted Plessy to the nearby police station, where, just as Desdunes had been, Plessy was booked, then released on bond the committee posted.

There is some disagreement among historians of the case as to how the conductor came to know that Plessy—who, after all, had been chosen because he could pass for white—was a colored man violating the law. This question would return throughout the litigation. According to one account, Plessy stated upon giving his ticket the words he prepared beforehand: "I have to tell you that, according to Louisiana law, I am a colored man." Other accounts claim the conductor asked him, "Are you a colored man?" and Plessy answered in the affirmative. The majority opinion for the Court in *Plessy* noted that Plessy was "of mixed descent, in the proportion of seven eighths Caucasian and one eighth African blood; that the mixture of colored blood was not discernible in him," but gave no details as to how the conductor or the High Court knew Plessy was colored. Indeed, why the detail of proportions of white and colored was a fact important enough to take space in the majority opinion (after all, it did not matter how colored Plessy was for him to have violated the letter of the law), or indeed why this fact, and not other facts about Jim Crow laws, commanded the attention of the High Court, is an important fact to consider. In any case, Louisiana law considered some portion of African ancestry as the definition of colored when color itself did not tell.

Besides leading to the dead-end discussion of how someone could be colored but did not appear to be, this confusion about Plessy's race would be a hurdle for Plessy's counsel to surmount. While the sheer arbitrariness of the law in determining race was of vital importance to their case, the committee and its lawyers could not adequately resolve the dilemma of how to get a person whose appearance would not arouse suspicion arrested on a charge of violating a law that was based almost entirely on appearance. Plessy's self-identification would have been the best solution. However, their failure to have this critical information entered into the record damaged their prospects for challenging racial distinctions on the basis of their vagueness.

Nevertheless, the litigation moved forward. As happens in most test cases, problems revealed themselves as the case unfolded. The committee's attorneys had to navigate the uncharted waters of both criminal and constitutional law in such a way as to maximize their chances for success. How they dealt with this daunting task is the subject of the next chapter.

CHAPTER 3

The Long Road to
the High Court

Litigating a test case was an expensive, difficult, and complex proposition. One had to recruit a defendant who could then appeal the conviction. One also had to arrange a conviction without seeming to resist too mildly. The litigant also had to raise the specific grounds for appeal at all stages of the litigation. His lawyers would have to construct persuasive legal arguments, mastering all of the relevant (and some not so relevant) precedents. These prior decisions, whether hostile or not, had to be either distinguished or analogized to the specific fact pattern of the test case. In *Plessy*, the litigation would not only be time-consuming and difficult, but conducted against a background of hostile case law. It would be an uphill climb.

As the Chinese philosopher Lao Tzu is reputed to have said about undertaking a journey of a thousand leagues, one must proceed step by step. Having secured the arrests of suitable defendants, the committee now had the actual controversy the courts required. Both Plessy and Desdunes were being prosecuted for crimes for which they were subject to criminal penalties: fines of $25, or "in lieu thereof," twenty days in the parish prison. The committee did not want their convictions to be overturned on technicalities in New Orleans. They wanted the case appealed all the way to the U.S. Supreme Court, and they wanted the High Court to strike down the Separate Car Act.

However, the two attorneys disagreed on the best route to take. Louisiana's appellate system was labyrinthine and its procedure complex. Walker doubted very much whether it would even allow for an appeal of such a minor sentence. He recommended seeking a writ objecting to the charge prior to trial. This would mean hearings before a trial court and then a direct appeal to the Louisiana supreme court. Both could be counted on to be hostile to the defendants' attorneys' objections to prosecution based on the argument that the Separate Car Act was unconstitutional.

Tourgée, on the other hand, favored a habeas corpus filing to federal court after trial. Habeas corpus is known as the great writ—one of the foremost and honored legal filings in the common law. The writ challenges detention: the sheriff is told to produce the offender and show cause for the arrest. Because of its common use in federal cases, Tourgée argued that it created the most favorable circumstance for federal review. It might also have been his favored course of action because of his familiarity with it, whereas he had little knowledge of Louisiana's procedures. Tourgée's position as lead counsel forced Walker to concede on this point, at least temporarily.

But Tourgée's understandable refusal to sacrifice his other interests or his health by going to New Orleans to work on the case complicated matters. Walker had to conduct a complex conversation about legal strategy and substantive legal issues by mail. Given that Tourgée's home in Mayville, New York, was far from the hub of any major metropolis, each piece of correspondence took up to a week or more. Despite this obstacle, Walker and Tourgée managed a collaboration that succeeded with the help, and sometimes the unwanted interference, of the committee that hired them. Like most test case subjects, Desdunes and Plessy, the actual defendants and supposed clients, had little say in the situation.

———

On July 9, 1892, Judge John H. Ferguson of section A of the New Orleans criminal court dismissed the charge against Daniel Desdunes. Without a written opinion, Ferguson ruled that the Louisiana supreme court's decision in *Abbott v. Hicks* made the charge unsustainable, essentially granting the defendant's lawyers' plea for dismissal. Though they had failed to overturn the law in court, Martinet wrote Tourgée that the committee was pleased with the outcome. He echoed these sentiments in the July issue of the *Crusader* when he declared, "The Jim Crow car is ditched and will remain in the ditch." A court had ruled that the Separate Car Act could not apply to interstate trains. Actually, the Louisiana supreme court had ruled slightly differently: that the law did not apply to interstate trains. Therefore, in all the ways that mattered, this was a defeat. The law still stood.

Whatever the Louisiana court's ruling on interstate train travel, the committee still had Plessy's case to litigate. Now the questions of race, racial identification, and the contest over fact and law began in earnest. All of the paradoxes of race and racial identification were present. They would have bewildered Solomon, and the Louisiana judges who heard the case were hardly Solomons. That may be forgiven, for the nation was just as bewildered by the indefiniteness of this most definitively applied legal test.

In 1893, Missouri's Mark Twain, already an internationally famous writer, made this problem the centerpiece of his *Pudd'nhead Wilson*. Set in pre–Civil War Missouri, the story culminates in a murder trial where the newfangled technology of fingerprinting causes a remarkable twist. The fingerprints on the murder weapon are those of a man whose fingerprints were taken when he was a baby. The twist comes from the fact that the baby whose fingerprints showed that he was the murderer is revealed to be the bastard son of a wealthy plantation owner and one of his female slaves, Roxy, who was herself the product of several such unions such that she had only one-sixteenth African American ancestry. Roxy had switched the baby after his fingerprinting with his half-brother—the heir—born roughly at the same time. Roxy had wanted a better life for her son, and she had had no trouble pulling off the deception as a result of the imperceptibility of race in her son's appearance.

Because of this revelation, not only is Roxy's son convicted of murder, but his status is switched with his half-brother, who himself has been raised as a slave and has none of the outward behavioral characteristics—education, manners, or speech—of a free man of great wealth. Roxy must see her spoiled son sent downriver to the harshest life imaginable—the very fate she had tried to avoid by the nursery-room switch. In this way, Twain exposed to his 1890s audience the artificiality of the slave versus free distinction based on a concept of race. Both as a reflection of what could pass muster in America in the 1890s and a substantive argument about race, *Pudd'nhead Wilson* supported the committee's central contention that race should not be the basis for any kind of discrimination.

It was not until October 13, 1892, that Assistant District Attorney Lionel Adams arranged for Plessy to be arraigned before the same district judge who had tried Desdunes, John H. Ferguson. Ferguson was a transplant from Massachusetts. Born there in 1837, he studied for and practiced law far from slavery and voted Democratic. At the close of the war, Ferguson heard reports from returning Massachusetts soldiers of the opportunities Northern men could have in the South, in particular New Orleans. Soon after he arrived in his new home, the Yankee from Boston married into a staunchly Unionist family and resumed the practice of law. He aligned himself not with Republicans, however, but with Democrats. When Nicholls first became governor, he arranged for Ferguson to enter the legislature. After one term, Ferguson returned to his legal practice. He reentered public service in June 1892, when Governor Murphy Foster, Nicholls's handpicked successor, rewarded Ferguson with a district judgeship for his many public speeches against the Louisiana Lottery Company. The *Plessy* case was to be his one claim to fame.

With the interstate aspects of the legal arguments now moot, Walker filed a slightly different fourteen-point argument in a plea against the charge against Plessy. Walker sought a write of prohibition—an order to suspend the prosecution of Plessy on the grounds that the Separate Car Act was unconstitutional. Walker's case centered on the violation of Plessy's rights under the U.S. Constitution, specifically the Thirteenth and Fourteenth Amendments. He made sure to mention Plessy's mixed background—a point Tourgée felt was critically important, particularly because it made the conductor's discretionary enforcement powers subject to a charge of being arbitrary. In oral arguments on October 28, Walker spoke for several hours on these points.

The newspaper reports noted that Adams responded more briefly. He alleged that the state of race relations and the noxious smells from colored people made the law reasonable. It is important to note the substance of this contention about reasonability. Although the U.S. Supreme Court had yet to establish the rational basis test for equal protection clause review, it was widely understood that states had to meet a burden of reasonableness even when they claimed a health or police power basis for legislation that restricted a person's liberty. For example, in 1897 in the case of *Gulf, Colorado & Santa Fe Railroad Co. v. Ellis*, the U.S. Supreme Court established that states had the right to exercise what the courts termed "the police power" as long as it bore a "rational relationship" with the "lawful objective" sought, a standard of review we know today as the rational basis test. Thus, it was critically important for those challenging a law not only to show that it impinged on a constitutionally protected right, but that it did so unreasonably.

While the term "strict scrutiny" lay in the future of constitutional jurisprudence, the High Court had already tested state legislation against the due process clause of the Fourteenth Amendment. In dissent in *Munn v. Illinois* (1877), Justice Stephen J. Field argued that a state regulation of grain elevator rates was an impermissible intrusion on constitutionally guaranteed individual rights. It violated the due process clause, and "if this be sound law, if there be no protection, either in the principles upon which our republican government is founded, or in the prohibitions of the Constitution against such invasion of private rights, all property and all business in the State are held at the mercy of a majority of its legislature." Field would have allowed state regulation necessary for the protection of life and health, but here, "the principle upon which the opinion of the majority proceeds is, in my judgment, subversive of the rights of private property, heretofore believed to be protected by constitutional guaranties against legislative interference." Whereas *Munn* was an economic regulation, the Separate Car Act affected the economics of the train companies and the value of the ticket purchased by a black rider. Constitutional adjudication operates by analogy, and the analogy of the grain elevator and the separate train car was hardly far-fetched.

Why the attorneys for Plessy did not argue for a higher standard of review of the statute than mere reasonability is a matter of speculation. Plessy's counsel must have realized that winning on the standard of review would be a giant step toward winning on the merits. For some reason, Walker and Tourgée never sufficiently addressed this point at this juncture. It is surely unfair to second-guess them. Constitutional challenges of this nature were unusual at this time. After all, this would be the first case involving an African American suing over segregation under the equal protection clause to gain attention of the U.S. Supreme Court since the *Civil Rights Cases.*

On November 18, 1892, as the defense team anticipated, Judge Ferguson issued his opinion denying Walker's motion on Plessy's behalf. According to the *Daily Picayune's* reprint of the judge's order, Ferguson dismissed any concern over the classification of Plessy as a person of color with the statement of fact: "There is no averment as to the color of the defendant." As for the idea that he could dismiss charges against a defendant because the policy behind the law was improper, he fell back to the concept of judge as the servant of the people: "Judges have nothing to do with the policy of particular acts passed by the legislature. The will of the law-giver being understood, nothing remains but to carry it into effect." Similar to recent U.S. Supreme Court justice nominees defining their jurisprudence as a matter of calling balls and strikes like a baseball umpire, Ferguson was denying responsibility for the law. He was also deferring to the legislature, a posture widely adopted by judges. Not only did it make sense for a political appointee like Ferguson to defer to the legislative majority, but also judges' deference to legislatures was a foundational principle of the Democratic Party.

Ferguson proceeded to dismiss each of Walker's points in turn. The argument against giving enforcement powers to conductors would not hold because trials could reverse the conductor's decision. Relying on the "equal, but separate" language and its enforceability against both whites and coloreds, he maintained that the law did not violate the equal protection clause of the Fourteenth Amendment: "There is, therefore, no distinction or unjust discrimination in this respect on account of color." Ferguson had bought into the mystification of race law: that discrimination based on a category was not necessarily unconstitutional so far as it did not entail unequal treatment. Per the common carriers practice in common law, Ferguson cited earlier cases to substantiate his ruling. Two circuit cases, *Logwood and Wife v. Memphis and City Railroad Company* and *Murphy v. Western and A. Railroad,* plus an unnamed admiralty decision made the point that "substantially like and equal accommodations" met the constitutional standard. He went on to cite the Louisville Railroad case from Mississippi involving that state's separate car law of 1888 to the same end. However, as his quote of the language of the U.S. Supreme Court made clear, the Court in that case was only considering whether the expense of maintaining a separate car resulting from the Separate Car Act was a constitutionally permissible state command: "This may cause an extra expense to the railroad company, but not more so than state statutes requiring certain accommodations as depots . . . and a multitude of other matters confessedly within the power of the state." Although Ferguson praised Walker for having "displayed great research, learning and ability," he ruled against him on grounds that he would hear over and over again.

Under Louisiana criminal procedure, when Plessy's legal team appealed Ferguson's denial of Plessy's motion, the case became known as *Ex Parte Homer A. Plessy to the Louisiana Supreme Court*, then *Plessy v. Ferguson to the U.S. Supreme Court*. "Ex parte" means for or on behalf of a party to a dispute, and it refers to a controversy where only one disputant is presented before the court.

The case went next on appeal to the Louisiana supreme court. There, in December 1892, in an opinion by Justice Charles E. Fenner (published in January 1893), the Louisiana supreme court upheld Ferguson. Fenner was one of the justices of the Louisiana supreme court, like former governor Nicholls (who was now chief justice), who were Democrats. Born in Tennessee, Fenner served the Confederate cause as a captain in a Louisiana artillery battery. Jefferson Davis was a family friend and spent many happy days visiting the Fenner family in their Garden District home. Davis died there in 1889. An attendee of the University of Virginia law school, Fenner had been on the court since 1880 and had a successful law practice after the war. In 1884, he spoke glowingly of Robert E. Lee's physical and moral attributes at the dedication of a statue to the Confederate commander of the Army of Northern Virginia in New Orleans in 1884. He would retire the year after rendering his opinion in *Plessy*, dying in 1911 a distinguished member of the bench and bar, and a member of the board of trustees of what would become Tulane University.

Three incidents shed some light on Fenner's thinking. They are suggestive rather than definitive. First, Fenner also fancied himself a scholar of the law. Displaying knowledge of classical Greek and Roman law and lawyers, he gave an address entitled "The Ancient Lawyer" to the Virginia State Bar Association in 1890. He did not address the issue of segregation and race relations, though both the Greek and Roman systems made provision for slavery, and disputes over slave ownership and otherwise involving slaves were a staple of ancient lawyers' practice. In fact, the very word *slave* was strikingly absent from the long presentation. We cannot know whether this was an attempt to stay away from controversy, or whether gentlemen of his caliber simply did not discuss such topics in public.

Second, in the weeks before the U.S. Supreme Court issued their judgments in *Plessy*, Fenner gave an address at the American Conference on International Arbitration in Washington, D.C., held on April 22 and 23, 1896. In it, he contradicted Herbert Spencer's letter on arbitration, which argued that war had "conferred upon the development and progress of the human race." "On the contrary," Fenner posited, "the progress of humanity consists in its elevation and advancement to a plane which enables it to dispense with such primitive institutions, and to substitute better ones." Fenner had seen war firsthand and had no illusions about it. Summarizing human history, he proclaimed, "Thus slavery, polygamy, irresponsible paternal and kingly power, governmental monopoly and control of land, and many other kindred institutions which, in their day, did necessary and efficient service, have been relegated to the limbo of effete and outgrown relics of the past, which the present discards and utterly condemns." Fenner had accepted the Confederacy's defeat, but this did not mean he believed slavery to be a mistake. Once it had been one of the foundations of a civilized society. The process of reconciliation would only be complete when those who advocated abolition and equality and those who would have died to save slavery accepted their mistakes.

In an introduction to a collection of memoirs published shortly before he died, Fenner called Reconstruction a time when "gross injustices which were being inflicted upon them [presumably whites] under the infamous regime of reconstruction . . . the infamies of reconstruction, and the widespread demoralization and corruption that prevailed after the war" were so widely recognized that no one could doubt them. He certainly did not.

As the legislature had planned when it passed the Separate Car Act, Fenner's opinion turned on the law's facially equal treatment of the races. Walker had argued "that the statute in question establishes an insidious distinction and discrimination between citizens of the United States based on race which is obnoxious to the fundamental principles of national citizenship, perpetuates involuntary servitude as regard citizens of the colored race under the merest pretence of promoting the comforts of passengers on railway trains, and in further respects abridges the privileges and immunities of the citizens of the United States and the rights secured by the thirteenth and fourteenth amendments of the federal constitution." Fenner was not persuaded.

Fenner dismissed counsel's Thirteenth Amendment position as argumentative—that is, without foundation in law. He cited the relevant passage in the *Civil Rights Cases*, the U.S. Supreme Court's voiding of much of the Civil Rights Act of 1875, which read in part: "The denial of equal accommodations in inns, public conveyances and other places of public amusements, imposes no badge of slavery or involuntary servitude upon the party, but, at most, infringes rights which are protected from State aggression by the XIVth Amendment." The use of this view to dismiss the Thirteenth Amendment claim might, in more sympathetic hands, have been the basis for crediting a Fourteenth Amendment claim, but Fenner was not sympathetic to that either. To reach that end, he could not rely on the *Civil Rights Cases*, because they conceded that state action (including a state law) might be held to violate minority rights under the Fourteenth Amendment. Instead, Fenner abandoned the *Civil Rights Cases* and turned to the Louisville Railroad case as controlling precedent. One expects this kind of mixing and matching of precedents, citing selectively from otherwise ill-fitting precedent, from counsel arguing a hard case. One does not expect it from an appeals court judge. Fenner then repeated Ferguson's tactic of applying a case involving a railroad's challenge on interstate commerce grounds with a case brought by an individual on equal protection, due process, and the Thirteenth Amendment's antislavery prohibition grounds.

But federal and state law were moving in the direction Fenner pointed, and he could rely on the plethora of federal circuit court and state supreme court decisions upholding segregation on railroads, schools, and other public places. Somewhat gratuitously, he also cited Massachusetts chief justice Lemuel Shaw's decision in the Massachusetts school segregation case of *Roberts v. Boston* in 1849. Shaw dismissed the idea that the school committee had forced any malevolent distinction onto the colored child: "This prejudice, if it exists, is not created by law and cannot be changed by law." From the supreme court of Pennsylvania, Fenner quoted a similar passage: "Law and custom having sanctioned a separation of races, it is not the province of judiciary to legislate it away."

Justice Fenner had done what clever lawyers do (and judges should not): he had analogized to favorable precedential language while ignoring the distinguishing facts of those cases. In the process, he mangled the subsequent history of cases, the actual holdings of the courts he cited, and the controlling context. For example, Massachusetts had overruled Shaw in 1855 after a considerable lobbying effort by one of the plaintiff's attorneys, the future abolitionist U.S. senator Charles Sumner. Pennsylvania's supreme court was not upholding a segregation law in *Philadelphia and Westchester Railroad Company v. Mary E. Miles* in 1867—quite the opposite. They were upholding an African American woman's suit against the railroad for violating her rights. In fact, the court held the railroad was a common carrier subject to the rules on that public interest. Although the court did admit that an equal accommodation would suit the ruling, they also denounced the railroad company's policies in no uncertain terms: "The whole genius of our Government and laws are opposed to such distinctions, but even in those countries where they are recognized and fostered, it has never been pretended that a carrier could make any distinction between passengers paying the same fare." It was true that segregation had become accepted practice in Louisiana, as the *Bertonneau* case made clear, which was why Fenner cited it, among others. But his attempt to bolster his decision with foreign citations was a feeble effort.

Fenner could have cited a number of cases from both North and South that upheld "equal, but separate" accommodations even before the U.S. Supreme Court declared most of the public accommodations provisions of the Civil Rights Act of 1875 unconstitutional. Judges in the lower courts found no right to ride in integrated accommodations, only a right not to be excluded. In this context, the

Louisiana supreme court's ruling was not unjustified, the quality of Fenner's legal reasoning and research notwithstanding. The growing prevalence of these judicial opinions can be read in a different light. Their occurrence after the close of Reconstruction indicates that segregation by law was replacing segregation by custom. Courts cited the latter, turning custom into common-law precedent. Rulings against African American litigants also indicated the abdication of the High Court's role in enforcing federal legislation. Instead, the Court seemed to be following inferior tribunals rather than directing them. The idea that the highest court in the land should follow inferior tribunals is contrary to accepted judicial practice, though not uncommon.

Fenner needed to justify the state of Louisiana's action not simply on the grounds that it commanded equal accommodations. He had to make the command a legitimate exercise of authority. In other words, he had to reconcile Louisiana's Separate Car Act with the demands of the *Slaughterhouse Cases.* He did this by using the grounds Justice Miller supplied for upholding the statute and separated it from Miller's view of the purpose of the Fourteenth Amendment. "The statute here in question is an exercise of the police power and expresses the conviction of the legislative department of the State that the separation of the races in public conveyances, with proper sanctions enforcing the substantial equality of the accommodations supplied to each, *is in the interest of public order, peace and comfort*" (emphasis added). Fenner argued that the state's blatant act of racial discrimination actually protected African Americans. It was therefore both a proper use of the police power and served the freedmen fulfilling the purpose of the Fourteenth Amendment, according to Justice Miller. Fenner even alleged that the failure of the record to state whether Plessy was white or colored showed the law's "fairness and equality."

In the process of dismissing the claim against the law's vesting of authority in train conductors and exempting them from liability, Fenner patronizingly critiqued the righteous outrage of those challenging the law as stemming from "some misconception." After all, if the legislature's white majority had such bigotry in mind, would it not be better for the colored people to accept segregation for their own protection? "It is certain that such unreasonable insistence upon thrusting the company of one race upon the other, with no adequate motive, is calculated, as suggested by Chief Justice Shaw, to foster and intensify repulsion between them rather than to extinguish it." Turning the reasonable test on its head, he opined that to insist on no racial distinctions in the law was "unreasonable." To desire that state law conform to the U.S. Constitution's demands was "no adequate motive."

On January 3, 1893, Chief Justice Nicholls denied Walker's petition for an additional hearing to go over factual issues Judge Ferguson had missed in the original trial. On January 5, Walker filed for a writ of error with the Louisiana supreme court to appeal its decision to the U.S. Supreme Court. Nicholls gave permission for the appeal the same day. The committee had achieved their objective: they now had an opportunity to challenge the law before the highest court in the land.

———

Practice before the U.S. Supreme Court is and was a rarefied art. It took great courage, mastery of the skills of appellate argument, and a familiarity with the Court's procedures to give a good account of oneself, let alone gain a favorable outcome. One also had to be admitted to practice before the Court—a special privilege granted to a select few. Tourgée knew he would need assistance in this regard. He did not have to look far. He selected an old friend from his days as a judge in North Carolina: the former U.S. solicitor general, now a Washington, D.C., attorney in private practice, Samuel F. Phillips.

Phillips was born on February 18, 1829, to the English mathematician James Phillips and his wife, Judith Vermeule Phillips, in New York City. From the age of two, Samuel grew up in Chapel Hill, North Carolina, where his father had become a professor at the newly established University of North Carolina. He graduated there in 1841 with highest honors, earning a master's degree in law three years later. After a brief stint as a tutor in the law department, he gained election to the state legislature in 1852 and 1854 as a Whig. From 1861 to 1862, he was on the court of claims, then served as state auditor from 1862 to 1864. He had objected to secession and participated prominently in the antiwar movement. In 1864 he regained a seat in the general assembly, where he became Speaker in 1866.

His support for equal rights for African Americans cut short his political career while bringing him into close contact with others of like mind such as Tourgée. Phillips greatly admired the judge and kept in correspondence with him as their career paths separated. After another term in the assembly from 1871 to 1872, President Grant appointed Phillips to be the second solicitor general. Phillips remained in that difficult post for the next thirteen years. He had the unenviable task of attempting to defend the Enforcement Acts and the Civil Rights Act of 1875 before an increasingly skeptical Court. Despite his general lack of success in these arguments, he did provide original lines of thought Justice John Marshall Harlan used in his dissents, as well as points his distant successors would use to great effect several decades later before more favorable courts. With his law partner, District of Columbia attorney Frederick D. McKenney, Phillips provided his own brief on Plessy's behalf to supplement Tourgée and Walker's. Both he and Tourgée were also able to make oral arguments before the Court.

———

In the midst of both sides' preparations, on July 4, 1892, Martinet communicated to Tourgée his cautious optimism about the situation. The Louisiana senate had temporarily killed the antimiscegenation bill—an attempt to prevent marriages between the supposed races. The Plessy litigation was also going forward. Martinet reported, "Of course I do not entertain the same favorable result as hopefully as in the Desdunes [case]. But perhaps it is best that the battle be fought." He cited favorable precedents and noted, "I rely, however, more on the fact that the Negro's right to travel interstate being recognized, & if maintained by him, it will throw the 'Jim Crow' car into disuse, as you say."

Martinet also explained to Tourgée his distress over the general tenor of the debate. "You wrote sometime ago that I was despondent. I don't know how you knew it, but you spoke right." He explained his dissatisfaction with the political situation and the divisions among the equal rights movement as follows: "The fight we are making is an uphill one under the best circumstances, and yet those for whom we fight make it still harder." Martinet was aware of the point he was separated from his natural allies by education, identity, and class regardless of the fact that he would share their fate.

Indicating both his sense of the moment and his insouciant optimism, Tourgée later wrote Martinet on October 31, 1893, that it might be a good idea to delay the hearing before the Court. His reading of the justices indicated that five out of the nine then on the bench would vote against Plessy's appeal. Though the membership of the Court was unlikely to change, they might be swayed by public opinion through his planned journal, the *National Citizen*. "Of course, we have nothing to hope for in any change that may be made in the court; but if we can get the ear of the Country, and argue the matter fully *before the people first*, we may incline the wavering to fall on our side when the matter comes up." Besides the inappropriateness of a lawyer suggesting that a litigant use public opinion to sway the supreme tribunal, it seemed presumptuous at best, and arrogant at worst, to think that his own publicity efforts might be worth more than a swift decision for his clients.

When arrangements finally moved toward a decision before the High Court in 1894, the committee had lost much of its fervor. Its advocates in state politics had either died or moved on. The successful passage of the miscegenation law prompted a protest but no legal challenge. One author has seen this lackluster response to these laws forbidding marriage among races, particularly against whites marrying those of other races, as the untold, critical part of the segregation movement. Besides the inherent problem in establishing who was a member of a race when there was no actual scientific evidence to substantiate the claim, especially the "one drop" standard of most laws, the state's official classification of people into racial categories and forbidding marriages among unrelated, consenting adults flew in the face of the equal protection guarantees of the Fourteenth Amendment. The laws' justification—the protection of the races, in particular the white race, from contamination—was a red flag of adverse discrimination if ever there was one. This was not just discrimination on the basis of race. It was the raising of white race to an elevated status and the viewing of another as a contaminant.

In many ways, the committee became resigned to defeat. Even the archbishop of New Orleans, the Dutchman Francis Janssens, had acquiesced in this violation of his flock's desire for equal treatment, setting up a black parish on Tulane Avenue. It bears emphasizing that the *gens de couleur libres* were Roman Catholic. They had given generously of their time and money to support Catholic institutions in New Orleans. However, even this tie had weakened under the oppression that was the increasingly segregated South.

As they awaited the outcome of their litigation before the U.S. Supreme Court, personal blows fell on committee members. In 1895, Aristide Mary shot himself to death at his dining room table. He had become increasingly frustrated with the setbacks of the preceding years, and his once-vigorous mind had been showing signs of senile dementia. Besides the loss of their leader, the remaining committee members also had to confront the obvious signs that the national Republican Party was abandoning them to their fate.

———

In between Plessy's arrest and the U.S. Supreme Court's decision in his case, the Democrats had taken full advantage of the Republican retreat from Reconstruction. Poll taxes, campaigns of intimidation, and the outright refusal to allow colored voters resulted in what became known as "lily white" Democratic majorities throughout the former slave states. Laws like Louisiana's Separate Car Act had become commonplace. Restrictions on what Negroes could do proliferated. In what the white supremacists described as laws to protect the integrity of the races, they outlawed interracial marriage. Though it took some time for courts to define what constituted white, colored, or Negro, their enforcement required that the classification of all those born in the state be officially noted on the birth certificate. The "one drop" rule—if you had a single African ancestor, you were a Negro—was the usual standard.

The Republicans made two last-ditch efforts in between losing elections in the U.S. House of Representatives: the Blair education bill and the Lodge federal elections bill, known by its derogatory name, the Force Bill. New Hampshire's Henry W. Blair wanted federal funds for public schools to each state to be provided on the basis of illiteracy. As controversial as this was in an era of laissez-fair attitudes toward government, what made the bill objectionable to the white supremacists was the provision of schooling to children of both races. As they had before the war, they saw this proposal as another attempt to interfere in their domestic affairs.

The Force Bill also came from a Northerner, then a congressman and later a senator, Henry Cabot Lodge from Massachusetts. It would have extended federal oversight to federal elections in the states of the former Confederacy. Because voter fraud was common even in New England, the Democrats might well have supposed that this was a partisan measure aimed at their new peculiar institution: the one-party state in which they represented persons whom they did not allow to go to the polls. Even with the brief hiatus of the one-term Republican hold on both houses and the presidency under Benjamin Harrison, the Republicans failed to muster majorities in favor of either measure. Other matters, like the tariff and the use of the gold standard, got in the way. Once Grover Cleveland and the Democrats regained control of the House and presidency in the election of 1892, both bills died.

———

As these events unfolded, Plessy's litigation awaited a hearing before the U.S. Supreme Court. In order to be heard by the court, both sides had to submit written arguments to the Court known in the law as briefs, even though they are usually anything but. These briefs had to convince the Court that it had jurisdiction; that there was an actual case or controversy upon which they could receive a remedy; that there was a justiciable federal issue; and that the appellant (Plessy) or the appellee (Louisiana) had a reasonable chance to win the appeal on the merits of their case. Both briefs were loaded with precedent—or, rather, readings of precedent, for the two sides read the precedents differently. Persuading the justices to overrule precedent, particularly their own prior holdings, was a much more difficult proposition than asking the Court to uphold its own precedents. But Plessy's counsel would argue that there was no precedent precisely on point.

Phillips and McKenney undertook the key task of making the initial procedural arguments. They then asserted the first of Plessy's constitutional arguments: in brief, that the Separate Car Act violated Plessy's rights under the privileges and immunities clause of the Fourteenth Amendment. While much of the procedural arguments were a walk-through—the state of Louisiana had conceded that Plessy had been arrested for violating the law and had faced trial, and that he had not been intoxicated, badly dressed, or disorderly—Phillips and McKenney did have to admit the record did not show whether Plessy was colored or white.

They attempted to make a virtue of this key omission by asserting that this made their case stronger. After all, in judging the case of a white sitting in a colored car or a colored sitting in a white car, "the constitutional liberty of the party so acted upon is as much offended in the first case as in the second." What was more, the statute was making an unequal discrimination inasmuch as it was reinstituting the racial verities of the antebellum period: "In either such case it is submitted as quite certain that the discrimination in question is along the line of the late institution of slavery, and is a distinct disparagement of those persons who thereby are statutorily separated from others because of a Color which a few years before, with so small exception, had placed them within that line." Phillips and McKenney, in other words, were alleging this was simply the Old South attempting to reassert itself, a "taunt by law." They were relying on the largely Northern-born justices to vindicate the Union's victory as well as the Reconstruction policies that followed.

Unfortunately for their cause, this line of assault did not properly take into account certain inconvenient truths. First was the fact that the statute mandated equal accommodations. Phillips and McKenney were proposing that discrimination in and of itself was necessarily adverse, even though the statute prescribed otherwise. Second, their argument missed the rather important point that their client's very identity defied the Separate Car Act's attempt to categorize him. In fighting Reconstruction over again in their brief, Phillips and McKenney committed a potentially fatal error: assuming the existence of the categories of white and colored. They admitted it to a degree when they wrote about the question of association between the groups as a "social matter" not fit for governmental regulation.

In prose that frequently waxed eloquent and cited the novels of Sir Walter Scott, Phillips and McKenney posited that the law could not discriminate on the basis of color—though outside of the law, such discrimination, much of it defamatory, it was widely accepted. They too seemed to accept a hierarchical ordering of the races. "Everybody must concede that this [sitting at the head of the table] is true socially of the White man in this country, as a class. Nor does anybody complain of that." The point was not to bring those social conventions into the law. "It is only when social usage is confirmed by statute that exception ought or legally can be taken thereto." Martinet and the rest of the committee would have been appalled at this casual acceptance of racism. More in keeping with the committee's sentiments was the point that discrimination against people of the "Celtic" race would be obviously wrong.

Phillips and McKenney did not stop there. They also took up valuable space in their brief arguing that train cars and common carriers were a different matter than schools and marriage in terms of state authority to regulate. By conceding these as precedent, they created an obstacle for themselves. Why was seating in a train car different from seating in a schoolroom? "Whether therefore two races shall intermarry, and thus destroy both, is a question of police, and, being such, the *bona fide* details thereof must be left to the legislature. In the meanwhile it cannot be thought that any race is interested on behalf its own destruction!" Having endorsed the repugnant notion that miscegenation was a genuine concern for both races, they decided to endorse segregated schooling. "In educating the young government steps '*in loco parentis*,' and may therefore in many things well conform to the will of natural parents. *Separate cars*, and *separate schools*, therefore, come under different orders of consideration." While we may interpret these noxious notions so contrary to the desires and programs of their clients as a tactic to avoid being rejected as advocating something too radical, Phillips and McKenney were certainly giving up a lot of ground to defend their client's basic civil rights.

Coming back to their main point about the Separate Car Act violating the privileges or immunities clause, they asserted the ability to travel in a common carrier without discrimination based on color was a privilege and an immunity. Further, it was not an incidental privilege or immunity, but because it was intrastate, it was primary and "absolute." Therefore, in considering the topic, "the court occupies a sort of *holy ground,* and must act under the influence of certain *favorable* presumptions." The portion of their brief concerned with common carriers and federal privileges concluded, they proceeded to explain how prior court precedents supported their client.

In *Railroad Company v. Brown* in 1873, the Court had upheld, among other items, a congressional command in 1863 that "no person shall be excluded from the cars on account of color." The justices interpreted this to mean that the railroad cars could not maintain separate cars and reserve one for whites and one for colored, even though the railroad company used the cars interchangeably. Although this case showed the Court was not hostile to the idea of prohibitions against "equal, but separate," the law at issue was not a government attempting to discriminate based on color, but a government attempting to prevent discrimination based on color. It had little to no value in the present set of circumstances because the Separate Car Act did not exclude Plessy; it merely ordered him to a separate car.

Phillips and McKenney also presented the case of *Crandall v. State of Nevada* from 1867 in which the Court had struck down the state tax on railroad passengers traveling outside of the state. The Court found that the tax impinged on the federal government's authority over interstate commerce, and, more important for Plessy's situation, travel between places of federal government business could not be impaired that way. Phillips and McKenney noted that New Orleans had a federal courthouse and other federal facilities, and Covington, Louisiana, Plessy's destination, had a post office. Again, it was not directly on point, but good lawyers always throw in as much as possible rather than too little.

Finally, they argued that the Court could not save the Louisiana law from itself by a creative construction of its provisions. They cited a passage in Justice Miller's opinion in the *Trade-mark Cases* in 1879 and to *Reese v. U.S.* in 1876 in support of this contention. It was a clever way around the problems *Reese* in particular caused their client. In *Reese,* the Court had voided the conviction of a poll worker in Kentucky under the Enforcement Acts, who had denied an African American a ballot in the election of 1872 even though he had presented proof of being duly registered. While *Reese* and the *Cruikshank* case decided on the same day had done great damage to equal rights, Phillips and McKenney now advanced the claim that these prior decisions aided Plessy's fight for his civil rights because, unlike in *Reese* and the *Civil Rights Cases*, the Separate Car Act was clearly state action. With that feat of legal legerdemain, they closed their portion of the brief.

Tourgée's section of the brief was a lengthy, multiple-point assault on the Separate Car Act. Because some of the points, questions asked, and refutations are duplicative, a look at them under their general headings is more instructive. First, he posited that the very discrimination on the basis of color violated the Thirteenth Amendment's prohibition on slavery. Putting people into different classes using a characteristic associated with bondage a generation ago was the equivalent of imposing the old caste system by other means. Second, the law vested too much authority in the hands of the conductors on trains. These private persons were not entitled to make judgments of this kind, not the least of which was determining to which category people belonged. Third, the law violated the strictures governing common carriers, in particular their duties of care, by limiting the liability of train conductors in their enforcement of the law. Fourth, the legislature and state of Louisiana had no justifiable purpose in making such distinctions among U.S. citizens. This went to the "reasonableness" of the act. Fifth, the law's exception for nurses of children introduced irreparable contradictions into its motivations, enforcement, and discriminations. Sixth, the law's categories were themselves unjustifiable divisions of people in an arbitrary manner. The law was overbroad and vague. In summary, Tourgée argued that the law violated the Thirteenth Amendment, as well as the privileges and immunities, the due process, and the equal protection clauses of the Fourteenth Amendment.

Tourgée also introduced some novel arguments. One was the idea that the law was depriving those it defined as colored of a piece of their property, namely their identity as just U.S. citizens. "Indeed, is it not the most valuable sort of property, being the master-key that unlocks the golden door of opportunity?" Whiteness was thus something tangible, of value, and recognized by all. It was a dangerous contention for someone to make on behalf of a client who was determined to challenge the very existence of such a classification, but Tourgée felt the need to put in everything he could. Property rights, after all, found a high level of protection from this Court.

In making this argument, he had to use the legal stratagem of arguing in the alternative. Barred in old English common law (one had to file a separate suit on each count of a common-law pleading), arguing in the alternative was permissible when defending a client in a constitutional case. Plessy's counsel had appealed to the U.S. Supreme Court on a writ of error, the gist of which was that the Louisiana courts had incorrectly read the federal case law and the amendments to the U.S. Constitution. Counsel sought a writ of prohibition from the High Court to the Louisiana courts in order to bar them from ordering Plessy to pay his fine or go to jail. Today, the High Court can take or leave any appeal. It has complete control over its docket. Then, the Court had to hear an appeal from a state's highest court when that court had ruled against a federal constitutional argument, as Fenner did in this case. Tourgée could thus argue in the alternative.

Tourgée next devoted some time to the proposition that "race-intermixture" had occurred to such a degree that state officials, much less train conductors, would not be able to determine the race without "careful scrutiny of the pedigree." Further, how was one to define someone of mixed ancestry? After all, looks could be deceiving, as they were in Plessy's case (by design, in order to raise this very issue). This argument tied in to his contention that the intent behind the law was not benevolent but malevolent, that it did not ensure equality but reinstituted slavery by another name. "The law in question is an attempt to apply this rule [color as a presumption of bondage] to the establishment of legalized caste-distinction *among citizens.*" This reasoning applied not only to the due process deprivation of property or liberty claim, but also to the privileges and immunities contention. "A law assorting the citizens of a State in the enjoyment of a public franchise on the basis of race, is obnoxious to the spirit or republican institutions, because it is a legalization of *caste.*"

Tourgée did not originate this language or concept, as we saw from the very start of the effort to overturn the Separate Car Act. The committee's initial statement in the *Crusader* in August 1891 made this point: "This obnoxious measure is the concern of all our citizens who are opposed to caste legislation and its consequent injustices and crimes." However, it did dovetail nicely with what he truly believed. Whether it would convince a majority of the justices presented a different matter entirely.

In this section of his brief, Tourgée reached high. He asserted that the privileges or immunities clause preempted the states' legislation and created "a *new* citizenship of the United States embracing new rights, privileges and immunities, derivable in a *new* manner, controlled by *new* authority, having a *new* scope and extent, dependent on national authority for its existence and looking to national power for its preservation." This was ambitious advocacy before a Court that had proven reluctant to recognize a "new" nation—quite the opposite.

Tourgée did not cite any precedent or authority for these propositions, unusual for a lawyer. He relied instead on the language itself, its context, and the general proposition he took from the case of *Prigg v. Pennsylvania* that federal constitutional law was superior to state law. It must have been with some irony that he quoted from that 1842 Justice Joseph Story opinion. After all, Story had invoked federal supremacy in order to reverse the conviction of a slave catcher who had kidnapped a Pennsylvania woman and her freeborn children so he could (and did) sell them in Maryland.

Tourgée then contended that the *Slaughterhouse Cases* and *Strauder v. West Virginia* (1880) supported his client's case. Although he dwelled on the minority opinions in *Slaughterhouse*, he made significant note of the fact that both majority and minority opinions agreed that, if the slaughterhouse law had affected persons of color, the Court would have used a different, perhaps stricter standard. In *Strauder*, the Court, through an opinion by Justice William Strong, held that West Virginia's command that no African Americans could serve on juries violated the equal protection clause of the Fourteenth Amendment.

Justice Strong posited that the purpose of the clause was "to assure to the colored race the enjoyment of all the civil rights that under the law are enjoyed by white persons, and to give to that race the protection of the general government, in that enjoyment, whenever it should be denied by the States." Tourgée believed *Strauder* lent itself to this interpretation of *Slaughterhouse*. This was in spite of the fact the *Slaughterhouse* majority opinion had sharply limited the national privileges or immunities to such a degree they harmed Plessy's case.

More important for the future opinions of the Court was Tourgée's assertion that the Reconstruction amendments to the Constitution now provided special protections against discrimination by states based on color. It amounted to an affirmative power, "but if it [the state action] imposes a greater burden or any inequality of privilege, upon the colored citizen, the general government is thereby vested with power to prevent or correct this inequality." This assertion went far beyond anything in the Court's opinions, particularly in light of the defeat of this very proposition by the Court's opinion in the *Civil Rights Cases*.

After all, the law at issue in the *Civil Rights Cases* was a civil rights act that Congress had passed, presumably under the enforcement clause of the Fourteenth Amendment. The Court disagreed, finding that Congress' attempt to desegregate restaurants, hotels, and other public accommodations was unconstitutional. However, Tourgée could have easily distinguished between the *Civil Rights Cases* and the present one merely by noting that this was a state legislature mandating segregation, not leaving the decision to the owners and operators of businesses open to the public. What was more, Louisiana's Separate Car Act was very much like the Black Codes the U.S. Congress tried to undo with the Reconstruction amendments.

At this stage in his argument, Tourgée left himself open to the counter that his view of the Fourteenth Amendment traversed his view of the Thirteenth Amendment—or, rather, that he had conflated the two. That is what Justice Miller did in the *Slaughterhouse Cases*. If, in fact, the reason Congress framed the Fourteenth Amendment was to retroactively protect the Civil Rights Acts, the language of the Fourteenth Amendment did not limit it to racial discrimination. In narrowing the application of the Fourteenth Amendment to the plight of the racially harmed people of color, Tourgée robbed it of its fullest potential. But all others who faced discrimination by state law were not his client. Only Plessy and those like him were.

Regardless of these obstacles, he moved forward with his call for equality. He analogized Louisiana's assertion of its right to promulgate a "police regulation" as upheld in *Slaughterhouse* to the Purim story in the Jewish book of Esther, when the evil Persian councilor Haman advised the Persian king to move against the Jews. Haman "did not set out the real cause of his zeal for the public welfare: neither does this statute," Tourgée explained. "He wanted to 'down' the Jew: this act is intended to 'keep the negro in his place.'" The exemption for colored nurses was proof positive. He concluded this section of the brief with a powerful statement: "Justice is pictured blind and her daughter, the Law, ought at least to be color-blind."

Perhaps reminded of the full potential of the Fourteenth Amendment by his analogy to a religious minority, Tourgée reversed course and insisted that the amendment was not a specific protection for those of color, but for all. As a result, the Separate Car Act did not pass muster with its special protections for both races. The Louisiana supreme court's decision made the Fourteenth Amendment "obnoxious to the severest opprobrium as *class-legislation of the rankest sort.*" The Fourteenth Amendment, properly read, mandated that all were to be treated the same without reference to color, not equal treatment that discriminated. The state's true motivation was, once again, adverse discrimination buffeted with states' rights reasoning. "It was the nurse and secured defence of slavery and excuse and justification of rebellion." He drew a straight line from the disfavored rebellion to Louisiana's discrimination on the basis of race.

Abandoning the strategy of reconciling with adverse precedents, Tourgée argued against both *Slaughterhouse* and *Cruikshank.* He ridiculed the latter's reading of the Fourteenth Amendment: "Truly, if this construction be the correct one, this section of the amendment is the absurdist piece of legislation ever written in a statute book." One justice who ruled on the 1875 case was still sitting on the bench, Stephen J. Field, no friend to black rights, and lambasting the Court was a dangerous course. Here Tourgée spoke not from the usual appellate stance of making legal points, but from his own wartime experience. The Fourteenth Amendment, a product of the sacrifices and ideals of that war, should not be rewritten by the Court. Likewise, "equal protection of the laws . . . is not a *comparative* equality—not merely equal as between one race and another, but a just and universal equality whereby the rights of life, liberty, and property are secured to all." Further, these rights "belong to a citizen in every free country and every republican government."

Besides the risk inherent in telling the justices that they were wrong, he was incorrect about the history. The Fourteenth Amendment had sprung from Congress's experience with Reconstruction, not the Civil War. He could have had a much stronger argument if he had brought forward the actual abuses of the freedmen and the complicity of presidentially reconstructed states before Congressional Reconstruction. However, he had a larger problem: the *Civil Rights Cases*.

Ignoring the majority's overturning of the public accommodations provisions of the Civil Rights Act of 1875, Tourgée saw in its demand for a "state action" a supportive precedent for his client. Louisiana had certainly acted. "It is an act of race discrimination pure and simple." The *Civil Rights Cases* limitation of the Fourteenth Amendment to state action put that precedent on his side. The Court, therefore, was entitled to rule on the question in favor of his client. Then he returned to his contention that the Separate Car Act was not a reasonable exercise of police powers. "The experience of the civilized world proves that it is not a matter of public health or morals, but simply a matter intended to re-reintroduce the caste-ideal on which slavery rested." Unfortunately, he was unable to escape the trap of racism himself when he posited, "The court will take notice of a fact inseparable from human nature, that, when the law distinguishes between the civil rights or privileges of two classes, it always is and always must be, to the detriment of the weaker class or race." Again, he admitted the existence of race in order to refute racist legislation.

Courts are reluctant to overturn their precedents outright. They prefer to distinguish a precedent they are departing from, leaving it to apply only to its specific facts as they go on to effectually overrule it. Asking the Court to renounce *Cruikshank*, a case that was not analogous to the present one, led to all manner of confusion. In that case, the Court overturned the Enforcement Acts on the same ground as the *Civil Rights Cases* knocked down the public accommodations provisions of the Civil Rights Act of 1875: the amendment only authorized Congress to pass acts that penalized state action. By citing *Cruikshank*, Tourgée undercut the point he had made about the *Civil Rights Cases*: "It is freely admitted that Cruikshank's case is squarely against us." Given that *Cruikshank* involved faulty indictments on a poorly worded section of the Enforcement Acts, it is hard to see how it related at all, much less went against Plessy's suit against a state law mandating discrimination based on race. Was Tourgée fighting old battles? Did his tortured way of thinking link the two cases in a way not easily seen? It would have been far easier and more advisable to distinguish between the two cases than to ask the Court to overturn precedent. Tourgée's intent is hard to discern, but he may have been seeking a sea change in the Court's jurisprudence on race. He had something of a Messiah complex, and it was affecting his ability to engage in sophisticated legal tactics.

Pulling back somewhat from this hard-line position, he asserted that Plessy was not seeking to dramatically limit state authority; "it merely asserts the right of the Federal Courts to pass upon legislative acts of the States touching such rights and the power of Congress to legislate in regard thereto, whenever it becomes necessary." This was the commonplace idea that the courts, with their power of judicial review, were the last line of defense for rights and liberties. It dated back to the English common law, and it had gained an exalted place in the United States.

Tourgée elected to prove the arbitrariness of the Separate Car Act by reference to the Court's decision in *Louisville, New Orleans, & Texas Railway Company v. Mississippi*. He read that opinion as stating that "the State may compel a railroad operated under its charter, to provide separate cars or compartments equal in character and accommodation, to be used by individuals of different races, if it sees fit to do so." This was a bizarre reading of the import of that case, in which a railroad challenged Mississippi's segregation statute as an unconstitutional infringement of the Congress's exclusive authority to regulate interstate commerce. Besides the fact that the plaintiff and cause of action were completely different from that of *Plessy*, Justice Brewer's majority opinion explicitly stated: "No question arises under this section as to the power of the state to separate in different compartments interstate passengers or to affect in any manner the privileges and rights of such passengers. All that we can consider is whether the state has the power to require that railroad trains within her limits shall have separate accommodations for the two races. That affecting only commerce within the state is no invasion of the powers given to Congress by the commerce clause."

Instead of quoting this distinguishing language, Tourgée used the occasion to lambaste the "equal, but separate" provision. He was going in circles. "The gist of our case is the unconstitutionality of the assortment; *not* the question of equal accommodation; that much, the decisions of the court give without a doubt." Had he just given away the entire case with this admission? What possibly could have been the point of this line of thought? He fulminated about the potential for abuse of allowing this kind of discrimination, using as his examples discriminating against redheads, requiring people to paint their houses the color of their race, and forcing people to use facilities of all kinds segregated according to color. It was a remarkably accurate forecast of Jim Crow America and Nazi Germany, but it did little to make up for his misreading of *Louisville.*

He went on to assert that the law's criminal punishment bore no relationship to whether the accommodations were truly equal. Not content with this important discussion of how to ensure equality, he decided to repeat his objection to the assignment of Plessy to the colored category despite his appearance as a white, ignoring the fact that Plessy himself called attention to his race. "Will the court hold that a single drop of African blood is sufficient to color a whole ocean of Caucasian whiteness?" He could not avoid his own bigotry. Plessy's ancestry went back several generations to the Louisiana Purchase. Even his African American great-grandparent's people had not been Africans for some time.

Tourgée then turned to the Thirteenth Amendment again. He asserted its purpose had been to end slavery and the legal status that went with it. "He [the slave] was a person without rights before the law, and all the other distinctive facts of his status, flowed from this condition." The amendment reversed this condition. "It meant to undo all that slavery had done in establishing race discrimination and collective as well as personal control of the enslaved race." The object was clear: the Court should strike down the Separate Car Act because it violated the Thirteenth Amendment's opposition to caste legislation.

After delineating the differences and implications of the words *right, privilege,* and *immunity,* in his twenty-third and final point, he contended the Declaration of Independence was "not a fable as some of our modern theorists would have us believe, but the all-embracing formula of personal rights on which our government is based and toward which it is tending with a power that neither legislation nor judicial construction can prevent." The Declaration had been the guiding star of generations of abolitionists. They argued it was incorporated in the Constitution. Even if they were right (a position that the High Court had rejected), surely the goals of the Declaration had been achieved by the Reconstruction amendments.

Denied a civil rights organization of national reach, a magazine for his cause to spread the word, and a political career to match his need, Tourgée used his appellate brief before the highest tribunal in the land to lay out his legal program. The Declaration of Independence had not been held to have any constitutional weight by any court, even though Justice Stephen J. Field might have wanted otherwise. However, Tourgée did not care about that. It supported the ideals he was pursuing, and it was part of the abolitionists' legal arsenal to which he had subscribed since his youth. The "pursuit of happiness" was "the controlling idea of our institutions. It dominates the national as well as the state governments."

He proposed that the justices should imagine themselves waking up with "black skin and curly hair—the two obvious and controlling indications of race" and consider the issues from that perspective. The Fourteenth Amendment, he claimed, would not stand a "Jim Crow Car" law if that were to happen. He was making a pointed argument about race and racial identity. If a little confused, it alluded to the hidden theme of the case: the problem race presented for the law.

Tourgée closed by excusing his somewhat informal legal writing style. "Legal refinement is out of place when it seeks to find a way both to avoid the plain purport of the terms employed, the fundamental principle of our government and the controlling impulse and tendency of the American people." He was uncompromisingly moral to the last, just like the abolitionists who were his ideological progenitors.

James C. Walker's section of the brief was much more circumscribed. He restricted himself to five main points, although each can be divided into distinct parts. In each, he always cited precedent. His first point was that the statute's empowering of train conductors to assign passengers to racial categories violated the due process rights of those singled out for the separate car. He noted that both state and federal courts held this kind of task to be a judicial one. Assigning this discretion to the conductors was especially problematic because the state of Louisiana had not defined race, and there was no consensus on what made a person belong to one race or the other. He quoted from statutes both North and South defining *colored* as anything from a quadroon (a grandparent was colored), to an octoroon (a great-grandparent), to the "one drop" rule. Unfortunately, this list also had the tendency to show the presence of belief in race as an objective legal category, if not one on which agreement had been reached.

The second part of his first point was that the statute was internally inconsistent. It allowed black nurses to travel with white children, but it did not allow mixed couples to sit together with their children. It was a neat example, though Louisiana law shortly eliminated that possibility by prohibiting mixed marriages. Nevertheless, it was a possible indication the law was, in legal terms used by Justice William Brennan in the second half of the twentieth century, unconstitutionally broad. When the language of a law encompasses too much, it violates the Constitution's due process requirement.

The third part of his first point argued that "the statute deprives the citizen of remedy for wrong, and is unconstitutional for that reason." Plessy had no opportunity to challenge the conductor's action. He could not have pleaded his case any better; he was without any legal process. He had a right to sit in the first-class coach for which he held a valid ticket. It did not matter. The statute had vested sole authority in the conductor. Fenner had replied to that argument in his opinion: a person wrongly segregated could always challenge the conductor's decision in a court of law. The problem was that such trials came long after the petitioner found himself or herself in the segregated train car.

What was more, Walker continued, the statute was not a reasonable exercise of the police power. "All police regulations are not necessarily constitutional; unconstitutional statutes are sometimes disguised in the habiliments of police regulations." Furthermore, they were subject to review. "Police regulations should be reasonable, and not involve the sacrifice of natural and inalienable rights, nor can they make a crime out of a natural right." Walker had hit upon the standard of review argument. He had found it wanting, inconsistent with the separation of powers that assigned judicial functions to courts. Unfortunately, he did not explain why the statute was unreasonable.

In his second point, Walker found fault with the "equal, but separate" justification for the statute because the conductor could assign a racial character to a passenger, then eject a passenger who was unwilling to move, regardless of whether the cars for the two races were actually equal. Again, he noted the conductor's exemption from liability under the statute. To the idea that white persons were subject to the same arbitrary authority, he scoffed. "Yes, when they are mistaken for colored persons." He continued, "After all, however, discrimination in the matter is evident, and whether for or against the white race, or for or against the colored race, it is by state legislation on account of race or color, and such discrimination is forbidden."

According to Walker's lights, this set of circumstances was exacerbated by the state's failure to designate Plessy as colored or white. For Walker, the factual classification was a constitutional matter—or rather, the Court should not take race into account. "Whether the petitioner, H. A. Plessy, is white or colored, or mostly white, or mostly colored, cuts no figure in the determination of the question of a court's jurisdiction or authority to hear and determine a case upon constitutional grounds." The law violated Plessy's right to due process and equal protection of the laws.

Walker's third point emphasized the vagueness of the law's specification of color and its assignment of sole authority to conductors. "The race to which the octoroon belongs is just where the state Supreme Court left it, to be decided by the railroad conductors." The state supreme court had ignored this important task, probably because they themselves could not define the racial categories. Walker stated, "When neither jurists, lexicographers, nor scientists, nor statute laws nor adjudged precedents of the state of Louisiana, enable us to say what race the passengers belongs to," how can there be duly executed laws on the subject?

Walker's fourth point centered on the legality of the indemnification provision. The Separate Car Act protected the railroads from suit for enforcing the statute. For Walker, this was an improper removal of liability because only courts could make the determination of whether someone was liable for his or her actions. "The legislature might with equal reason," Walker analogized, "undertake by anticipation to say that the courts shall not condemn a policeman for clubbing an unresisting prisoner in his custody." Although it sounded absurd on its face, it was actually common practice for states to exempt their officers from liability for their actions. It was not the sovereign immunity—that is, "the sovereign can do no wrong"—that protected the state itself from suit (reinforced by the Eleventh Amendment to the federal constitution), but rather official immunity, a more limited protection of a state employee or officer acting within the prescriptions of the law and his or her official duties.

In his fifth and final point, Walker assailed the state supreme court's ruling that conductors had no final authority in the assignment of passenger cars based on race. It was as plain at the statutory language itself. It made conductors unappealable judicial officers. After quoting Fenner's opinion's label of "necessary discretion" to describe conductors' powers, Walker asked, "What idea do these words convey? Neither more nor less than what we say ourselves." With this, he concluded his section of the brief. It was now the state of Louisiana's turn.

———

There were three attorneys for the state of Louisiana: Milton J. Cunningham Sr., the attorney general; Lionel Adams, the district attorney for New Orleans; and Alexander P. Morse, local counsel. Milton J. Cunningham was born in Louisiana in 1842 and served in the Confederate army. He sat in the state senate in 1879 and participated in the state constitutional convention of that year. He served his first term as Louisiana's attorney general from 1885 to 1888. He began his second stint in 1893 and would serve until 1900.

Alexander P. Morse was a noted District of Columbia attorney who specialized, like Phillips, in appellate law. His treatise on citizenship, published in 1904, was much cited by those wishing to challenge Barack Obama's eligibility to be president as a natural-born citizen. Morse also distinguished himself in international law, arguing the case for the United States in a dispute with Venezuela in 1894 and 1895. He was among the first enrollees in Georgetown Law Center in 1870 and graduated on June 27, 1872. Born in Louisiana, Morse was probably brought onto the case because of his long-standing relationship with Louisiana cases and Cunningham. Later, he was the sole Louisiana representative at oral argument.

After providing a seventeen-point summary of their arguments, the state of Louisiana's attorneys included a statement of facts, the state court briefs of Tourgée and Walker, Judge Ferguson's opinion, and the response to their appeal of his decision. They then proceeded to lay out their case before reproducing Justice Fenner's opinion. They dedicated the first part of their argument to the contention that Plessy's race could not be introduced into evidence because the trial court had made no mention of it. It is an established doctrine of appellate practice today that an issue not raised at trial cannot be contended in an appeal. Courts in the nineteenth century did not feel bound by this doctrine, however. Louisiana counsel made this point in order to whitewash, as it were, the prosecution of Plessy. U.S. Supreme Court precedent in cases like *Slaughterhouse* and *Strauder* indicated that the Court would look suspiciously at any prosecution of a colored man because he was colored. They needed to make the law, as well as its enforcement, look neutral.

The next section of their brief referred to prior cases to support their position. They used the precedent of *Louisville, New Orleans, & Texas Railway Company v. Mississippi* to deal with any interstate commerce clause objections. They admitted Mississippi's law had inspired theirs, "from which our own is borrowed." Then they used the *Civil Rights Cases* to briefly dismiss any "badge of slavery" claims stemming from the Thirteenth Amendment, Fenner's sleight of hand. After that, they cited *The Sue* (1885), a Maryland case in which Chief Judge Morris found in favor of several African American women who had sued a steamboat company for forcing them into a separate cabin, despite their having first-class tickets. Louisiana's lawyers cited it because Morris found separation by race consistent with the common law so long as the accommodations were "equally safe, convenient, and pleasant." In the case itself, Morris, however, found that the accommodations were not so, and awarded $100 to each plaintiff.

The second case they cited, *Logwood and Wife v. Memphis & C.R. Co.* (1885), was another federal judge instructing a jury, in this one a Judge Hammond in Tennessee. Using instructions from *The Sue*, Hammond stated, "Equal accommodations do not mean identical accommodations. Races and nationalities, under some circumstances, to be determined on the facts of each case, may be reasonably separated." However, he too commanded "in all cases the carrier must furnish substantially the same accommodations to all, by providing equal comforts, privileges, and pleasures to every class." Whether or not those cars were equal was a matter of fact for the jury. Cunningham, Adams, and Porter were moving too fast through their brief to note these specifics.

In the third federal court case they referenced, *Murphy v. Western & A.R.R. and others* (1885), an African American passenger sued the railroad, the conductor, a brakeman, and another passenger for forcibly removing him from the first-class car. Judge Key instructed the jury to put their racial affiliations aside. He also made an observation that "those who are most sensitive as to contact with colored people, and whose nerves are most shocked by their presence, have little to be proud of in the way of birth, lineage, or achievement." Louisiana's lawyers were probably relying on Key's ruling that "a railroad may set apart certain cars to be occupied by white people, and certain other cars to be occupied by colored people, so as to avoid complaint and friction; but . . . it must furnish, substantially, like and equal accommodations." However, Key was not ruling in favor of a segregated car. He was determining that, like Morris and Hammond, railroads could not charge first-class fares and relegate people to second-class cars "simply because they are black."

Despite lukewarm support from cases not directly on point, Cunningham, Adams, and Porter plowed on with their defense of the Separate Car Act. Dealing with Plessy's attorneys' assault on the use of "color," Cunningham, Adams, and Porter asserted, "The term color in the sense employed in the statute presents none of the scientific and legal difficulties contemplated by counsel." They then cited the *Century Dictionary* and Anderson's *Dictionary of Law* for the proposition that race not only existed, but was universally agreed upon to compose "all persons descended wholly from African ancestors, but also those who have descended in part only from such ancestors, and have a distinct admixture of African blood," per Anderson's dictionary.

This argument possessed two very real problems. First, it was assumed that "distinct admixture of African blood" applied to Plessy and others similarly situated when in plain fact it could not. Plessy, after all, had passed for white. Second, they also assumed having African ancestors was unique to the colored. Scientifically speaking, all peoples came from Africa. Though not widely known at the time, a lawyer doing even a superficial investigation would have found the scientific fossil evidence directly contrary to any other notion. Were the Bible the source of their terminology, in it all men were descended from Adam and Eve. Color variation came later. Citing dictionaries, which themselves were based on unsettled law, was evidence only of diverse opinion regarding social notions of race. The court was not bound to notice any of it.

To counter the charges concerning the authority vested in conductors, Louisiana's lawyers maintained that the law did not vest authority in conductors. After all, the statute stated that the conductor merely reported the passenger's "insisting on going into a coach or compartment to which by race he does not belong." The conductors were just acting in a "ministerial" capacity, for race was easily known in most cases. "But as a rule, there is no question as to which race a man belongs, it requires no exercise of judicial powers to determine that question, and when a conductor directs a passenger to a given coach, he does not arbitrarily consign the passenger to a particular race."

In other words, the attorneys for Louisiana were arguing that conductors were not determining race when they forcibly removed passengers they adjudged were in the wrong car. In the words of future Justice Oliver Wendell Holmes Jr., this was a distinction without a difference. The conductors were necessarily determining who was colored and who was white in order to carry out the law that not only compelled them to enforce the order, but removed liability from suit for doing so.

Before largely reprinting Justice Fenner's opinion, they concluded this part of their brief by arguing "equal, but separate" applied to both races. Therefore, it was not discriminatory. It applied to both whites and to the colored races. Why any white, or those passing for white, would want to go into the colored car they left unstated. Oddly, they closed with an excuse for their brevity and for reprinting Fenner's opinion. "The notice that this case was about to be reached came to the Attorney-General so unexpectedly he could not devote the time to it he had intended." Given the case had been in the works for over two years, it was a curious rationale for not writing a more expansive, diligent brief.

Morse did not offer any such excuses. His effort, though not as long as Tourgée's or Walker's, covered much the same ground. He began by noting that, procedurally speaking, the Court could not take notice of any evidence relating to Plessy's racial status because the trial record failed to do so; nor could the Court hear any evidence as to the equality of the accommodations on the railroad. It had to be assumed to be "of the *same class and of equal accommodation* as those to which he had been refused admittance." This relegated the Court's judgment to the question of whether the state's discrimination by race alone violated Plessy's rights.

Morse then proceeded to lay out his case in three major points. First, by providing for "equal" accommodations, the law did not create an inequality. Second, the statute did not "unfairly" discriminate. Third, it was "within the police power," and therefore a legitimate exercise of state authority. Morse justified the reasonableness of the "safety and comfort" goal by alleging that the law was meant for the rural and sparsely populated areas where "the danger of friction from too intimate contact" was greater than for the "thickly populated centres" where "the white and colored races . . . enjoy a more advanced civilization." He gave no support for this contention, other than the fact that the law exempted streetcars.

Morse was on much more solid ground with the extensive case law he cited to support his reading of what was a reasonable exercise of the police power, which included the *Slaughterhouse Cases*. Again, he made much of the fact that the law itself provided for equal accommodations. He trotted out the familiar precedents of the *Civil Rights Cases* and *U.S. v. Cruikshank* to sustain the propositions that there was no badge of slavery in mere discrimination and that the states should be granted a wide berth to provide their own criminal laws, respectively. But he also distinguished the *Railroad Co. v. Brown* and the *Crandall v. Nevada* cases from Plessy's.

He went on to attack the argument that somehow public schools and common carriers were of a different order than marriage—Phillips's contention. Morse gave a long list of precedents in which various states and federal courts had upheld segregation in public schools and common carriers. In short, "It appears from the reasoning in several of the cases that this power is committed to the authority of the local State governments for the reason that they are the appropriate judges of the policy, occasion, and extent of its exercise." Finally, he noted that the District of Columbia had segregated schools from 1862 to the present, "and the constitutionality of this provision has not been questioned." Even the Congress enacting the Thirteenth and Fourteenth Amendments had supported segregation (although by their inaction on the custom rather than explicit action). Shorter than every other contribution, Morse's brief tersely, effectively countered the wordier, more sophisticated briefs of his opponents. Sometimes, less can be more.

––––––

Though they discussed miscegenation statutes, none of the briefs mentioned *Pace v. Alabama* (1883). As a result, it did not appear in the opinions of any of the courts involved in the *Plessy* litigation. *Pace* concerned two provisions of the post-Reconstruction Alabama criminal code that provided penalties for adulterous relations. Alabama proscribed a maximum penalty of two years for single-race couplings but a penalty of two to seven years in prison for mixed-race couples. The couple in the litigation was an African American man and a white woman, according to the statements introduced in the proceedings. In a brief unanimous opinion by Justice Stephen J. Field, the U.S. Supreme Court held that Alabama's discrimination on the basis of race did not violate the equal protection clause of the Fourteenth Amendment. In the words of Field, "Whatever discrimination is made in the punishment prescribed in the two sections is directed against the offense designated and not against the person of any particular color or race. The punishment of each offending person, whether white or black, is the same."

The distinction between the offense and the person was clever, much like the use of the word *equal* in the state's defense of the separate car law. In fact, the offense did not exist in the abstract. It existed as a fact of social and cultural life. Without people, there was no offense. Only people could cohabit, fornicate, or marry. Abstract legal terms did none of these proscribed offenses. Field and the Court had found no discrimination because members of both races would be punished for intermingling. The justices missed or ignored the underlying offense that Alabama prosecuted in its miscegenation statute—the factual intent of the law was the polluting of the purity of one race by sexual contact with another. What was more, Alabama was not only designating its population as belonging to one group or the other. It was dramatically limiting the interactions—the liberty—of all persons in the state. In this sense, then, the law did not discriminate. Anyone who crossed the color line was liable to criminal penalties. The Court's handling of abstractions was very much a precedent for "equal, but separate."

———

There was one final act of the litigation drama for counsel to play: oral argument before the Court. In 1849, the Court limited counsel to two hours and required a written summary of points and case law in advance of argument. Attorneys could no longer duplicate the days-long harangues of Daniel Webster and others of his generation. Though more and more Gilded Age attorneys worked in offices and avoided litigation, lawyers of great stature were still great orators like William M. Evarts, whose sophisticated declamations were models of rhetoric as well as legal erudition. To come before the highest tribunal was an advocate's greatest privilege. It was also a potential nightmare: one's carefully prepared arguments could be derailed by a skeptical, or even worse, a hostile, justice's questioning. Tourgée now had his chance to join the elite of his profession—or suffer one of its most embarrassing occasions.

On April 13, 1896, Tourgée and Phillips appeared before the Court. They prepared their presentation in advance. Although we do not know what Tourgée actually said before the justices, a set of note cards in his personal papers has survived. Although it encompasses the arguments he made in the brief, their transformation into an oral argument appears to have freed him from elaborate legal shackles he never particularly liked. It is also possible Tourgée's thought crystallized further after he wrote his section of the brief.

Tourgée's notes fall into three main categories. The first centers on the exemption from liability for train conductors and their employers' enforcement of this law. Tourgée maintained that under *Allen v. Louisiana*, the statute was fatally flawed and thus prosecution under it void. The idea was that the conductors had to make findings as to the race of the passengers without proper evidence or procedures, or a usable definition as to what constituted colored or white. "It is a new ethnology by prejudice based on the lessons of slavery, [and] does not stop at trifles." After all, the legislature had ignored all the other "ordinary scientific terms" such as "Caucasian, Mongolian, Indian, Negro." Again, in making a case against racism, Tourgée admitted evidence in support of race's existence.

The second section of the notes focused on the intent of the statute: discrimination on the basis of race in order to favor one over the other—an unconstitutional discrimination. "The machinery of the statute is intended only to promote one object." In other words, "equal, but separate" was a lie to hide its true purpose of preventing the commingling of the races. Tourgée presented no evidence to support this claim, only the inherent illogic of the statute's provisions. As well as any other person, he knew the virulent racism that ruled recently "redeemed" states like Louisiana. Yet he presented none of that history.

The third and last portion of his prepared statement made the claim that the statute was void for "uncertainty"—what we would today call vagueness. Louisiana had not only failed to define what belonging to a race consisted of, but it also could not. Here, Tourgée came the closest to encompassing his clients' most heartfelt wish. He declared that one should not have to belong to a race defined as inferior, accepting the most dreadful designation one could have. What was more, the post–Civil War amendments forbade such designations, in particular the Fourteenth. It was the "law of human nature" for one race to try and dominate the other, and for the other to resist. Progress in human society came with the end of this kind of contest.

This was the point he really wanted to make—a point about human relations rather than artificial laws. It was a point that emboldened him to wax eloquent. He cited the problems of the Jews in Spain and Russia, the principles of the Declaration of Independence, and the difficulties of a legal regime that countenanced race. He rejected a reading of the Fourteenth Amendment that restricted it to just preventing discrimination against African Americans. He posited a new constitution with a new idea of citizenship. "The NEW citizenship of the United States, has nothing to do with race or descent, but is determined solely by the place of birth, 'Born or naturalized in the United States.'" He believed that the amendment set up equality without reference to race.

Tourgée himself had not plumbed the full depths of this final section, for he himself accepted the existence of race. Even in the course of pointing out the difficulties of assigning race, he gave it credence. "How shall a man who may have one-eighth or one-sixteenth colored blood know to which race he belongs?" Tourgée asked. "The law does not tell him; science decides perhaps one way and common repute may decide the other." These terms accept race as a category at the same time Tourgée wanted the justices and the law to not use it. On what scientific basis could anyone classify Homer Plessy as colored? On what customary basis could he be classified? The answer from the state of Louisiana was obvious: the "one drop" rule. This placed everyone into one race or the other on the basis of an arbitrary discrimination that was not possible if the law had rejected those categories outright. It was a subtle, minor opening that Tourgée had given his opponents, but it proved to be an important one.

Plessy's attorneys did what any good lawyer would do: they used every precedent, law, and constitutional argument they could. They were zealous advocates on behalf of what they believed to be their cause. They neither stinted nor shied away from making unpopular points or challenging the justices to rule in their favor. They distinguished cases that were hostile, and they made analogies to cases that were favorable. They looked to intent and meaning in the language of the Constitution using enactments of the time and plain-language analytical tools. They effectively humanized their clients and presented solid evidence for the problems with the state of Louisiana's policy decision to discriminate on the basis of race. However, they did not make the argument that might have thrown the case wide open: the nonexistence of race, and hence the impermissibility of a state making judgments on that basis.

Though Tourgée and Walker's reading of the meaning of the Civil War and Reconstruction's contribution to American law was eminently supportable, it led them into a trap of mammoth proportions. It is not hard to understand why they fell into it. Despite their relatively radical continuing commitment to equal treatment for all regardless of race and their opposition to racial segregation by law, they were still people of their time. Racism was so deeply ingrained in America's history, society, culture, and law even a fervent antiracist like W. E. B. DuBois accepted its existence. In this fashion, racism is not necessarily adverse discrimination based on a concept of peoples separated by outward physical differences like skin color, hair type, physiognomy (the shape of facial features like noses and lips), and continent of ancestral origins. Racism is merely the thinking about identity in those terms.

What Tourgée and Walker failed to do was to recognize what their clients truly wanted, represented, and constituted in their very persons for the legal debate over race in America. Homer A. Plessy, like Desdunes, Mary, and Pinchback, as well as the other members of the Comité des Citoyens, was a category breaker. His statement to the conductor about Louisiana's definition of him as colored spoke volumes about the arbitrary nature of race. The *gens de couleur libres* had not fought racism for generations because they were seeking equal treatment between Negroes, African Americans, coloreds, and whites. They were seeking equal treatment as individuals. Their pronounced defiance of racial categories was not just a political stance, but a reflection of their own unique identity. In short, they were seeking the abolition of race in America. Their lawyers' inability to escape the racial concepts of the time was largely inevitable, but it was also a disservice to their clients and, in a larger way, to the country.

———

The final blow to the committee came in the form of the U.S. Supreme Court's ruling in *Plessy v. Ferguson* on May 18, 1896. Plessy and all similarly situated had not only lost their case, but had also lost their cause. Perhaps the deck was stacked against the petitioner, the committee, and Plessy's lawyers. Perhaps as they gathered up their notecards and watched the justices retire behind the curtains at the back of the raised bench, counsel knew who had won and who had lost. But the decision of the Court went far beyond upholding the Separate Car Act. It gave the High Court's seal of approval to state-mandated segregation and to the racism that underlay all Jim Crow statutes.

CHAPTER 4

A Segregated Court

The Supreme Court that reviewed the arguments in *Plessy v. Ferguson* was a far cry from the courts of *Cruikshank, Reese, Slaughterhouse,* and the *Civil Rights Cases.* All but two of the justices arrived after the Compromise of 1877 ended Reconstruction. Only two were from the South, and only three were Cleveland Democrats. One might have expected a Court of this makeup to sympathize with a Republican-themed argument. One would have been wrong. This generation of justices, save one who dissented from his brethren, had not fought in the Civil War. They were not of the "Bloody Shirt" ilk who possessed the spirit of that battle standard. Although a good many Radical Republicans were lawyers, most members of that profession possessed a rather different view of how the law should work. Once the Republicans who at least had participated in the fights over Reconstruction had gone into retirement, those who took their places had little sympathy for an activist project.

Added to the lawyer's natural conservatism was the concept that law was not rule by force of arms—"rule by bayonet," in the unsympathetic nomenclature of the times. Law, much like the people who interpreted its meaning, was a restrained, consensus-driven entity. One historian has called this era's jurisprudence "legal orthodoxy." Others have called it "formalism." The judges, justices, and jurisprudential writers asserted they were not so much interpreting law as discovering it in a scientific fashion. They did not look to the legislative records to ascertain what the legislators thought about their work. They examined the language and looked to basic understandings of how societies and law worked to find what later generations called "original intent."

Mystifying to those present-day seekers after truth who would consult, at the very least, the *Congressional Globe* or the *Congressio-*

nal Record to find the official record of the debates on congressional enactments, the justices of this era consulted nothing but their own understandings of what law was. This process was seemingly anti-democratic—and, quite possibly, intentionally so. But some present-day legal historians argue that these justices were just as politically sensitive to the zeitgeist as their forebears and successors. Although there is no consensus as to their hidden motives, their careers do shed some light of what their personal proclivities may have been.

————

In chronological order of appointment, the justices of the U.S. Supreme Court who heard and decided on *Plessy* were Stephen J. Field, John Marshall Harlan, Horace Gray, Chief Justice Melville W. Fuller, Edward D. White, Rufus W. Peckham, Henry Billings Brown, and George Shiras Jr. Although David Brewer was a member of the Court at the time, he did not participate in the decision. We will deal with them each in turn, except for the opinion writers, Brown and Harlan, whom we will treat in more detail.

Born in 1816, Stephen J. Field came from a distinguished Connecticut family. His father was a minister who moved the family to Stockbridge, Massachusetts, shortly thereafter, where Stephen would grow to manhood. His brother, David Dudley Field Jr., became one of the most successful attorneys in New York City, a man who made his own mark on the law in the United States with his project to create a civil code for the state of New York. Their nephew, David Josiah Brewer, would join Stephen on the Supreme Court. Another brother, Cyrus, became an extraordinarily wealthy merchant, notable for being behind the laying of the first transatlantic cable.

Field traveled to Turkey and Greece when he was thirteen, gained a degree from Williams College in 1837, and studied law in his brother David's office, where he practiced until 1848. In 1849, Stephen decided to go west with the other forty-niners seeking wealth in the gold rush fields outside of San Francisco, California. He established a prosperous practice there, was elected to and served as chief justice of the state's supreme court from 1859 to 1863, and helped write California's first state constitution. A lifelong Jacksonian Democrat, he had no difficulties excluding free African Americans from the state by law (in a provision of the constitution he wrote) while at the same time espousing the strongest democratic, egalitarian principles.

When Congress decided to add a tenth justice to the U.S. Supreme Court in 1863 in order to give Lincoln and the pro-Union forces a majority on the bench, Lincoln tapped the Californian for the post. This made sense in terms of the new judicial circuit Congress had created out of Oregon and California, as Field would be at home there as well. For the remainder of the conflict and for a time thereafter, Field was a solid vote for the Union cause, but he reverted to his Democratic states' rights, racist, and antiregulation views on almost everything else in his thirty-four years on the Court—the second longest term in the Court's history to this date.

Field based his jurisprudence on the "inalienable rights" in the Declaration of Independence, which he only felt obligated to apply to white men. He is often credited with inventing the doctrine of substantive due process, which the Court would adopt after his death most notably in the case of *Lochner v. New York* in 1905. In the women's rights cases, he, like his brethren on the Court, found ways to bring gender into the Constitution where it did not appear. When it came to the rights of African Americans, he found that the Reconstruction amendments did not modify the prior pieces of the document, reversing the normal rule of statutory interpretation that holds what is later in time modifies what is earlier. In the Chinese exclusion cases, he saw no contradiction in government contravening basic rights on the basis of race, going so far as to compare the situation with that of African Americans in the South. Per his opinion in *Chae Chan Ping v. U.S.* in 1889, "The control of local matters being left to local authorities, and national matters being entrusted to the government of the Union, the problem of free institutions existing over a widely extended country, having different climates and varied interests, has been happily solved." It was "happily solved" for white men of property, perhaps, but not so much for others. He was as unlikely to agree with Plessy's attorneys as anyone on the bench.

Born March 24, 1828, to a prominent Boston family, Horace Gray was the resident legal historian of the Court. After graduating Harvard College, he attended Harvard Law School and was admitted to the bar in Massachusetts. In 1854, he became the reporter for the supreme judicial court of Massachusetts. While there, he gained valuable experience and knowledge in precedents both current and ancient. These he would cite when his judicial career began as a justice of that court in 1864 at the record-setting young age of thirty-six. In 1873, he became chief justice, a post he held until 1881. In that year, President Chester A. Arthur honored recently assassinated James Garfield's intent to place Gray on the U.S. Supreme Court.

Noted for his citation-laden, heavily researched opinions, Gray also initiated the practice of hiring recently graduated law students as clerks. He used his own salary to do so because Congress had not yet funded these positions. Gray's clerk while chief justice in Massachusetts was future justice Louis D. Brandeis, who graduated first in his class at Harvard Law School. Gray's brother, John Chipman Gray, was a professor at Harvard Law School and supplied Gray's clerks on the Supreme Court. So began the tradition of premier law schools with connections to the Court providing clerks for the justices who might themselves go on to become justices.

Gray's jurisprudence was conservative, though he on occasion did break with his colleagues to uphold state regulation of business for health and safety reasons. Although he too made no efforts to arrest Jim Crow, he did author the majority opinion in *United States v. Wong Kim Ark* in 1898, finding that the Fourteenth Amendment guaranteed so-called birthright citizenship against acts of Congress.

Melville W. Fuller had been chief justice since President Cleveland had plucked him from the Chicago bar and placed him in the center chair in 1888. It was a controversial appointment, in part because it came four months before Cleveland was to go down to defeat against Republican Benjamin Harrison. Besides a stint in the Illinois legislature, including a trip to the state's constitutional convention in 1863, Fuller won no place of public authority. His practice as an attorney had brought him before the Supreme Court to argue cases, usually to victory, at least every year for the sixteen preceding his elevation to the Court. And that took some doing. With a Republican-controlled Senate and the hostility of the chair of judiciary committee, Vermont's George F. Edmunds, Fuller's pronounced Democratic record came under verbal fire.

Fuller, like most Democrats, walked a fine line during the Civil War between patriotism and party politics that detracted from the

Republican-led war effort. Fuller was not even from a Southern-leaning part of the country; he was from Maine, a Phi Beta Kappa graduate of Bowdoin College, and a student for six months at Harvard Law School before he picked up and moved west. During the war, Fuller had opposed emancipation, any interference with slavery, and efforts to give full political and civil liberties to African Americans. What was more, he had joined with other Democrats, like presidential aspirant George McClellan, in calling for a peace conference in 1864. Nevertheless, Fuller had a defendable, if not unimpeachable, record as an attorney and the support of the Illinois elite, including two Republicans, former senator Lyman Trumbull and current senator Shelby M. Cullom. Playing some role in the 40-to-12 confirmation was the Republicans' concern that, if they blocked the nomination, they would look like they were trying to extend their domination over the courts, an appearance they wished to avoid.

Given Harrison's eventual victory and Fuller's ability to win over the court to his conservative, states' rights views, this Republican concession worked out poorly. Although Fuller's court may not have been the most restrictive one on record, it came close. Fuller did not always get his way with his fellow justices, but he did help them toward a flock of decisions that restricted the powers of legislatures to regulate business, eviscerated civil rights claims, and imposed injunctions on organized labor. The Fuller Court, with a few exceptions, was no great friend to the poor and unfortunate.

Edward D. White was a native Louisianan who was extremely familiar with the local context of *Plessy*. White became chief justice when Fuller died in 1910. Born to Catholic parents on a plantation just outside of Thibodaux on November 23, 1845, White attended Catholic schools until the outbreak of the Civil War interrupted his freshman year at Georgetown. One year later, he ran away from home at seventeen so he could join the Confederate army. He did not serve long: the arrival of Union forces in Louisiana led to his capture at Port Hudson. In prison camp for enough time to develop severe illness, he was paroled and spent the rest of the war recovering at home and preparing to enter the law like his father, Edward Sr., a distinguished former congressman and governor.

White was a servant of the sugar interests and managed quite well for them in his New Orleans practice, winning a substantial number of victories that protected their interests against the Reconstruction government's attempt to regulate them more closely. Not all of his activities were confined to the strictly legal. He was an active member of the white supremacist militia and participated in the successful coup d'état of 1874 against the Republican government of Governor Kellogg. Only the arrival of federal troops delayed White and his Redeemer cohorts' eventual victory. A prominent member of the antilottery forces and Governor Nicholls's two administrations, White served on the Louisiana supreme court from 1879 to 1880, then gained election by the state legislature to the U.S. Senate in 1888 for a term to begin in 1891. His stay there was brief because Grover Cleveland appointed him to the Supreme Court in 1892. He was there as chief justice until his death in 1921.

The legal philosophy he brought to the Court was one of unrelenting, inveterate states' rights conservatism. Although most of his opinions were so antithetical to the needs of the country that they were overturned and neglected after 1937, White exercised a powerful influence while on the bench. There was no chance he would sympathize with African Americans and their attorneys' claims that the Civil War and Reconstruction had wrought a significant change in the United States' legal landscape. In 1912 at a banquet, he summarized his views with the exclamation, "The blue and the gray, thank God, are one." The Union forces had preserved the nation, nothing more.

Rufus W. Peckham was perhaps the greatest champion on the Court for its emerging commitment to substantive due process. Like its other adherents, Peckham did not particularly care about legislatures when they acted against minorities unless those minorities were well-to-do or business owners. Born in Albany, New York, in 1838, to a lawyer and state supreme court judge father, he lost his mother when he was nine. After graduating from Albany Academy, a private school, he studied law in his father's office, entered upon ten years of legal practice after passing the bar, and gained election to a series of public offices: district attorney from 1869 to 1872, counsel to the city, a trial judge on the New York Supreme Court, then the supreme court of New York, the state's court of appeals, from 1886 until President Cleveland made him his last appointment to the U.S. Supreme Court in 1895.

When he was not in public office, Peckham had a lucrative practice serving railroads and real estate moguls. Active in New York Democratic politics, he was a confidant of the wealthy and powerful, both in Albany and New York City. His jurisprudence did not, however, always reflect these connections. It fell to his pen to author *Lochner v. New York* in 1905, although he sided with those who protected Chinese Americans in the exclusion cases and upheld the actions of Chicago health inspectors who destroyed contaminated food in the case of *North American Cold Storage v. Chicago* in 1908. He also favored an interpretation of the Sherman Anti-Trust Act of 1890 that protected small business owners from large corporations. His sympathies did not extend to African Americans as he joined the majorities who rejected pleas for the Court to invalidate Jim Crow.

George Shiras Jr. was born in Pittsburgh, Pennsylvania, on January 26, 1832, where, except for three years in Dubuque, Iowa, he would practice law for the steel industry and railroads until President Benjamin Harrison nominated him for the U.S. Supreme Court in 1892. As of this writing, he is the only justice never to have held any public office. A lifelong Republican, he was a dependable pick for the conservative Harrison, proving his worth to the Fuller Court with his authorship and agreement with all of the decisions invalidating state regulation of business, but noticeably quiet on race with one exception. On the same day the Court decided *Plessy*, May 18, 1896, he wrote for a unanimous court in the case of *Wong Wing v. United States* that an alleged alien could not be sentenced to hard labor without a trial: "It is not consistent with our theory of government that the legislature should, after having defined an offense as an infamous crime, find the fact of guilt and adjudge the punishment by one of its own agents."

Justice Henry Billings Brown, who wrote the majority opinion in *Plessy*, was as unlikely a suspect in the construction of Jim Crow as one is likely to find. He was a New Englander by birth and youth, and a Republican throughout his career. Born to an owner of several lumber mills in South Lee, Massachusetts, on May 2, 1836, he was an industrious boy who, according to his memoir, had "a natural fondness of machinery and was never so happy as when allowed to 'assist' at the sawing of logs and shingles and the grinding of grain in father's mills." He entered Yale University when he was sixteen; youth made his adjustment to college life difficult. After graduating, he took a year off to take the European tour fashionable among the sons and daughter of elite families in America, then attended Yale Law School for nine months and Harvard Law School for six months, without earning a degree from either.

Like Field, Brown decided to pack up and go west, settling in Detroit in 1859. Letters of introduction from family in the East eased his way into the profession, and he became a member of the bar in 1860. At the firm of Walker & Russell, he began a long, distinguished career in the primary business of the area—admiralty law. (Detroit was a Great Lakes shipping port.) Again using family connections, he secured the position of deputy U.S. marshal for Eastern Michigan. He acknowledged later that this employment gave him advantageous contacts that he could then use in his practice: "[The position] was out of the line of professional advancement, but I had no hesitation in accepting it, as it not only gave me an immediate income, but also brought me into connection with vessel men of all classes who naturally gravitate toward the Marshal's office whenever any question arises as to 'tying up' a vessel to secure a claim."

In 1863, Brown received another in his long line of appointments, assistant U.S. attorney for Michigan's eastern district. After his father-in-law died, leaving Brown and his wife a substantial fortune, he was able to pursue public office. Starting in 1868, he began a brief stint on the Wayne County circuit court in Detroit. He failed to gain the permanent post in the subsequent election as a result of the Democratic turnout in the district. Brown's fortunes did not suffer. His private practice with the admiralty firm of Newberry & Pond flourished to such an extent that he became a named partner. Although professional success was a boon to his finances, Brown often found the practice of law demeaning: "How sad it is to think that prosperity generally grows fat upon the miseries of the rest of the world." In 1875, when the sitting judge for the U.S. district court for Eastern Michigan died, Brown lobbied successfully to be his successor.

For fifteen and a half years, Brown served on the bench before receiving his appointment to the U.S. Supreme Court. Not coincidentally, he gained a reputation as the nation's expert on admiralty law. His 1876 treatise on the subject, *Brown's Admiralty Reports*, was well received, and his docket increased immensely as litigants sought to come before him to try their cases in that area. He was a conservative judge, reluctant to establish new law, although his friend, Charles Kent, wrote of him, "Perhaps his greatest fault was an ambition to understand a case and express his opinion too early in the argument."

While on the bench, he became friends with circuit judge Howell E. Jackson from Tennessee. Jackson had been a friend of Benjamin Harrison when they were both in the Senate, and he recommended Brown to Harrison when Justice Samuel Miller died on October 13, 1890. It might seem odd that Brown would be on friendly terms with a southern Democrat, but Brown was no radical Republican, nor had he served in the war. Like many a well-off member of the bar, he had bought a replacement to do his fighting for him. Similarly, many Democrats and conservative Republicans like Brown were probusiness, pro–states' rights, and fiscally conservative. Brown would return Jackson's favor by recommending to Harrison that Jackson join him on the Court, which he did in 1893, though his death in August 1895 ended his term on the Court shortly thereafter.

Brown fondly remembered Memphis, Tennessee, during his time on the circuit court there. "Indeed we found ourselves the favoured recipients of the most refined hospitality. Dinners and receptions were given with prodigality, and our rooms at the hotel were constantly thronged by callers." He and his wife even had the pleasure of dining with Jefferson Davis, the former president of the Confederacy, and his family. Brown enjoyed that too. "I then appreciated for the first time that an honourable, conscientious man, removed as far as possible from the criminal classes, may be guilty of treason—a most flagitious crime when committed by an officer of the army or navy in time of war, but in civil life and in time of a general peace, often involving little more than a radical difference of political opinion." Gone at the dinner table was the vast gulf between the regions. Gone was the rebellion that had cost over 300,000 U.S. military personnel their lives. All that was left was the sense that these two men belonged to the same class of people. Brown never mentioned Reconstruction or its violence in his autobiography.

As a stolid, conservative Republican with a solid judicial reputation and influential friends from the other side of the aisle, Brown met with little difficulty gaining confirmation from the U.S. Senate in December 1890. Oddly enough for the future author of *Plessy*, Brown brought with him to serve as a bailiff an African American, a former slave by the name of Richard Bush, the first African American bailiff in Supreme Court history. They were buried in the same cemetery in Detroit—something that could not have happened in the Jim Crow South.

With the notable exception of his opinion in *Plessy*, Brown made little impression on the Court, writing on admiralty and other technical subjects, and fading into the majority in the Court's conservative jurisprudence. Brown entirely sympathized with an agenda that protected economic or property rights of individuals (including, according to the Court, corporations) under the due process clause. Although he never gained a reputation as one of the Court's leading lights, he created a favorable impression among his fellow justices. Justice William R. Day, who served with him for part of that time, wrote that Brown was "a capital judge and a genial and loveable companion, free from littleness, rejoicing in the good fortune of his brethren, and at all times upholding the honour and dignity of the Court."

Brown was comfortable with concentrations of wealth and power. It is natural for those who are fortunate to believe that they are deserving of their fortune. It is also common for the fortunate to look down on those who are less fortunate, believing that, correspondingly, the less fortunate must deserve that fate as well. In a paper for the American Bar Association meeting in 1893, Brown expressed these ideas plainly: "Education may do something to equalize men, and to soften the asperities of character, but inherent defects can never be wholly remedied, nor inherent virtues wholly suppressed. In the words of the maxim which so well expresses the popular idea, 'Blood will tell.'" Although he was arguing against income taxes, government regulations of business, and so-called social legislation, he also revealed an incipient racism.

Much has been made of the social science and biological sciences literature of this time in terms of its influence on the outcome of *Plessy*, but it is also inescapable to conclude that, besides the writings reflecting the society that produced them, these sentiments were far from new. Charles Lofgren and others have definitively shown that racism pervaded almost all corners of the academic world, popular literature, and politics. Those who were not racist were in the distinct minority. The scientists of the time, their predecessors, and their successors proved not only the existence of race, but the inferiority of the so-called Negro race. The late Harvard biologist Stephen Jay Gould has shown the despicable methods these men used to buttress their own prejudices, but their shoddy science, riddled with easily disprovable presumptions, were readily accepted even by prominent African Americans like Booker T. Washington. In all, Brown was typical of the appointments that comprised the membership of the Fuller Court. Suspicious of government, except when it reflected the Redeemed South, they represented the most conservative elements of the bar, if not the country.

However, there was one member of the Court who dissented in *Plessy*. Justice John Marshall Harlan had already staked his claim to being the most sympathetic of the justices to the Plessy committee's cause. Whether or not he contributed financially to their litigation is a matter of some dispute, but there could be no doubt his dissent in the *Civil Rights Cases* supported their claims.

Harlan has been justly described as an enigma. It would be one of the great ironies of *Plessy* that the New Englander who had gone to the upper Midwest and was a founding member of the Republican Party and the former slaveholder from Kentucky would be opposing sides of the race question, with the Kentuckian as the more radical of the two. A part of the explanation lies in his journey to the U.S. Supreme Court.

Born in 1833 to a respected, long-standing Kentucky family, Harlan graduated with honors from Centre College in Lexington, then, following his lawyer father's advice, studied law at Transylvania University. He joined with a friend to practice law and became active in Whig politics. He served as adjutant general in the state until the demise of the Whig Party in the mid-1850s. He then joined the anti-immigrant American Party, the Know-Nothings, but found little traction for himself as a vote getter. With the outbreak of the Civil War, he became a staunch Unionist, formed a regiment, and fought in the war's western theater of operations along the Mississippi. In 1863, when his father died, he resigned his commission to return home so he could provide for his family.

In that same year, he reentered politics and ran successfully for attorney general. Although he vigorously advocated for the Union cause, he also spoke out against emancipation and suffrage for African Americans, going so far as to promote the prosecution of U.S. army officers who aided and abetted runaway slaves. He lost his bid for reelection as attorney general despite his outspoken campaign for Democratic presidential candidate George McClellan in 1864. However, by 1868, he had switched sides in the debates roiling the country over Reconstruction and joined the Republican Party. Failing to win office both in 1871 and 1875 in his campaigns for governor, he nevertheless stayed the course and worked vigorously on behalf of Rutherford B. Hayes in 1876 after his former law partner and Grant's anti–Ku Klux Klan solicitor general Benjamin Bristow's bid fell short.

When Justice David Davis became one of Illinois's senators in 1877, a grateful Hayes nominated Harlan to the court over the objections of many stalwarts—those who had stuck with Grant in 1872—who argued that Harlan could not be trusted because he was so recently a Republican. Had they taken a closer look at Harlan's evolution over the previous thirteen years, they would have seen a man substantially altered in his views, especially his understanding of the changes the war and Reconstruction had brought to the country and its laws. In brief, John Marshall Harlan had begun as a citizen of the federal union, and ended up as a citizen of the nation.

This transformation did not mean Harlan was a liberal in the modern sense—far from it. However, it did mean he had accepted certain principles, among them the equality of all before the law. There may have been a link between these principles and his devout adherence to his Presbyterian church, where he was a trustee at his vacation home and taught Bible classes every Sunday, but it is only a matter of speculation.

Even after *Plessy*, Harlan did not always side with African Americans against segregation. In *Cumming v. Richmond County Board of Education* (1899), Harlan agreed with the majority that a Georgia county could eliminate the colored high school and not provide any higher education facilities for nonwhites, though the county had a high school for whites. Harlan declared that no state was obligated to provide an education for all its youth, even though it was providing one for some based on their race. It was a curious position for the man who had penned the righteous dissents in the *Civil Rights Cases* and *Plessy*. A clue to this mystery may lie in an evening of storytelling his wife recounted years later. It was about 1901 or 1902, and he was waxing nostalgic about his Civil War days, in particular his attempt to catch the Morgan raiders in Kentucky. One of his guests, federal judge Horace H. Lurton of Tennessee, later a Taft appointee to the Court, exclaimed, "Harlan, is it possible I am just finding out *who* it was that tried to shoot me on that never-to-be-forgotten day?" The justice responded, "Lurton, do you mean to tell me that *you* were with Morgan on that raid? Now I know *why* I did not catch up with him; and thank God I didn't hit *you* that day."

Besides having been pleased he had not shot this Confederate, Harlan and his wife were pleased at the conviviality among the former opponents; as his wife recalled, "The whole company was thrilled by the belated but dramatic sequel to my husband's story, as they realized afresh how completely the wounds of that fratricidal war had been healed." Reconciliation was complete. The old battles were now war stories to be shared between men who were comrades in arms, if on opposite sides. Mrs. Harlan observed further, "For there were those two men, fellow citizens of the one and united country, serving together as Judges on the Federal Bench. It was as if there had been no Civil War." A great many African Americans might have agreed with that conclusion.

————

The decision in *Plessy* that came down on May 18, 1896, had several parts. The first was the summary of the case written by the clerk of the Court. The second was a majority opinion by Justice Henry Billings Brown, which all but Justice Harlan signed. In brief, it upheld the judgment of the supreme court of Louisiana that the Separate Car Act did not violate the U.S. Constitution, but took issue with the liability provisions. Justice Harlan's dissent filled the third part of *Plessy*.

In the summary of the petition of the case that accompanied the opinions, the terms that described Plessy's status—"a citizen of the United States and a resident of the State of Louisiana, of mixed descent, in the proportion of seven eighths Caucasian and one eighth African blood: that the mixture of colored blood was not discernible in him"—gave the litigants both a victory and a defeat. They had successfully gotten Plessy's identity into the record, but in so doing, they had also gotten the language that accepted race into the conversation. There was and is no such thing as African blood, save the blood of Africans. Nor was Plessy African in any sensible parsing of the word. Plessy's ancestors went back a century or more to the time when the territory of Louisiana was a French possession. Arguing that one-eighth of Plessy was African was akin to maintaining that he was seven-eighths English and Dutch—a fact that the reporter of the case neglected to mention. Yet these were the terms of the time, and there was no escaping their import.

A procedural recounting preceded Brown's majority opinion. Plessy's attorneys had done their procedural job well. Even a Supreme Court hostile to their cause had to admit the constitutionality of the Separate Car Act was properly before it. The recounting also noted that "the respondent [the state of Louisiana] made answer . . . asserting the constitutionality of the law, and averring that, instead of pleading or admitting that he belonged to the colored race, the said Plessy declined and refused, either by pleading or otherwise, to admit that he was in any sense or in any proportion a colored man." Unfortunately for Plessy's cause, Brown did not realize the significance of this dispute. How to define a person was as much at issue as whether those discriminations were permissible.

Brown dismissed the Thirteenth Amendment arguments asserting that it was "too clear for argument" that abolishing slavery and involuntary servitude had nothing to do with separating out people by race on railcars. He cited the *Slaughterhouse Cases* and the *Civil Rights Cases* to buttress his point, even though those cases had little or nothing to do with segregation by state law. He quoted Justice Bradley from the latter more to reflect his own rejection of the Thirteenth Amendment's use than as an actual precedent: "It would be running the slavery argument into the ground to make it apply to every act of discrimination which a person may see fit to make as to the guests he will entertain, or as to the people he will take into his coach or cab or car, or admit to his concert or theatre, or deal with in other matters of intercourse or business." Brown had confused the state action doctrine with the meaning of the Thirteenth Amendment. He did not know or willfully ignored slavery's inextricable links with racism.

Brown dismissed the Thirteenth Amendment contention. In the process, he revealed an almost casual racism: "A statute which implies merely a legal distinction between the white and colored races—a distinction which is founded in the color of the two races, and which must always exist so long as white men are distinguished from the other race by color—has no tendency to destroy the legal equality of the two races, or reestablish a state of involuntary servitude." In a few words, he had communicated a mouthful.

First, Brown's assertion that telling where people could and could not sit on a railcar solely on the basis of their perceived race was "merely a legal distinction" betrayed a certain indifference to real people's feelings. Although Brown cannot be condemned for a lack of empathy, his attempt to turn it into a legal principle is noteworthy. Nothing that is a legal distinction and properly before the Court can be dismissed as minor. The very legality of the distinction is what the Court is attempting to weigh. Second, his contention that the "color of the two races" is the source for the discrimination ran afoul of the text of the law and the fact that Louisiana did not provide such a definition. This is a distinction that does show a difference. Race was on Brown's mind—racial differences and the need to scaffold the differential treatment of the races by law. Ironically, Brown thus had to ignore Plessy's uncertain status under the Separate Car Act. Plessy appeared white and thus could not be distinguished on the basis of his color. Brown's definition of what is white and what is colored did not apply in Plessy's case, or in the case of anyone similarly situated.

Third, the "tendency to destroy the legal equality of the two races" is a factual determination that Brown did not bother to investigate. If he had, he would have found that everywhere segregation had taken place, both cases and common everyday experience revealed there was invariably inequality. To be generous, one would conclude that Brown, an appellate court judge, thought that facts had no place in his opinion. But the opinion itself was grounded and hedged around with the facts that race mattered and that racial differences could be the basis of legal differences.

Brown spent the rest of his opinion dealing with the Fourteenth Amendment argument. He prefaced his entire discussion by assuming that the *Slaughterhouse Cases* had established that the amendment's "main purpose was to establish the citizenship of the negro; to give definitions of citizenship of the United States and of the States, and to protect from the hostile legislation of the States the privileges and immunities of citizens of the United States, as distinguished from the States." He further stated: "The object of the amendment was undoubtedly to enforce the absolute equality of the two races before the law." Thus far, he might have taken his text from Plessy's counsel. But he did not stop there. He contended on the basis of no law whatsoever, "but in the nature of things it could not have been intended to abolish distinctions based upon color, or to enforce social, as distinguished from political equality, or a commingling of the two races upon terms unsatisfactory to either." Where in the law did "the nature of things" appear? For Brown, this was a fact that trumped all legal argument.

The Fourteenth Amendment nowhere mentioned race. Its provisions refer to citizens and persons and make no mention of color, race, or any other distinction. The exact wording is: "nor deny to any person within its jurisdiction the equal protection of the laws." To find that the Fourteenth Amendment's provisions are solely about guaranteeing Negro equality is to read into the amendment language that its provisions simply do not support. The Court in the *Slaughterhouse Cases* had opined, in a dictum (that is, a statement not necessary to the decision in the case), that the historical purpose of the amendment was to protect the rights of the newly freed men and women. But it is one of the well-established rules of interpretation to assume the use of particular words and not others was intentional. The framers of the Fourteenth Amendment did not include race.

The second line of reasoning Brown used departed even farther from the text of the law. Declaring that the Fourteenth Amendment could not command commingling or "enforce" social equality reversed the Court's actual duties under the Constitution. The Court was reviewing a state law that commanded separation of persons according to color, not a state or the Fourteenth Amendment commanding a mixing of two distinct groups of people. Brown had reversed the imperatives of the equal protection clause.

One possible answer is that Brown was assuming that segregation was natural as well as legal. For all his time in the District of Columbia, he had lived with and grown accustomed to seeing segregation. He might have been positing that to deny Louisiana the authority to segregate by law was to force the state's whites and blacks to commingle. The two were opposites, at least in his mind. Therefore, to prevent the one became to command the other. In practical terms, if Louisiana did not segregate, whites would be forced to sit next to Negroes.

To his aid in this logical and sociological sleight of hand, he summoned a list of the various situations, laws, and court decisions that had upheld segregation. Brown declared that segregation laws "do not necessarily imply the inferiority of either race to the other, and have been generally, if not universally, recognized as within the competency of the state legislatures in the exercise of their police power." The modifier "necessarily" was the keyword. He was announcing a standard of review in effect, which held laws based on race to a low level of scrutiny. "Do not necessarily" gives the benefit of the doubt to the legislatures, a deference to legislatures that the Court often practiced.

The source for these racist laws lay in large measure before the Civil War, before the emancipation of the slaves, and before the Reconstruction amendments. In his "string" citation, many of the cases he cited were not directly on point. More important for students of the opinion, none of the state laws that discriminated on the basis of race derived from the legislators' belief in the equality of the races. All the evidence of state legislative activity on public accommodations reveals that the legislators thought the darker races inferior to the lighter ones. The lily-white legislators had enacted Jim Crow because the members disliked, feared, and wanted to subjugate a group of people different from themselves.

Brown then assayed a brief history of racial segregation in America going back to Lemuel Shaw's opinion in *Roberts v. City of Boston* largely duplicating Justice Fenner's opinion point by point. Pointing out that these laws segregating schools and public areas "have been generally, if not uniformly, sustained by the courts," he made the case that segregation was prevalent, accepted by many lower courts, and sustained by his own Court, though not on grounds of benefit to all parties. Instead, he implied that segregation laws were within the police powers of the states. The failure of Plessy's counsel to at least consider introducing argument for a higher standard of review of these police regulations was here a grievous missed opportunity. When far less committed and able counsel made the argument against a New York state law regulating baker's hours, it won the day (though the Court's majority opinion in *Lochner v. New York* [1905] has not fared so well in later legal scholarship).

Brown defended his view of the train car laws by reference to marriage laws. These laws "have been universally recognized as within the police power of the State." Again, the adverb was crucial. "Universally" was misleading. There were states and municipalities that did not segregate on the basis of race. Segregation was not mandated by nature or nature's law. It was a custom that was becoming law in some jurisdictions. To imply by the word "universally" that a custom was everywhere a rule was based on the assumption that segregation was rooted in nature—the same assumption that opened the infamous "in the nature of things" terminology. If race-based slavery was universally legal in the antebellum South, did it imply (as it must, following Brown's specious logic) that all people of that race must be suited for slavery? In fact, that was the assumption that legal apologists for the South's "peculiar institution" like Thomas R. R. Cobb and Chief Justice Roger B. Taney made. As Cobb put it in his widely cited *An Inquiry into the Law of Negro Slavery in the United States* (1858), "In this view, is Negro slavery consistent with the law of nature? . . . His black color peculiarly fits him for the endurance of the heat of long continued summers . . . the mental inferiority of the Negro has been often asserted and never successfully denied . . . they have at no time formed great political states . . . a want of judgment . . . improvement never enters into his imagination . . . he never originates a single [musical] air, nor invents a musical instrument," and in freedom is invariably "idle, insolent, and profligate." Brown was not defending slavery, and it is somewhat unfair to link his view of the "nature of things" to those who did, but his idea of the universality of racial distinctions is the very same that Cobb promoted.

Brown distinguished between the "political equality of the negro" and social equality in "schools, theatres and railway carriages." By this tactic, he could assert that the various jury cases such as *Strauder v. West Virginia*, which forbade racial discrimination in the selection of jurors, did not apply to railroad discrimination. He also attempted to use *Hall v. DeCuir*, as Fenner did, to rule out an interstate commerce claim. Brown reached for Justice Bradley's opinion in the *Civil Rights Cases* in order to show a distinction between political and social equality. However, the section of Bradley's opinion he quoted showed that the *Civil Rights Cases* supported Plessy's claim against Louisiana, not the reverse. Bradley stated in part that the Fourteenth Amendment "does not invest Congress with power to legislate upon subjects that are within the domain of state legislation; but to provide modes of relief against state legislation, or state action, of the kind referred to." Brown mistook the command of the Fourteenth Amendment to not allow for racial distinctions for a requirement to protect the Negro in certain areas of American life. In this, he rejected the Republicans' very purpose in framing the Reconstruction amendments and the legacy of Congressional Reconstruction: to give all people of the states of the former Confederacy, including African Americans, full equality in all aspects of life. Only then could the Republicans hope to have a viable party in the South. But by 1896, only a few dared to dream that dream.

Brown then analogized the Separate Car Act for intrastate train travel in Louisiana to the Court's decision in *Louisville, New Orleans, & Texas Railway Company v. Mississippi.* He conceded that the Louisville railroad had little or nothing to do with *Plessy*: the plaintiff in the former was a railroad company, and the Court only considered the case as a matter dealing with a state's regulation of interstate train travel. The citation did allow Brown to introduce the various state court decisions upholding segregation on railroads. None of those state cases was dispositive, however, for none of the state courts could determine the meaning of the Fourteenth Amendment (though state court judges could interpret it as they chose).

Brown also conceded that the question of whether the conductor could act as judge and jury in the matter of determining the race of a passenger and the statute's granting of immunity from suit created a problem area: "Indeed, we understand it to be conceded by the State's attorney, that such part of the act as exempts from liability the railway company and its officers is unconstitutional." Nevertheless, the Court, as per his opinion, deemed that the issue did not "properly arise upon the record in this case" because Plessy was only challenging the constitutionality of the act. He silently rejected Tourgée's well-reasoned proposition that this represented a fatal defect in the law itself.

In the most tortured portion of his opinion, Brown dealt with Tourgée's contention that Plessy was being deprived of his property right without due process. Brown found "if he be a colored man and be so assigned he has been deprived of no property, since he is not lawfully entitled to the reputation of being a white man." Not only was this circular reasoning, but if reputation was a form of property, then it was protected by the Fourteenth Amendment. If it was not, then no one had it, whatever their ancestry. Brown was indifferent to the distinction. Brown saw no contradiction in simultaneously holding that a white reputation was equal to a colored one, and that whites' reputations were superior to blacks'.

In American culture, reputation was based on an individual's conduct in the eyes of his or her peers. Shameful conduct diminished reputation. Honorable conduct enhanced reputation. What Brown was conceding (or perhaps defending) was the assumption that in everyone's eyes—just by looking at an individual—dark color meant a lesser reputation than light color. Nothing could have been a more obvious indicator of his casual racism than this assumption. In purely legal terms, however, if being assigned to one race rather than another was important enough to incur a debility in reputation (that is, to be treated shamefully), then the assignment of racial distinctions clearly did harm one's reputation.

Brown next considered whether Louisiana had exercised its police power reasonably. He ruled that Tourgée's bizarre examples of discrimination on the basis of hair color or nationality, leading to requirements to paint your house that color or walk only on one side of the street, would not meet the standard. Brown stated, "The reply to all this is that every exercise of the police power must be reasonable, and extend only to such laws as are enacted in good faith for the promotion for the public good, and not for the annoyance or oppression of a particular class." This was a circular definition of reasonable, simply accepting that the Redeemer majority in the state legislature acted according to their own lights—"good faith"—was enough. How did separating blacks from whites actually promote health and safety? Standing in the way of this conclusion was *Yick Wo v. Hopkins* (1886), in which a San Francisco municipal regulation effectively closing Chinese laundries violated the owners' due process rights. He summarized the findings of that landmark civil rights case as follows: "It was held to be a covert attempt on the part of the municipality to make an arbitrary and unjust discrimination against the Chinese race." In order to violate the Fourteenth Amendment, therefore, the regulation or statute needed to be "covert," "arbitrary," and "unjust." Prudently, the Louisiana law was on its face nondiscriminatory.

Having just set the bar of reasonableness or rationality very low for Louisiana, Brown gave the state even more latitude: "There must necessarily be a large discretion on the part of the legislature." Although it is difficult to discern his precise meaning, we can place the remark in context. He clarified with his next sentence that what he meant was to give the state legislature a great deal of discretion in local matters: "In determining the question of reasonableness it [the legislature] is at liberty to act with reference to the established usages, customs and traditions of the people, and with a view to the promotion of their comfort, and the preservation of the public peace and good order." This was a kind of Redemption-era judicial deference of a kind that was lacking in the Court's decisions about economic matters, however.

What is more, Brown implied that if customs violated the Fourteenth Amendment requirements, the latter must fall. Some of the customs predated the passage of the amendment. Some predated the Civil War. Brown's reasonableness standard might thus include customs rooted in slavery. He never gave a rule for which customs were so established that the postwar amendments did not apply to them. Why did the Court need to be deferential toward the local traditions when they violated the U.S. Constitution's guarantees of due process and equal protection?

Brown concluded his opinion for the Court with a consideration of what racial equality meant. He found comfort in the state of Louisiana's clever use of the word "equal" in its segregation statute. After all, Louisiana had commanded "equal, but separate" cars for the two races. To Brown's way of thinking, there was nothing inherently adversely discriminatory in the segregation by race. The "badge of inferiority" did not exist in the law, he reasoned. "If this be so, it is not by reason of anything found in the act, but solely because the colored race chooses to put that construction upon it." As Professor Charles Black of Yale Law School commented in the *Yale Law Journal* in 1960, "The curves of callousness and stupidity intersect at their respective maxima." Brown had put the onus of the effect of the law's discrimination upon its intended victims.

After a fashion, Brown was quite right to do so. The state of Louisiana was attempting to create a racially segregated society that let one race know it was not fit to mix with the other. The message to the colored race would be loud and clear. Brown did not take judicial notice of how the law was going to work in practice. The colored cars were always in worse condition, less convenient, and noticeably inferior. Though facts "in the nature of things" mattered to him, facts of life in New Orleans' public transportation did not. Brown might have been on surer factual ground if he had found, on the basis of preserving order and for public safety, that it was reasonable to segregate railcars. He could then have cited evidence of racially based conflict in racially mixed cars. Later courts would find such facts a surer foundation for upholding Jim Crow legislation.

As to the underlying facts in the nature of things, of who was colored and who was white, Brown abdicated any federal court role. He noted that North Carolina used the "any visible admixture of black blood" rule, that Ohio used the "preponderance of blood," and that Michigan and Virginia declared that "white blood must only be in the proportion of three fourths." He dismissed the idea that such variations of what constituted belonging to one race or the other meant that there was no valid basis for it: "But these are questions to be determined under the laws of each State and are not properly put in issue in this case." Therefore, he left Plessy's status to be determined by Louisiana.

If in the nature of things race was a defining characteristic of men and women, the legal test for race should have been uniform across the country. The fact that jurisdictions did not agree on a test for race should have suggested that custom and culture dictated the definition of race, not nature. If race was so frequently hard to determine that courts and legislatures had to engage in arbitrary, varying, and contentious contortions to render it a useful category, how could it be assumed that the category existed in the natural world?

One cannot enter the mind of a judge who lived over a hundred years ago any more than one can enter the minds of today's justices. But Brown left a clue to his underlying beliefs in the last sentences of his opinion. He wrote, "The argument [of Plessy's counsel] also assumes that social prejudices may be overcome by legislation, and that equal rights cannot be secured to the negro except by an enforced commingling of the two races." Tourgée, Walker, and Phillips's brief did not advocate legislation to force two groups of people to sit together when they did not want to do so. They did not argue for integration. They were contending that it was wrong for a state government to force them to sit apart. Brown did not misread their arguments, though he did mischaracterize them, for he had other facts in the nature of things on his mind.

He was weary and wary of the legislative program of Congressional Reconstruction. He had not fought in the war that ended slavery; nor had he sacrificed anything of his own in that effort. He viewed it from the safe distance of a law office. From that less than exalted perspective, he could see that no court was going to change what Redemption had achieved. He could have been a little more candid, as soon to be justice Oliver Wendell Holmes Jr. was in *Giles v. Harris* (1903), denying a black Alabama voter's petition to the Court: "The [petitioner's] bill imports that the great mass of the white population intends to keep the blacks from voting. To meet such an intent something more than ordering the plaintiff's name to be inscribed upon the lists of 1902 will be needed. If the conspiracy and the intent exist, a name on a piece of paper will not defeat them. Unless we are prepared to supervise the voting in that State by officers of the court, it seems to us that all that the plaintiff could get from [a court order] would be an empty form."

But it does not take too much imagination or the exercise of too much authorial discretion to read these motives into Brown's final words: "If the two races are to meet upon terms of social equality, it must be the result of natural affinities, a mutual appreciation of each other's merits and a voluntary consent of individuals." He then cited from a case from the highest court in New York, the court of appeals, *People v. Gallagher*, and went on to declare, "Legislation is powerless to eradicate racial instincts or to abolish distinctions based upon physical differences, and the attempt to do so can only result in accentuating the difficulties of the present situation." In his view, the Republican effort to provide political, civil, and legal equality for the Negro had only resulted in violence, disorder, and the Redeemer governments. "If the civil and political rights of both races be equal one cannot be inferior to the other civilly or politically. If one race be inferior to the other socially, the Constitution of the United States cannot put them upon the same plane."

Or perhaps Brown's view was largely political. One notes the intentional inclusion of Northern states cases in his brief survey. Like many Northern Republicans, he was concerned with what might happen in the North if events stemming from disputes in the South affected their equally racist Northern counterparts. Might blacks move north and demand equal treatment there?

Was it equally possible that he regarded the white South as an uncontrollably violent, bigoted, largely unlawful region? In other words, that his opinion in *Plessy* did not respect the Redeemed region so much as consign it to an unredeemable land of bigotry and backwardness? "Equal, but separate" was the best African Americans could hope for from this benighted area.

———

In his dissenting opinion, Justice John Marshall Harlan refuted Brown's position so thoroughly that it secured Harlan's reputation as "the great dissenter." Although he certainly demolished the rest of the Court's decision in *Plessy*, it was not so much an original argument as the refinement, a distillation even, of what Plessy's attorneys had argued in their briefs and oral argument, and the problems with Brown's own treatment of case law and racial distinctions. Harlan's dissent also made clear that much of Brown's opinion was taken from the state of Louisiana's brief and oral argument. With all this understood, Harlan's dissent is not that of a man free from racism, a man apart from his time, or a paragon of jurisprudential rectitude.

Harlan began with his own summary and quotations from the Separate Car Act. He almost immediately focused on the exemption for nurses. He wondered why a "colored servant" or a "colored maid" was not exempt. He continued with a short statement of the law's purpose: "Thus the State regulates the use of a public highway by citizens of the United States solely upon the basis of race." For him, the public safety and comfort motive was irrelevant. All that mattered was that the state of Louisiana had enacted a discrimination based on a forbidden category. He posited that even the fairness of the issue was not relevant: "However apparent the injustice of such legislation may be, we have only to consider whether it is consistent with Constitution of the United States."

Harlan based at least some of his reasoning on common carrier law. Reaching back into the English common-law inheritance, the common carrier law held such businesses to a higher standard of care and duty than other entities. Quoting from a Supreme Court decision in *New Jersey Steam Navigation Co. v. Merchants' Bank*, Harlan noted, "A common carrier was in the exercise 'of a public sort of public office, and has public duties to perform from which he should not be permitted to exonerate himself without the assent of the parties concerned." He went on to quote from other Court common carrier decisions to emphasize the point that common carriers, which included railroads, were public. He was doing this in order to show that this was no minor, private matter, but an interference with a basic right.

But Harlan took common carrier law a step further when he declared, "In respect of civil rights, common to all citizens, the Constitution of the United States does not, I think, permit any public authority to know the race of those entitled to be protected in the enjoyment of such rights." In parallel with, if not taken directly from, Tourgée's brief, he was making a case for the elimination of race as a permissible category of distinction for law. He also applied this to courts: "But I deny that any legislative body or judicial tribunal may have regard to the race of citizens when the civil rights of those citizens are involved." This was not about the Reconstruction amendments' protection of Negroes. Harlan rejected that view of their purpose. "Indeed, such legislation, as that here in question, is inconsistent not only with that equality of rights which pertains to citizenship, National and State, but with the personal liberty enjoyed by every one within the United States." The guarantees of the Fourteenth Amendment were for all citizens.

Harlan also rejected Brown's dismissal of Plessy's Thirteenth Amendment claims. In his mind the Thirteenth Amendment was not only apposite but dispositive. "It not only struck down the institution of slavery as previously existing in the United States, but it prevents the imposition of any burdens or disabilities that constitute badges of slavery or servitude." For him, slavery and race were intertwined. The Fourteenth Amendment thus supplemented the Thirteenth. It "added greatly to the dignity and glory of American citizenship, and to the security of personal liberty" with its provisions on citizenship, due process, and equal protection. In summary, "These two amendments, if enforced according to their true intent and meaning, will protect all the civil rights that pertain to freedom and citizenship." He rejected Brown's contention that they were only there to end slavery and protect the Negro, respectively.

To support this interpretation, Harlan cited Supreme Court decisions overturning racial restrictions for juries: "They [the Thirteenth and Fourteenth Amendments] removed the race line from our governmental systems." In addition, "They declared, in legal effect . . . 'that the law in the States shall be the same for the black as for the white; that all persons, whether colored or white, shall stand equal before the laws of the States, and, in regard to the colored race, for whose protection the amendment was primarily designed, that no discrimination shall be made against them by law because of their color.'" And, finally, from the case of *Gibson v. Mississippi*, "All citizens are equal before the law." These decisions "show that it is not within the power of a State to prohibit colored citizens, because of their race, from participating as jurors in the administration of justice."

Harlan rejected the contention "in argument" that the "equal, but separate" provision of the Separate Car Act made the statute race neutral. "Every one knows that the statute in question had its origin in the purpose, not so much to exclude white persons from railroad cars occupied by blacks, as to exclude colored people from coaches occupied by or assigned to white persons." He was most likely referring to something in the oral argument that the state of Louisiana's attorneys introduced to defend their law. They succeeded with the other seven justices, but not Harlan. "The thing to accomplish was, under the guise of giving equal accommodation for whites and blacks, to compel the latter to keep to themselves while travelling in railroad passenger coaches." Contrary to the conclusion of his brethren, "No one would be so wanting in candor as to assert the contrary." At stake was not the desire of one race to mix with the other, but what Harlan termed "personal liberty"—the freedom to mix if one so desired. He asserted that if a "white man and a black man" wanted to sit together, "no government proceeding alone on grounds of race, can prevent it without infringing the personal liberty of each."

Harlan was doing two kinds of adjudication that Brown had not. First, Harlan was looking at the legislative record to see what purpose Louisiana had in passing the law. Finding that the state wanted to impose segregation rather than to ensure equality, he was able to dispose of the "equal" in the text of the law as a sham—indeed, it was an affront to the Court. Second, he was looking behind the law in the briefs to find the impact of the law on the everyday lives of those it affected. This kind of judicial activity would be the basis (and the bane) of civil rights adjudication after *Brown v. Board of Education II* (1955).

Unlike Brown, who had placed the onus for wanting to mix the races with Plessy, Harlan placed the burden for separating them solely on the state of Louisiana: "It is quite another thing for government to forbid citizens of the white and black races from travelling in the same public conveyance, and to punish officers of railroad companies for permitting persons of the two races to occupy the same passenger coach." With an prescience that came from a truer understanding of the object of white supremacists, he proceeded to predict coming segregation in sidewalks, streetcars, courtrooms, and public assemblages. He considered those possibilities to be as absurd as segregating on the basis of "native and naturalized citizens" or "of Protestants and Roman Catholics." Some jurisdictions had not only allowed segregation, but before the adoption of the Constitution's first amendment, they had set religious qualifications for office.

Harlan next rejected the reasonableness standard of review for state exercise of the police power: "But I do not understand that the courts have anything to do with the policy or expediency of legislation." He decried a look into the rationality of the legislature as a violation of the separation of powers. "There is a dangerous tendency in these latter days to enlarge the functions of the courts, by means of judicial interference with the will of the people as expressed by the legislature." His judicial deference was even stronger than Brown's. He proclaimed the limits of judicial review as follows: "The courts best discharge their duty by executing the will of the law-making power, constitutionally expressed, leaving the results of legislation to be dealt with by the people through their representatives." Here was the doctrine announced in *Carolene Products* in 1938, footnote four, in which Justice Harlan F. Stone indicated that courts must give deference to legislatures except when their actions infringe upon the constitutionally protected rights of "discrete and insular minorities." In other words, Harlan declared that "if the power exists to enact a statute, that ends the matter so far as the courts are concerned." This was with the understanding that legislatures did not have the power if it violated the Constitution.

However, Harlan completed his refutation of Brown's countenance of racist legislation with a declaration of his own racialist faith: "The white race deems itself to be the dominant race in this country. And so it is, in prestige, in achievements, in education, in wealth and in power." With some expression of pride in his own racial identity, he declared, "So, I doubt not, it will continue to be for all time, if it remains true to its great heritage and holds fast to the principles of constitutional liberty." It was an odd sentiment considering the heritage of slavery, bigotry, and violence that he had just laid out, but Harlan was expressing the sentiment of the time. It had already formed an emerging profession's history of the United States, expanding over time into the histories we learn to this day. It is the familiar story of the nation being founded as bastions for religious, economic, and political liberty. It was already shaping the story of the Civil War as a "new birth of freedom." It ignored slavery, the true purpose of the Puritan community, and the lack of freedom in politics, economics, and society except for white men—and sometimes not even them. But it was a popular narrative, not least because it allowed people to take comfort in a happier tale of struggle, opportunity, and triumph.

Harlan then turned away from this expression of racial pride to resume the task of constitutional adjudication. "But in view of the Constitution, in the eye of the law, there is in this country no superior, dominant, ruling class of citizens. There is no caste here." This was the democratic experiment of American exceptionalism: a nation apart from the Old World of feudalism, inherited ranks, and oppression. Taking his cue from Tourgée, he pronounced, "Our Constitution is color-blind, and neither knows nor tolerates classes among citizens. In respect of civil rights, all citizens are equal before the law." He repeated the law's ideals, at least according to those who held that law was something more than the diktat of the state. "The humblest is the peer of the most powerful. The law regards man as man, and takes no account of his surroundings or of his color when his civil rights as guaranteed by the supreme law of the land are involved." It was certainly a high principle. But Harlan knew he was a minority of one in asserting it that day. "It is, therefore, to be regretted that this high tribunal, the final expositor of the fundamental law of the land, has reached the conclusion that it is competent for a State to regulate the enjoyment by citizens of their civil rights solely upon the basis of race."

Harlan saved his best salvos for last. He condemned the majority opinion: "In my opinion, the judgment this day rendered will, in time, prove to be quite as pernicious as the decision made by this tribunal in the Dred Scott case." This was harsh language. The Court had taken a beating over that case over the years, if not at the time, in particular Chief Justice Roger B. Taney's opinion that denied that African Americans could ever be citizens as per his unsupportable, odd reading of the Constitution. Harlan correctly noted that the Reconstruction amendments had "eradicated these principles from our institutions." However, Harlan saw a defeat for those enactments in the *Plessy* ruling. "The present decision, it may well be apprehended, will not only stimulate aggressions, more or less brutal and irritating, upon the admitted rights of colored citizens, but will encourage the belief that it is possible, by means of state enactments, to defeat the beneficent purposes which the people of the United States had in view when they adopted the recent amendments of the Constitution."

Again, Harlan was correct in this prediction. What was more, he believed, quite rightly as it turned out, that violence would continue. "What can more certainly arouse race hate, what more certainly create and perpetuate a feeling of distrust between these races, than state enactments," he opined, "which, in fact, proceed on the ground that colored citizens are so inferior and degraded that they cannot be allowed to sit in public coaches occupied by white citizens?" He produced another accurate prediction of the effect of *Plessy*: the undermining of the whole Reconstruction project. "State enactments, regulating the enjoyment of civil rights, upon the basis of race, and cunningly devised to defeat legitimate results of the war, under the pretense of recognizing equality of rights, can have no other result than to render permanent peace impossible, and to keep alive a conflict of races, the continuance of which must do harm to all concerned." He alone had not been fooled by the state of Louisiana's deceptive use of the word "equal" to describe their racial segregation.

The solution for Harlan to the "race problem" was simple. "The sure guarantee of the peace and security of each race is the clear, distinct, unconditional recognition by our governments, National and State, of every right that inheres in civil freedom, and of the equality before the law of all citizens of the United States without regard to race." Despite his own acceptance of the existence of such things as a white race and a colored race, he adhered to the possibility that Tourgée had laid out before him of a color-blind law.

Harlan then disposed of Brown's distinction between social and political equality. "That argument, if it can be properly regarded as one, is scarcely worthy of consideration," he wrote dismissively, "for social equality no more exists between two races when travelling in a passenger coach or a public highway than when members of the same races sit by each other in a street car or in the jury box, or" political assemblies, the streets, registering to vote in the same room, or vote in the same place. He was quite right to compare railroad car segregation to segregation in these other areas of life, both political and social. However, as he had noted earlier in his opinion, the ultimate goal was to segregate everywhere to enforce a system of oppression against the colored race. The argument of reductio ad absurdum—taking a position to its extreme in order to discredit it—only works if your opponent is not seeking the extreme.

Harlan's next example was even more tenuous: "the Chinese race." After relating the history of anti-Chinese legislation and prejudice, he questioned why a Chinaman should be allowed to ride with whites when coloreds, "many of whom, perhaps, risked their lives for the preservation of the Union, who are entitled, by law" to full political and civil rights, "are yet declared to be criminals, liable to imprisonment, if they ride in a public coach occupied by citizens of the white race." If the easy answer came that the Chinese were not present in Louisiana in substantial numbers, he might pointedly make the case that this was the proof positive that this was racially targeted. Unfortunately, Harlan did not proceed in that direction, even though the precedent of *Yick Wo* was immediately before him in Brown's majority opinion.

Harlan was moving too fast towards his coda to pay attention to these nuances. He reiterated the Thirteenth Amendment claim as his own, borrowing from his dissent in the *Civil Rights Cases*. "The arbitrary separation of citizens, on the basis of race, while they are on a public highway, is a badge of servitude wholly inconsistent with the civil freedom and the equality before the law established by the Constitution. It cannot be justified upon any legal grounds." Louisiana's position that public safety and comfort required it found no sympathy here: "If evils will result from the commingling of the two races upon public highways established for the benefit of all, they will infinitely less than those that will surely come from state legislation regulating the enjoyment of civil rights upon the basis of race." There was no difference between political and social rights. They were all civil rights. The possible discomfort and threat to public order did not outweigh the violation of these rights. Harlan had weighed, measured, and examined the Separate Car Act and found it wanting.

He concluded, "The thin disguise of 'equal' accommodations for passengers in railroad coaches will not mislead any one, nor atone for the wrong this day done." Again, he predicted the outcome of *Plessy* quite well. "May it not now be reasonably expected that astute men of the dominant race, who affect to be disturbed at the possibility that the integrity of the white race may be corrupted, or that its supremacy will be imperiled, by contact on public highways with black people, will endeavor to procure statues requiring" the partition of juries? He continued, "I cannot see but that, according to the principles this day announced, such state legislation, although conceived in hostility to, and enacted for the purpose of humiliating citizens of the United States of a particular race, would be held to be consistent with the Constitution." Before we consider Harlan to be a seer of incredible accuracy, we should remember that Southern legislatures had already enacted such a system before, and not for slaves. The so-called Black Codes, until Congressional Reconstruction destroyed them, created just such a system. Oddly enough, as Harlan pointed out, the Thirteenth and Fourteenth Amendments were supposed to prevent such things in the future. The Congress had not reckoned on Redemption and the U.S. Supreme Court.

Harlan lamented this future as "mischievous" and worse. "Such a system is inconsistent with the guarantee given by the Constitution to each State of a republican form of government, and may be stricken down by Congressional action, or by the courts in the discharge of their solemn duty to maintain the supreme law of the land, anything in the Constitution or laws of any State to the contrary notwithstanding." He was referring to Article Four, Section Four, of the Constitution. This little-used clause might have been a powerful weapon against undemocratic regimes if the Court had but availed itself of it. Like Brown and the majority in *Plessy*'s restrictive interpretation of the Thirteenth and Fourteenth Amendments, it declined to do that as well.

So ended one of the most remarkable dissents in the history of the U.S. Supreme Court. It was flawed in some ways. Harlan did not develop his points for either the Thirteenth Amendment or equal protection as fully as he could have. He did not properly distinguish the majority opinions in the *Civil Rights Cases*, the *Slaughterhouse Cases*, or *Louisville, New Orleans, & Texas Railway Company v. Mississippi* from the case at hand. Moreover, he demonstrated his own acceptance of racial categories while not assiduously questioning the state standards for what constituted a race. He thus missed a golden opportunity to destroy racial legislation.

However, Harlan did introduce to American jurisprudence several important arguments about how the Constitution should be read, the law applied, and the kind of society that could result in post–Civil War America. He popularized Tourgée's concept of the color-blind Constitution. He laid out the foundations for what would become known as strict scrutiny for suspect legislation. He also gave a full meaning to the intent of the attempt by the Reconstruction Congress to reform American law in light of the aftermath of emancipation. The revival of segregation, the Ku Klux Klan, and the society of violence, hatred, and tyranny demonstrated that Harlan's commitment to the actual rule of law instead of one of prejudice, oppression, and overreaching hidden behind lies and sophistry to be the better philosophy.

Harlan's dissent made one other enduring impact on American law. It, and not Brown's majority opinion, introduced the enduring phrase "separate but equal" into the popular lexicon. This reversed the Louisiana Separate Car Act's formulation of "equal, but separate," as well as the Court's underlying rationale for upholding it. Harlan's formulation placed the emphasis on the segregating rather than the supposed neutrality of the racial discrimination. In so doing—so successfully that his phrasing became the dominant one—he gave those challenging *Plessy* a kind of high ground.

———

When, on May 18, 1896, both opinions in the case of *Plessy v. Ferguson* came down, the public reaction to the decision in *Plessy* was mixed and muted. For a case that would come to symbolize an era of American law and society, it did not receive much attention at the time, barely getting a mention in the judicial columns of the major newspapers. Not surprisingly, the *New Orleans Daily Picayune* applauded the decision in an editorial on May 19, 1896: "Equality of rights does not mean community of rights." To do otherwise "would be absolute socialism, in which the individual would be extinguished in the vast mass of human beings, a condition repugnant to every principle of enlightened democracy." The inherent contradiction between opposing socialism—the state-imposed system of communal property—and favoring state imposed segregation was lost on that particular writer.

The *Democrat and Chronicle* from Rochester, New York, an old Republican standard-bearer, expressed a different view in an editorial on May 20, 1896. It agreed with Harlan's dissent that Brown's opinion was the equivalent of arguing "that it would be just as reasonable for the states to pass laws requiring separate cars for Protestant and Catholics or descendants of those of the Teutonic race and those of the Latin race." Further, it was a betrayal of the "principles of the republic." Certainly, there could be no mistaking the impact. "It puts the official stamp of the highest court in the country upon the miserable doctrine that several millions of American citizens are of an inferior race and unfit to mingle with citizens of other races." The *New York Daily Tribune* agreed in a piece the day before: "It is unfortunate, to say the least, that our highest court has declared itself in opposition to the effort to expunge race lines in State legislation."

The *Washington Post* gave the case a brief story largely describing the opinions without comment, though it mentioned Brown's opinion was "very brief." It also described Plessy as a mulatto—a term for someone of mixed racial ancestry. The *Central Law Journal* gave the decision more space but favored Brown's opinion reporting that it "shows very clearly that the distinction between laws interfering with political equality of the negro and those requiring the separation of the two races in schools, theaters, and railway carriages has been frequently drawn by that court." It went on to list the major cases (and misspelled "Strauder" as "Strander"). It described Harlan's manner in his dissent as "vigorous."

The Springfield, Massachusetts, *Republican* took a more sardonic tone: "The law may now be expected to spread like the measles in those commonwealths where white supremacy is thought to be in peril." It wondered, "Did the southerners ever pause to indict the Almighty for allowing negroes to be born on the same earth with white men?" It concluded, "We fear it was the one great mistake in creation not to provide every race and every class with its own earth." This editorial's musings gave new meaning to the phrase "to each his own."

A writer in *Donahoe's Magazine* lamented the current state of affairs: "It is more than thirty years since Appomattox; time enough assuredly for race prejudice against the negro to have died from the heart of the white man under influence of the Constitutional Amendments in his favor." There was only one unfortunate conclusion. "With legislation against the negro backed up by the highest tribunal in the country (just as if the Dred Scott decision had not passed into lasting infamy, and as if there had been no Civil War)," amid all the other pieces of prejudicial legislation, "the United States presents to the world a sad spectacle of inconsistency and contradiction." It was a state to be condemned not countenanced.

Other publications accepted the decision as appropriate for local conditions. The Duluth, Minnesota, *News Tribune* opined on May 22 that "the necessity for such a law exists only in the South and the statue would never have been enacted but for conditions which made the separation of the races in railroad travel apparently unavoidable in order to secure the comfort of all concerned." The Richmond, Virginia, *Dispatch*, added the day before, "Some colored people make themselves so disagreeable on the cars that their conduct leads white men to ponder the question whether such a law as that of Louisiana is not needed in all the Southern States." One wonders whether the writer had the same treatment in mind for the disagreeable whites.

The *New York Journal* agreed with the *Dispatch* and added on May 20, "Colored persons are entitled to all the common rights which pertain to any other persons, but they frequently exaggerate a denial of special privileges, not necessary to them, though hurtful to others, into rights." Perhaps they thought being free from the threat of lynching for being too close to a white woman was a privilege.

––––––

Of the two opinions in *Plessy v. Ferguson*, Brown's has come to be regarded as the most representative of this time in the nation's history. As historians David W. Blight, Edward J. Blum, Nina Silber, and Drew Gilpin Faust, among others, have written, the 1870s, 1880s, and 1890s saw a host of events that changed the memories of the Civil War from one of bitter contest to a titanic struggle between reconcilable narratives. In religious revivals, the yellow fever epidemic of 1878, and the crusades of organizations like the Women's Christian Temperance Union, Americans made common cause with one another across the sectional divide, but at the cost of Northerners acceding to Southern whites' demands for racial exclusion and segregation. In memorializing the dead to the reunions that led to reenactments, both Union and Confederate veterans found ways to come together by the end of the century, largely to the exclusion of even African American veterans. Union veterans and their relations could celebrate the preservation of the Union. Their former opponents commemorated the Lost Cause in which they had merely defended their homes against invasion. Gone was the vengefulness and the commitment to emancipation wrought by the strenuousness of war.

At the same time, the nation went through a grieving process in which national cemeteries, burial practices, and mourning underwent significant changes. Holidays honored the bravery of both sides and the sacrifice of the two regions, and lamented the horribleness of war. Amateur psychologists might be tempted to apply, more rigidly than is merited, Elisabeth Kübler-Ross's stages of grief to the nation's traumatic losses in the Civil War, namely denial, anger, bargaining, depression, and acceptance. Though these stages roughly fit the timeline of Presidential Reconstruction (denial of the Confederate South's commitment to rebellion and white supremacy),

Congressional Reconstruction (anger at the Black Codes and election of former Confederates), the Compromise of 1877 (bargaining to reduce tensions), Redemption (the depression of those fighting in the courts for African American rights), and Jim Crow (the ruling in *Plessy* and acquiescence to the establishment of a racist South), one should probably regard analyses of how individuals cope with loss as a metaphorical rather than a literal basis of comparison to a national phenomenon of incredible complexity.

The aftermath of *Plessy* in the law was complex. *Plessy* did not herald the imposition of a system of racial segregation. In fact, some scholars have decided that the decision did little except recognize a system already proceeding apace. Other scholars argue that segregation came to the United States one case at a time, with *Plessy* as but one of the precedents. Regardless, Jim Crow America was coming. It was just a question of how fast and what shape it would take.

CHAPTER 5

Plessy's World

As Brown's opinion indicates, the law in Plessy represented the currents of contemporary thought. At the same time, it provided the foundation for another round of segregation—this one much more severe than what had preceded it. *Plessy* rearranged the conversation about segregation from one of legal categories to one of evidence, social science, and psychology. In summary, *Plessy* gave a window of opportunity for litigants to challenge Jim Crow on the basis of actual inequality of facilities, funding, and treatment. The case law that followed *Plessy* provides evidence for all of these statements.

The first mystery, doctrinally speaking, is how Harlan's dissent's phrasing of the doctrine "separate but equal" became generally accepted over the Court's and the Separate Car Act's phrase "equal, but separate." Dissenting opinions have no precedential value. There was no legal reason for Harlan's phrasing to gain credibility. With only a few exceptions, an examination of the case law after *Plessy* does not show state legislatures adopting the Harlan formulation either. They either used "equal, but separate" or mandated "separate" facilities and that they be "equal." But then Associate Justice Charles Evans Hughes accepted the "separate but equal" phrase as an accurate summary of the holding in *Plessy* in his majority opinion in *McCabe v. Atchison, Topeka & Santa Fe Railway Company* in 1914. Furthermore, headnotes—the publisher-provided keys to decisions—in the West Law compendiums of cases began to routinely use the "separate but equal" language to describe the provisions of state statutes and the holding of various courts, including the U.S. Supreme Court, whether or not those words appeared in the decisions themselves. Besides a quiet acceptance that Harlan was right to put the emphasis on the segregation, it is possible that his phrase was just easier on the ear than its competition.

Although *Plessy* was not the clarion call for states to institute Jim Crow laws, it certainly gave the go-ahead. Regardless of whether state legislatures were looking for the U.S. Supreme Court's imprimatur, a flurry of segregation laws followed. As a result, the South in particular became a visibly and unbridgeable divided society. These laws covered everything from cradle to grave. The signs appeared, literally, all over the region. Signs reading "Whites Only" and "Colored Only" instructed everyone that there were two groups, and you either belonged to one or the other. Colored facilities were never the equivalent of those for whites. Besides instituting a scramble to have oneself placed into the favored category—after all, it was obvious which one was better—Jim Crow states made sure to go through the extra expense of providing two different facilities for each race. As the system spread, the obvious inequality of segregation became clear for all to see. Vastly inferior schools, bathrooms, entrances, cemeteries, and water fountains, sometimes side by side, sometimes hidden, sometimes not, were provided for the colored. The facts of Jim Crow soon demonstrated the hollowness of de jure equality.

States as far afield as Wyoming, New Mexico, Arizona, and Oklahoma joined the South in nullifying marriages and prohibiting marriages between whites and Negroes. Arizona's statute went even further: "The marriage of a person of Caucasian blood with a Negro, Mongolian, Malay, or Hindu shall be null and void." (As for whether Arizona understood that Hindu was a religion, not an ethnicity, that subject is debatable.) Alabama legislators concerned themselves with recreation: "It shall be unlawful for a negro and white person to play together or in company with each other at any game of pool or billiards." Louisiana made sure the separation was sizable even in the selling of tickets to the circus: "The said ticket offices shall not be less than twenty-five (25) feet apart."

That these laws reflected the old antebellum concerns that African American men and white women would form social alliances became obvious with such laws as Alabama's concerning nurses: "No person or corporation shall require any white female nurse to nurse in wards or rooms in hospitals, either public or private, in which negro men are placed." Georgia extended its concerns to hair cutting: "No colored barber shall serve as a barber [to] white women or girls." Just as the Black Codes reflected the former slave states' need to reestablish a form of slavery, so Jim Crow before and after *Plessy* reflected the same racial concerns as before the war.

The U.S. Supreme Court did little to nothing to stem this tidal wave of segregation, cleaving instead to its de jure review of the text of laws in a series of cases following *Plessy*. On December 18, 1899, Justice Harlan wrote for a unanimous court in *Cumming v. Richmond County Board of Education* that the county was not obligated to provide a high school for colored students as well as a high school for whites. He noted that the plaintiffs were not challenging the Jim Crow school law, only the board of education's decision not to open a high school for African American children while it converted their high school to one for whites on the grounds that the limited funds meant it was a choice between a high school for African Americans and primary and secondary schools. "We are not permitted by the evidence in the record to regard that decision as having been made with any desire or purpose on the part of the Board to discriminate against any of the colored school children of the county on account of their race," Harlan reasoned. Although he may not have seen the racism in providing a high school education only for whites in the pleadings, the effect of this decision was to create an exception to equal education that white supremacists could drive an entire convoy through.

On December 3, 1900, in the case of *Chesapeake and Ohio Railway Company v. Kentucky*, Justice Brown had an opportunity to revisit the Court's decision in the *Louisville* case in which the Court had held that Mississippi's separate car law was not an infringement of Congress' authority to regulate interstate commerce. The Kentucky supreme court had read the statute as to limit its intent to railway travel within the state even though the legislature made no effort to do so. Brown upheld this construction as a matter of deference: "It is scarcely courteous to impute to a legislature the enactment of a law which it knew to be unconstitutional." Why Brown thought courtesy had anything to do with the U.S. Supreme Court's review of a state enactment is a worthy question. One might suppose he meant deference. Courts were supposed to salvage laws resorting to a declaration they were unconstitutional only when absolutely necessary. The unanimous court did not seem to think this was one of those cases, the *Hall v. DeCuir* precedent notwithstanding. Integration was a burden to interstate commerce while segregation was not.

On November 9, 1908, the Court, in an opinion by Justice Brewer, who had been unable to participate in *Plessy*, upheld a Kentucky law that made teaching or schooling the two races together a criminal offense even though the college in question was a private school, in *Berea College v. Commonwealth of Kentucky*. The law discriminated on the basis of race. It forbade the private, voluntary intermingling of people from different races. A more clear-cut violation of equal protection could not be found. Brewer made up for his inability to bar Plessy from a railroad car with a justification for a state government interfering with private association that went beyond the Louisiana case: "Again, the decision by a state court of the extent and limitation of the powers conferred by the State upon one of its own corporations [the college] is of a purely local nature." Because the state of Kentucky and its laws were racist, the U.S. Supreme Court was duty bound to defer to its state court in determining whether one of those laws violated the U.S. Constitution.

Although Justices Oliver Wendell Holmes Jr. and William Henry Moody concurred in the judgment only, Harlan was able to get Justice William R. Day to agree with his dissent this time. Just as in *Plessy*, Harlan found the deference of the Court to a state legislature baffling given the purposes of the Fourteenth Amendment: "In my judgment the court should directly meet and decide the broad question presented by the statute." It was, after all, the Court's role in the constitutional framework. "I am of opinion that in its essential parts the statute is an arbitrary invasion of the rights of liberty and property guaranteed by the Fourteenth Amendment against hostile state action and is, therefore, void."

On May 31, 1910, Justice Joseph McKenna wrote for a nearly unanimous court that a railroad company's regulation separating passengers on an interstate line by race was a reasonable exercise of their authority in the case of *Chiles v. Chesapeake and Ohio Railway Company*. For the proposition that a community's prevailing racism could justify such an action he cited Brown's opinion in *Plessy*, which established the standard of reasonableness review now plainly based on the prejudices of the majority and the legal incapacities of the minority: "It is true the power of a legislature to recognize a racial distinction was the subject considered, but if the test of reasonableness in legislation be, as it was declared to be, 'the established usages, customs and traditions of the people' and the 'promotion of their comfort and the preservation of the public peace and good order,' this must also be the test of the reasonableness of the regulations of a carrier, made for like purpose and to secure like results." Further, McKenna proclaimed, "Regulations which are induced by the general sentiment of the community for whom they are made and upon whom they operate, cannot be said to be unreasonable." Besides his confusion of a community with the politically powerful in that community, there is the odd notion that federal law does not hold sway over local sentiments. Harlan dissented without writing an opinion to this diminishment of the Union's victory over states' rights. Justice Hughes applied the supposed *Plessy* standard of "separate but equal" to an Oklahoma statute in the 1916 case of *McCabe v. Atchison, Topeka & Santa Fe Railway Company*, and found that the challenge was not appropriately before the Court because the plaintiffs had not properly arranged to purchase tickets, then be arrested after the passage of the statute.

But there were indications that *Plessy* would not determine the outcome of every appeal. The next year, in the case of *Buchanan v. Warley* (1917), the Court, in an opinion by Justice Day, held that a local Kentucky ordinance forbidding the sale of certain houses to colored people violated the Fourteenth Amendment. While conceding the broad scope of a state's police power, Day declared that "it is equally well established that the police power, broad as it is, cannot justify the passage of a law or ordinance which runs counter to the limitations of the Federal Constitution; that principle has been so frequently affirmed in this court that we need not stop to cite the cases." He added, "The federal Constitution and laws passed within its authority are by the express terms of that instrument made the supreme law of the land," and this included the due process clause of the Fourteenth Amendment. Day allowed for local custom. "That there exists a serious and difficult problem arising from a feeling of race hostility which the law is powerless to control, and to which it must give a measure of consideration, may be freely admitted. But its solution cannot be promoted by depriving citizens of their constitutional rights and privileges." As for why this segregation ordinance was different from the others the Court had upheld, including the one in *Plessy*, Day had little to fall back on except that those enactments included a mandate for other equal facilities and that Day's court was upholding a white man's right to sell to a colored man, not the colored man's right to buy. However, this was also a property right—something near and dear to this era's jurisprudence.

On November 21, 1927, in the case of *Gong Lum et al. v. Rice et al.*, chief justice and former president William Howard Taft put his weight behind the opinion that someone of the "Mongolian or yellow race" was "colored" for the purposes of segregation. Mississippi's post-Reconstruction constitution mandated separate schooling for whites and colored people. Though the Mississippi constitution was solely aimed at keeping African Americans away and below whites, Taft and a unanimous court had no difficulty lumping together those of an entirely different ancestry, continent of origin, and outward appearance: "Most of the cases cited [including *Plessy*] arose, it is true, over the establishment of separate schools as between white pupils and black pupils, but we can not think that the question is any different or that any different result can be reached, assuming the cases above cited to be rightly decided, where the issue as between white pupils and the pupils of the yellow races." With such civil libertarians as Oliver Wendell Holmes Jr., Harlan F. Stone, and Louis D. Brandeis in agreement, Taft was able to reconcile Mississippi's brutal segregation with the requirements of the equal protection law merely by referencing the Court's long history—*Buchanan v. Warley* and *Strauder v. Virginia*, among others, aside—with arbitrary segregation regimes. At least with regards to hues other than white, the Court truly was color-blind.

———

As for the subjects of this legal regime, African Americans shouldered the brunt of the twin and mutually supporting evils of the denial of the franchise and the reduction to at best second-class citizenship. The experience of Jim Crow could be a gut-wrenching one. One of the more poignant stories comes to us from its end in the late twentieth century. A white second-grade teacher related her first encounter with an African American student. On the last day of classes, she had the students file by for their customary good-bye hug. "And do you know, that little colored boy came, too, holding his arms out to me, just like the rest. And I just had to push him away. All the other children were watching. I just had to." Racism claimed more than just one more victim that day. The teacher and the children observing the scene, drawing their own conclusions, as well as the little boy who, expecting equal treatment, was denied the affection given to others, all learned the cruelty of that system.

That young boy suffered what many African Americans had feared: integration would bring them nothing but trouble, derision, and distaste from their fellow Americans. People like Delores Thompson Aaron, who lived her whole life in New Orleans in the mid-twentieth century, adjusted to life in the segregated South, imbibing its values and making them their own. With a hint of nostalgia, Aaron recalled what it was like to go to school in the morning: "During my young years it was very *common* to have white folk living next door to you, who would speak to you, be very polite with you, would walk to school with you and continue on to their school because all of us knew the schools were segregated."

Even when she thought about her relationships with white schoolchildren, it was one of amiable separation: "I remember how we used to compare lessons; we compared book, and that's how we knew they got new books. I never remember one of the Longeau children displaying a book at the beginning of the year because you want to know what book you're in." She explained the rivalry as follows: "That competitive spirit came from our parents, and also our Sunday school teachers. Our Sunday school teachers were always preparing us to do a better job and always using white people as the standard." This was how race became ingrained in everyone's mind. It was not just white supremacist whites, but African Americans teaching white supremacy to their charges. At the same time, there were exceptions: African Americans and whites who taught a different way of looking at the world, nonracist or black pride approaches.

Then there was the obvious inequality of the separate treatment detailed in countless photographs, studies of funding, and testimonies like that of someone seeking medical care from the only doctor in town. "But I remember at the time they had separate waiting rooms when you went to the doctor, and they'd serve all the white patients and then serve all the black patients. The last white patient might be served, and then they'd serve blacks." Justice Harlan's prediction about the probable outcome of segregation proved correct largely everywhere the law sanctioned separation.

This also led to a warped relationship between African Americans and police officers. Violence against an African American—even a rape of a young girl—by a white could not be reported because, more often than not, the assailant was either connected with the police, would receive police sympathy because it was just a Negro, or was the police. Ferdie Walker, born and raised in Fort Worth, Texas, in 1928, remembered an incident when she was eleven years old. Waiting for a bus to take her to church on a Sunday afternoon, "these policemen would harass me as I was standing on this corner waiting for the bus to come. . . . They'd drive up under there and then they'd expose themselves while I was standing there, and it just really scared me to death." Reporting the crime to the authorities, including the FBI under the racist director during most of the twentieth century, J. Edgar Hoover, was an exercise in futility.

Besides the ordinary violence of harassment, there was always lurking in the background the lynch law, a vicious form of mob justice. The term probably originated from either Charles Lynch or Captain William Lynch's actions in Virginia during the Revolutionary War as they arranged for vigilante justice against suspected loyalists. In Jim Crow America, for even accidentally brushing a white woman, an African American man would be threatened with being hanged from a nearby tree, and, frequently, publicly dismembered to the cheers of the crowd, as one World War II veteran nearly experienced upon his return to his native Alabama. White photographers captured the incidents and made postcards out of them. The cards sold well. The Tuskegee Institute, building on the courageous and pioneering work of Ida B. Wells, recorded the grim statistics: from 1882 to 1968, lynch mobs, with at least the tacit support of—and sometimes active participation of—the police, murdered 3,437 African Americans. The usual accusation was that an African American man had raped a white woman. Sometimes there had been a sexual interaction; often there was none. Wells, among others, revealed the obvious truth that African American men were having relationships with white women the same way white men were having relationships with African American women. America's racial boundaries were just as porous, sexually speaking, as they had been before emancipation.

The lynchings themselves were often something of a public spectacle, with all the accompanying merriment of a Fourth of July celebration. The following is a description of a lynching in Duluth, Georgia, on June 21, 1920: "The [alleged] murder of the beautiful young woman was avenged in a manner that ought to strike terror to those who might be tempted to commit a similar crime. After his body had been mutilated, while he was alive, the Negro was saturated with gasoline and burned, and while he was burning his body was literally riddled with bullets and buckshot." The newspaper report went on to tell of the witnesses and participants to the crime: "The execution of the negro was witnessed by hundreds of persons, and many thousand who were in the crowd literally fought to get close enough to see the actual details." It was not just men who behaved this way. The genteel ladies of the area played their part too. "Four young women from the crowd pushed their way through the outer rim of the circle and emptied rifles into the Negro." To complete the day's events, "They stood by while other men cut off fingers, toes, and other parts of the body and passed them around as souvenirs."

These quasilegal proceedings, which former Justice Brown condoned as natural responses to justice delayed, bespoke another important aspect of the world *Plessy* helped create. If the law was on its face constitutional, its practical impact, the real-world execution of it, and the patina of legitimacy it placed on racial discrimination gave racism licensed a de facto world of bigotry. Two painfully honest, self-demeaning jokes that circulated among African Americans in the South reflected their experience of Jim Crow. The first concerns an African American boy who was asked what he wanted to be when he grew up. His answer was, "A white man. Because my mother told me negro men are no damn good." The second joke involved a chief of police who explained the murder laws thusly: "If a nigger kills a white man, that's murder. If a white man kills a nigger, that's justifiable homicide. If a nigger kills another nigger, that's one less nigger." The guarantees of "equal protection of the laws" were hollow indeed when this is the commonly understood meaning of how law works in the Jim Crow world, both North and South.

The nationalization of popular culture soon spread this Southern institution to the rest of the country. The racism, whether crude or benign, of novels like *The Clansman* and *Gone with the Wind*; the blockbusters of the silent era like *Birth of a Nation* in 1916, and the consolidation of movie theaters and moviemakers that gave the segregated South a veto over motion pictures, brought to life the distorted picture of race that Brown had taken for granted. Few were the movie companies that wanted to forfeit the Southern moviegoer as a ticket buyer. African Americans were relegated to secondary roles in the movies usually playing into racial stereotypes that originally appeared in minstrel shows and literature before the Civil War. Ticket buyers in the rest of the country rarely objected to the racial stereotypes or the rewriting of history in films like *Birth of a Nation, Gone with the Wind,* or even light comedic fare like the Shirley Temple films, *The Littlest Rebel* or *The Littlest Colonel* in the 1930s. The image of the little girl with curly blonde hair tap-dancing beside her supportive servant, played by the accomplished African American performer Bill "Bojangles" Robinson, was permissible. The consensual union of whites and blacks was still not permissible. One film scholar has gone so far as to note that the only roles available or portrayals of African Americans in movies were those of the unthreatening "coon" and "Uncle Tom" and "mammie" or the "tragic mulatto" or the evildoer "Buck"—an African American man who was more beast than man, and the horror film character of his day.

In 1934, when the Hays Motion Picture Production Code took effect, the rules regarding race became enshrined in a censorship regime so comprehensive it rivaled anything the antebellum South used to suppress abolitionism. To some extent modeled on the Roman Catholic Church's list of banned books and materials, the code—so the joke ran—served white Protestants, was written by Catholics, and was enforced by Jews, who were the magnates of Hollywood at the time. The Hays Office even had a specific rule that any mulatto portrayed in a movie had to come to an unhappy end so that miscegenation would not be promoted. Americans went to the movies in huge numbers during this period, and only a scattered protest greeted these virulently racist portrayals.

And why would they object? Even the history textbooks of the period adopted the white supremacist version of Reconstruction. During the last years of the nineteenth century and the first two decades of the twentieth centuries, William A. Dunning at Columbia University trained an entire generation of historians of the South who turned the propaganda of the militias and Democratic papers into academic histories. Soon, even American schoolchildren using the Old Left textbooks of Charles and Mary Beard were learning of the greedy carpetbaggers who invaded the prostrate South, the scalawags who aided and abetted them, and the rapacious, unruly, unlettered, shiftless Negroes who were their pawns and out-of-control lackeys, depending on the demands of the moment. President Andrew Johnson regained a measure of popularity in this retelling as the martyred hero of reconciliation opposed by the conniving radical Republicans like Thaddeus Stevens. The 1942 movie *Tennessee Johnson* glossed over Johnson's actual role in Reconstruction.

From this gross distortion of history came not only the support for Jim Crow, but a delusional, virulent nostalgia for the Old South that extended into the 1950s with movies like *Tammy and the Bachelor.* Television shows like *Amos 'n' Andy,* based on the popular radio show of the late 1920s and 1930s, kept the stereotypes of the earlier period alive. Though the *Amos 'n' Andy* daily serial radio show was not the vicious kind of racism that *The Clansman* and *Birth of a Nation* exhibited, it did showcase minstrelsy and held African Americans up to ridicule.

The cartoonish depiction of African Americans often took their most vicious form in children's books, print advertising, and billboards, as well as in the cartoons that so permeated American culture that their legacy lives on, practically unnoticed, in such characters as Bugs Bunny, Mickey Mouse, the Little Rascals, and the French cartoon heroes Asterix and Obelix's adventures in the days of Julius Caesar. Although these were not the only nasty caricatures of the time period (the Charlie Chan movies played the same role for Chinese Americans), the large noses and bulbous lips of African American stereotyping became so widespread that one may wonder whether *Plessy* could have possibly had such a large influence over something as ubiquitous as it was insidious.

————

Nevertheless, there is some debate as to whether Henry Billings Brown recanted his opinion in *Plessy,* possibly in light of the hideousness that was Jim Crow. The one critical piece of evidence is a piece Brown wrote in the *American Law Review* on the dissents of John

Marshall Harlan upon the latter's death in 1912. Speaking to Harlan's reading of the intent of the Louisiana legislature, which Brown's opinion had found to be reasonable and without malice, "He assumed what is probably the fact, that the statute had its origin in the purpose, not so much to exclude white persons from railroad cars occupied by blacks, as to exclude colored people from coaches occupied or assigned to white persons." However, there is a fair bit of contrary evidence as well.

After retiring from the Court in 1906 because of his failing eyesight, Brown made some after-dinner remarks at an event honoring him by the Bar Association for the District of Columbia. In the course of lamenting the inefficiency of the criminal justice system, he argued that lynching was a sign of the community's commitment to swift justice for criminals. Beyond the fact that these were odd words for someone who, as a judge and attorney, was supposedly committed to the rule of law and not mob action, it also displayed an ignorance of what lynchings actually were. In addition, in the same *American Law Review* piece on Harlan's dissents, Brown noted that the Court had many reasons to overturn a precedent: "But there comes a time when even the court which pronounced them is compelled by the pressure of public sentiment to correct them." In acknowledging a role for popular opinion, he was conceding a thread of his own jurisprudence on minority rights—that he was attuned to local concerns as much as he was to the dictates of law at least outside of that of property rights.

In a 1903 letter to his friend, Charles Kent, Brown wrote: "I know of nothing more ineradicable than racial antipathy, except, perhaps, national antipathy. My experience has taught me that the natural position of two nations toward each other is one of hostility, to which there are very few exceptions." In a speech in 1910 to the Ladies' Congressional Club in Washington, D.C., describing how giving women the vote would be impracticable, he analogized the situation to the Fifteenth Amendment's guarantees of African American suffrage: "The amendment has been generally disregarded in the South, and a serious attempt to enforce it by the military arm, if persisted in, would probably have resulted in another civil war." That his and the previous Court's rulings had done much to limit what effort there was to enforce the law of the land he did not acknowledge.

In another letter to Kent on May 26, 1913, Brown slipped into pejoratives. "There are always a few in the District who are clamouring for a change to a popular government, but the phantom of negro suffrage stands inexorably in their path. No suffrage without nigger—no suffrage, no nigger." Thus, we may safely conclude that far from renouncing his opinion in *Plessy*, its author was convinced of its rightness for the same reasons he tried to put forth at the time.

———

The Comité des Citoyens and their newspaper, *The Crusader*, were gone by 1897, but resistance to Jim Crow did not die with them. Across the segregated South, those defining themselves as African Americans or, in the parlance of the times, Negroes, organized to resist the onslaught of legalized racism. Perhaps the most vivid of these protests was the streetcar boycott in New Orleans in 1902.

The boycott stemmed from the experience of the African American community in the race riot in New Orleans in late July and early August 1900 featuring a series of killings and assaults thereafter. The spark for this particular scene of white mob violence against African Americans was struck when a thirty-four-year-old African American migrant to New Orleans named Robert Charles refused a police officer's command that he leave the sidewalk outside a house where he was waiting for his girlfriend. When he resisted capture and injured the officer, a manhunt began that the police seemed incapable of concluding. Taking their frustration at Charles's success in escaping Jim Crow justice, white mobs formed, taking their vengeance on whatever African Americans they could find. At least six African Americans were lynched and dozens assaulted, including women and children. In a grave threat to the community, mobs also targeted African American schools.

Charles himself managed to kill seven white men, including four police officers, before being gunned down in the two weeks that followed, but the African American community did not resist so violently. Many simply chose to migrate north. The reason the governor finally sent in the state militia to quell the violence was that African American protests made the actions of the white mobs so notorious that outside investors—so vital to Louisiana's economy—were reluctant to risk their money in such a lawless environment. If any silver lining can be discerned in this tragic period, it was the demise of the proposal to segregate New Orleans's streetcars. In 1902, the proposal came back and became law in July. With the large-scale elimination of African American votes in the Crescent City after 1900, African Americans had little choice but to conduct mass action and hope the negative attention would again kill the idea.

In response to the streetcar act, a key division between dissenters, who wanted to bring a test case in the courts, and the majority, that wanted to mount an economic boycott, weakened the overall movement. The test case failed in 1903 when, in the case of *Pearson v. State*, the Louisiana Supreme Court relied on *Plessy* in ruling that streetcar segregation did not violate the equal protection clause. This was in spite of the fact that the large screen the law required separated off a vastly inferior section of the streetcar. The boycott was also unsuccessful, though it garnered a great deal of attention. Again, the cancellation of several events adversely affected the streetcars and the tourism business. Unfortunately, African American economic pressure on the city and the traction companies was not significant enough to have the sufficient impact required, at least for that time.

The boycott in Richmond, Virginia, in July of the next year was much more successful. It initiated a wave of similar actions in Tennessee, Florida, and Georgia. The Richmond boycott garnered greater support because it incorporated working-class African Americans as well as the better-off. The leaders of the boycotts also made sure to properly instruct the black community. They were not to provoke in any way, or likewise cause an incident. Though the code of behavior was more demanding for the protesters than for anyone else, including the armed conductors of the streetcars, their cause had to take into account the tinderbox of race relations in the South's fifth largest city.

After nearly two years of boycotts, the Virginia Passenger and Power Company was forced into receivership, although this result was at least in part due to the poor management of its owners, the son and daughter of financier and stock swindler Jay Gould. As their newspapers claimed victory, the boycotters faced a severe defeat in the form of a new segregation law mandating separation, as opposed to the prior law, which left it up to the railroad company. Nevertheless, their near triumph inspired others. Meanwhile, suits in both state and federal courts failed as the courts cited the *Plessy* decision to uphold the increasingly legally segregated South.

In these two instances of mass protest, we can see both the baleful and benevolent effects of racism. Jim Crow, stemming from white racism, forced those determined to be colored or Negro to ally with one another. In this shared experience, they found community. They founded their own newspapers and their own social organizations; they attended their own churches; they organized among themselves. There were divisions along class lines, but common pains brought these different people together.

—————

At the same time, Jim Crow solidified the concept of race in the minds of people of color. This formation of an African American identity, though advantageous in many respects, was also the intent of the white supremacists—people like those the Comité des Citoyens had tried to fight. Racism was becoming deeply ingrained not just in the majority culture, but in the minority one as well.

Again, the Republican Party proved of no use. In fact, one of its leading lights, President Theodore Roosevelt, proved an unreliable ally. At the same time he took the political heat for inviting Booker T. Washington to the White House for a meeting, he also demonstrated his own long-standing prejudice against African Americans. In 1906 in Brownsville, Texas, a group of African American soldiers were accosted by a white mob. In the turmoil that followed, it was impossible to determine whether the townspeople's allegations of African American soldiers discharging their weapons in the town were true or if they were concoctions to revenge themselves on uppity African Americans. Roosevelt, as was his wont, shot from the hip and dismissed all 168 "with dishonor." He disregarded their service in the horrific struggle that was the suppression of the insurrection in the Philippines.

The African American community should not have been surprised at Roosevelt's action. He was a prolific writer of history along the lines of race theory, arguing that humanity belonged to different races, just as there were different breeds of cattle and dogs. He naturally reserved all the best qualities for his own particular race—the Anglo-Saxons. What he neglected to mention was that although his father was a tolerant descendant of the original Dutch settlers of New York, his mother was one of the Bullochs from Georgia, who proudly displayed the Confederate flag outside the family's townhouse in New York City during the Civil War and told stories of the South, complete with her impressions of various slaves. Young Teddy's enthusiasm for taxidermy had mixed with his mother's virulent racism and love of the antebellum South to form a vicious concoction of quasiscience, reconciliation history, and inveterate bigotry. In all of his appointments to the Court, even that of the much-celebrated Oliver Wendell Holmes Jr., he exercised similar judgment.

When Woodrow Wilson became president in 1913, even the federal government's mild commitments to employing African Americans in positions other than that of a servant ceased. Wilson was a true son of the South, born and raised in Virginia, North Carolina, and Georgia. Wilson's boyhood memories of Reconstruction were of the lost cause variety, viewing the presence of federal troops to keep the peace as a violation of the rights of the South. Conveniently ignoring all African American Southerners, he appointed a virtually completely lily-white Democrat cabinet who had no difficulty enforcing Wilson's orders to segregate every aspect of the executive branch, including all of Washington, D.C. When prominent African American leaders protested, he appeared to be genuinely flustered by their opposition. "The purpose of these measures was to reduce the friction. It is as far as possible from being a movement against the Negroes. I sincerely believe it to be in their interest," he proclaimed. His paternalism extended so far as to make intermarriage a felony in the nation's capital.

———

The failure of the *Plessy* litigation did not mean that the struggle was lost for all time. A combination of circumstances, larger societal and economic changes, and the impact of two world wars on the home front set the stage for greater success. However, that effort, while more celebrated, also brought with it seemingly insurmountable problems. One might have thought that the issue of segregation was forever settled by *Plessy* and its progeny despite the contrary precedents of *Yick Wo, Strauder,* and *Buchanan.* But one would have been wrong. Brown's opinion had provided an opening in its focus on local customs, traditions, and practices. Harlan's dissent reinforced this pragmatic approach to judging the constitutionality of a statute based on its real-world impact. If plaintiffs could demonstrate that the effect of the enactment was not, in fact, equal, the Court might very well find the enactment fell afoul of the equal protection clause of the Fourteenth Amendment.

Adding to this potential was a development in a different area of litigation, though one that also implicated reasonableness review of state laws. The so-called Brandeis brief proved that even the *Lochner* Court could be persuaded of the correctness of a state legislature regulating private business. Louis D. Brandeis had assembled such a brief for the Court in the case of *Muller v. Oregon* in 1908 on behalf of the state of Oregon. It was filled with a huge amount of data to support the state's claim that limiting the working hours of women protected their health. Even though Justice Brewer's opinion was filled with condescending sexism, it upheld the Oregon statute.

Similarly, in the case of *Missouri ex rel. Gaines v. Canada, Registrar of the University of Missouri, et al.* in 1938, a group of lawyers persuaded the Court of the manifest inequality of the state of Missouri's system for providing legal education. Lloyd Gaines was a successful graduate of Lincoln University in Missouri, the university set aside for African Americans under the state's Jim Crow education laws. But as an African American, he was denied admission to the only public law school in the state, the whites-only University of Missouri Law School. Missouri allowed for African Americans to attend law schools in neighboring Kansas, Iowa, and Illinois, but the Court, in an opinion by Chief Justice Hughes, agreed with Gaines that this was not the same as attending Missouri's only law school. "The basic consideration is not as to what sort of opportunities other States provide, or whether they are as good as those in Missouri, but as to what opportunities Missouri itself furnishes to white students and denies to negroes solely upon the ground of color." The Court's conclusion, unanimous except for Justice James Clark McReynolds, who dissented (McReynolds had little use for minorities of all stripes), was to order Gaines's admission to the law school.

By April 28, 1941, in the case of *Mitchell v. United States et al.*, Chief Justice Hughes's opinion for the Court indicated *Gaines* was the beginning of a possible shift in the Court's jurisprudence. It reversed a finding of the Interstate Commerce Commission. In this incident, a railroad company relegated a first-class passenger, who happened to be African American congressman Arthur W. Mitchell, to a second-class compartment when the train entered Arkansas on a trip from Chicago. "The denial to appellant of equality of accommodations because of his race would be an invasion of a fundamental individual right which is guaranteed against state action by the Fourteenth Amendment" under the precedents set by *McCabe, Missouri ex rel. Gaines*, "and in view of the nature of the right and of our constitutional policy it cannot be maintained that the discrimination as it was alleged was not essentially unjust." The railroad company had fallen afoul of the "equal" side of the mandate as well as the command of the Interstate Commerce Act forbidding unreasonable discriminations. The Court, now made up of a large contingent of New Deal liberals, was willing to entertain factual evidence of the inequality of these separate accommodations. Also worthy of note was the fact that the chief justice's opinion did not mention *Plessy*, though the appellees certainly did.

The Court's reasoning in cases like *Buchanan* and *Gaines* laid the groundwork for a reversal of *Plessy*. This was no accident. A new legal effort had taken the place of the moribund Comité des Citoyens. A new group of litigants had taken up the cause in the form of the National Association for the Advancement of Colored People (NAACP), a biracial organization formed in 1909 to undo the oppression of African Americans. The NAACP represented the post-Reconstruction generation's contribution to the civil rights struggle. Among its founders was the editor of its newspaper, *The Crisis*, W. E. B. DuBois.

DuBois, like the litigants in *Plessy*, was descended from Creoles on his father's side, although his mother was the descendant of free slaves in Massachusetts. With the help of relatives and people in his community, he was able to attend Fisk College, a black college in Tennessee, then Harvard College, from which he graduated cum laude in 1890. With a scholarship from the John F. Slater Fund for the Education of Freedmen, he attended the University of Berlin in

Germany, then became the first African American to earn a Ph.D. from Harvard in 1895. In addition to his work for civil rights, he was an accomplished historian, who refuted the work of the Dunning School, and an able criminologist. In 1905, he cofounded the Niagara Movement, an organization dedicated to eradicating bigotry of all kinds. When the movement broke down over disagreements about integration versus a go-it-alone approach, he helped found the NAACP.

———

While DuBois edited the newspaper, wrote columns publicizing the cause of equality, and debated Booker T. Washington on the proper course for African Americans in the face of Jim Crow, the NAACP moved toward a litigation strategy to fight inequality. With financial assistance from the Garland Fund, they hired a legal team to pursue a refutation of *Plessy*. Though the Great Depression severely constricted their funding, the NAACP committed itself to litigating an end to segregation with the hiring of Charles Hamilton Houston to succeed the able but overcommitted Nathan Margold in May 1934.

The transition to Houston signified more than the hiring of perhaps the nation's foremost African American attorney and educator. The organization was committing itself to a court-based opposition to segregation. DuBois had broken with the NAACP over this very matter, forcefully asserting that integration might well damage African American independence by harming their institutions like the historically black colleges and universities. Although it may seem strange for the supposed champion of integration against Booker T. Washington's seemingly more accommodationist leanings, DuBois had become much more separatist as the effort ground on, and his own identity became firmly entrenched as an African American. DuBois may have lost his dispute with the executive board of the NAACP, but his concerns live on to this day. Racism and race consciousness claimed more than just the white supremacists.

Charles Hamilton Houston reconciled these competing claims— race consciousness and the search for equality—in a manner appropriate for someone with a deep commitment to the law: he pursued the overturning of segregation while sponsoring the achievements of his fellow African Americans. In one of those odd coincidences that are sprinkled throughout history, Charles was born in 1895 just a few blocks from the Court in Washington, D.C. He was one of the Negroes who Justice Brown saw every day in the capital in his large mansion, paid for with his wife's substantial inheritance. The young Houston benefited from his parents' extraordinary sacrifices to give him the best education possible. His hairdresser mother and lawyer father sent him to Amherst after making sure he enrolled in the precollegiate M Street High School for African Americans. Houston graduated Phi Beta Kappa after a rocky start that was largely due to his isolation as the only African American in the 1915 class. He later recalled that he had "few friends in town and rarely paid a social visit." Amherst life was dominated by fraternities, and they did not admit nonwhites.

After teaching school, Houston joined the American Expeditionary Force in France in World War I. His experiences there and with the racism of his officers' training program back home before his departure convinced him of the evils of institutionalized segregation: "The hate and scorn showered on us Negro officers by our fellow Americans convinced me that there was no sense in my dying for a world ruled by them. I made up my mind that if I got through this war I would study law and use my time fighting for men who could not strike back." A near mass lynching in France when a white officer resented a French woman stepping out with an African American made the injustice of the system plain. Military justice was a farce. None of the whites guilty of this severe infraction of the Military Code of Justice were even charged. Upon his return from France, Houston saw that gallant military service by African Americans did not result in any positive gains. In fact, 1919 witnessed some of the worst racial violence against African Americans since Reconstruction. But this time, the substantial movement of African Americans into Northern cities during the wartime boom made the issue a national one. Incidents in Chicago and Washington, D.C., were particularly bloody, but all of them demonstrated, at least to Houston, the inequities of America's legal system.

In the fall of 1919, he enrolled in Harvard Law School, where he did so well that he became the first African American member of the *Harvard Law Review* staff, perhaps the most distinguished law journal in the country. He then pursued his doctorate in juridical science, making research trips to North Africa, where, for the first time, he was able to envision a world outside of Jim Crow. He saw that part of the problem rested with the lack of African American attorneys in the South—the people most likely to serve that oppressed community. As a teacher, then dean, of Howard Law School, an African American school in the District of Columbia, he dedicated himself to creating this group of professionals. From 1929 until he joined the NAACP's legal effort full time, he turned Howard into a premier law school, but with a higher purpose: to fight for true equality.

To Houston's way of thinking, lawyers were more than just their clients' hired guns. They were social engineers. In effect, Houston turned Howard into the nation's first public interest law school, albeit for a more narrow purpose: the overturning of segregation and fighting for African American civil rights. This strategy sought equal treatment but accepted race as a category. Houston created a law school for African Americans to fight for African Americans. In this racial objective, he succeeded marvelously. One of his many recruits was Baltimore-born Thurgood Marshall. The son of a railroad porter and the descendant of former slaves, Marshall had excelled at the Frederick Douglass High School and Lincoln University in Pennsylvania before graduating first in his class from Howard Law School. Marshall from the first was close to the dean of the school, going so far as to copy his mentor's sayings and mannerisms. This served Marshall well in the still-segregated courts of *Plessy's* America. Houston's abilities were not of the combative, vituperative style of his opponents; he was sure-handed, respectful, and highly committed.

Houston's premature death from illnesses related to his cigarette smoking in 1950 prevented him from seeing the ultimate victory, but the precedents he and his protégés from Howard, like Thurgood Marshall, had won laid its groundwork. The first of these victories was in Maryland in *Murray v. Pearson* in 1935. Maryland had provided only one law school for the state, which it reserved for whites under their separate schooling laws. Houston and the NAACP's legal team, separated from the NAACP and rechristened the Legal Defense Fund (to protect the NAACP's tax status), persuaded a majority of that state's supreme court to acknowledge that merely providing scholarship aid for African Americans to go to law school out of state was inconsistent with equal protection under the Fourteenth Amendment. This was not a contraction of the doctrine in *Plessy*. Rather, it was consistent with Brown's holding that there needed to be equal facilities if the state was to separate them.

The *Gaines* case was a natural successor to *Murray*, only this case went to the U.S. Supreme Court when Missouri's supreme court refused to honor *Plessy*, as Maryland's had. The victory in *Gaines* came at a high cost for its putative litigant. Although Gaines had gotten the U.S. Supreme Court behind his admission to Missouri's law school, he disappeared before Houston's legal team could get the local court to order his admission. Given the notoriety and the accompanying death threats Gaines had to endure during the long course of this nationally publicized case, much speculation still exists as to his fate. Without Gaines, the white supremacists had prevented integration, but not the additional crack in *Plessy*'s armor.

In 1946, the Houston strategy, as carried out by Thurgood Marshall and William Hastie, claimed another victim in the form of a refutation of the Court's doctrines regarding segregation and interstate commerce in *Morgan v. Virginia*. Seemingly consistent with *Hall v. De Cuir*, but problematic for *Louisville, New Orleans, & Texas Railway Company v. Mississippi*, Justice Stanley Forman Reed's majority opinion declared Virginia's statute segregating passengers on an interstate bus line was an unconstitutional burden on interstate commerce: "As there is no federal act dealing with the separation of races in interstate transportation, we must decide the validity of this Virginia statute on the challenge that it interferes with commerce, as a matter of balance between the exercise of the local police power and the need for national uniformity in the regulations for interstate travel. It seems clear to us that seating arrangements for the different races in interstate motor travel require a single, uniform rule to promote and protect national travel." Justice Felix Frankfurter concurred in the result but argued that Reed had gone too far in his opinion. The ever-cautious Frankfurter would have limited the case to upholding *Hall v. DeCuir*. Justice Burton dissented, finding that it was inappropriate for a private passenger to complain about a burden to interstate commerce.

Irene Morgan initiated the case when, as Rosa Parks was to do eleven years later, she refused to sit in the back of a Greyhound bus.

The ruling in the case also spurred the Congress for Racial Equality to launch the pathbreaking Journey of Reconciliation, an ancestor and inspiration for the Freedom Rides of 1961. The Reconciliation riders met a similar fate of arrests and mob violence, but without the notoriety the Freedom Riders generated. Although not a direct refutation of "separate but equal" and *Plessy*, it was another precedent hostile to Jim Crow.

In June 1950, two months after Houston died, the strategy he did so much to enact bore fruit in the form of the twin cases of *Sweatt v. Painter* and *McLaurin v. Oklahoma State Regents*, which expanded on the per curiam (unsigned and unanimous) opinion in the *Sipuel v. Board of Regents of University of Oklahoma* in 1948. Although his failing health dictated that he leave the litigation in the capable hands of his successors in 1940, his imprint on the two cases was fairly clear. In *Sipuel*, Thurgood Marshall successfully argued for Ada Sipuel's admission to Oklahoma's only and exclusively white law school on the same grounds as Houston had for Gaines.

In *Sweatt*, Robert L. Carter, the NAACP's lead attorney for this case, convinced the Court to confront the situation of another African American who attempted to get into the state's only law school. However, this time the state of Texas attempted to create a colored law school to match their whites-only law school at the flagship state university of University of Texas at Austin. This new Houston, Texas, school was put together in the six months' delay the lower courts afforded the defendants. The U.S. Supreme Court, in a unanimous opinion by Chief Justice Fred Vinson, was not impressed with the supposed equality of the schools. The numbers and qualitative factors simply did not support the letter of the law. UT at Austin Law School had sixteen full-time and three part-time faculty members, UT at Houston had five full-time faculty; UT at Austin had 850 students, UT at Houston 23; UT at Austin 65,000 volumes in the library, UT at Houston 16,500; UT at Austin had moot court facilities, UT Houston a practice room; UT at Austin had the prestigious Order of the Coif Society and a network of hundreds of graduates admitted to the bar, UT at Houston had no honor society and only one graduate who was a member of the bar. If there was one thing the justices of the U.S. Supreme Court understood, it was the importance of the law school you attended to your future: "What is more important, the University of Texas Law School possesses to a far greater degree those qualities which are incapable of objective measurement but which make for greatness in a law school. Such qualities, to name but a few, include reputation of the faculty, experience of the administration, position and influence of the alumni, standing in the community, traditions and prestige. It is difficult to believe that one who had a free choice between these law schools would consider the question close."

In the *McLaurin* case, the issue was the same but the facts differed in George McLaurin's attempt to obtain a doctoral degree in education. The original suit resulted in a favorable ruling from the lower federal courts, but there was no command to integrate. Oklahoma responded by integrating the graduate school in as reluctant a manner as could be conceived. McLaurin had to take his classes by using a desk in the hallway outside the door of the classroom. He had to eat at his own special table in the cafeteria. His access to the library was confined to a table in the balcony from where he could study and request books. After additional court orders, Oklahoma educators removed the bar and sign in the classroom saying "Reserved for Colored," but McLaurin was still kept in a row separated from his white classmates.

Vinson's opinion for another unanimous Court found these restrictions particularly problematic if McLaurin was to go on to educate others: "Their own education and development will necessarily suffer to the extent that his training is unequal to that of his classmates. State-imposed restrictions which produce such inequalities cannot be sustained." The conclusion, therefore, was inescapable. "We hold that under these circumstances the Fourteenth Amendment precludes differences in treatment by the state based upon race. Appellant, having been admitted to a state-supported graduate school, must receive the same treatment at the hands of the state as students of other races." Inasmuch as the Court had found the segregation of professional and graduate education a violation of the equal protection clause of the Fourteenth Amendment, it might have appeared that the Court had partially overruled *Plessy*. This, however, would have been a premature conclusion at best.

However, *Sipuel*, *Sweatt*, and *McLaurin* were grounds for celebration. Even if they had not overturned *Plessy*, they had certainly contradicted the principle, if not the case, of *Richmond*. If the *Richmond* Court had decided these cases, the outcome might very well have been different. What happened? Many scholars argue that World War II effected a sea change in American attitudes toward race and racism. The abhorrent regime of the Axis powers, particularly Nazi Germany, were now almost universally recognized as evil, and the war waged to defeat the Axis was well on its way towards its current reputation as the "good war." Adolf Hitler's racism had resulted in a conflict in Europe that had led to massive destruction and the loss of tens of millions of lives, including twelve million (six million of them Jewish) in a program of mass killing that introduced the world to the term "genocide." There were also the unmitigated horrors of killing, rape, slave labor, and live experimentation on Jews. All this combined to form the Holocaust, known in Hebrew as the Shoah. Even before the war, when Jesse Owens beat Hitler's Aryan supermen at the Olympic Games of 1936 in Berlin, Americans celebrated Owens even though he was as unable to dine, live, or be buried with whites in Jim Crow America as he would have been in Nazi Germany.

The Nuremburg Trials for Germans accused of war crimes may not have been all that effective in prosecuting the defendants, but they did publicize their actions, including those Germans in the judiciary who became willing accomplices to the Nazi regime of segregation, then dispossession and mass killing. The fact that many of the provisions of the Nuremburg Laws that had begun this process were direct copies from Jim Crow America was not lost on everyone participating in the trials, like Supreme Court justice Robert H. Jackson or the considerable audience back home. Wartime propaganda had emphasized the true evil of Hitler and his racist regime alongside the atrocities that accompanied his and his allies' rise to power and what they did when in possession of foreign lands. This propaganda effort, combined with the ensuing patriotism that comes from waging an immensely taxing, violent, and unified effort against racism overseas, could not have but affected racial attitudes back home.

In addition, thanks to the more enlightened but still segregationist policies of the Franklin D. Roosevelt administration, African Americans once again proved their valor, patriotism, and steadfast desire for equal treatment by fully participating in all aspects of the war effort to which they were allowed to contribute. The Tuskegee airmen were but a few of the tens of thousands of African Americans who put their lives on the line, sometimes never to come home, just like other Americans. Although we cannot be sure of the effects of this meritorious service, on occasion not properly recognized with medals until long after the fact, we can be sure that this sacrifice did not go completely unnoticed. It played a significant role in many of the military's highest-ranking officers agreeing to President Harry S. Truman's order to desegregate the U.S. armed forces. This decision in and of itself is a story of struggle, resistance, and consequences, including the Dixiecrat revolt of Strom Thurmond against Truman in the presidential election of 1948, but it certainly reflects a significant shift in the political winds regarding segregation under law in the United States. For the first time, the federal government at least seemed to be re-interested in civil rights for African Americans.

The war also affected the political makeup of the United States by bringing millions more African Americans north and west to work in war industries. This second wave of migration out of the South (the first followed the end of the Civil War) created a substantial number of urban African American voters for Democrats to court if they wanted to counter the increasingly conservative Republican Party, whose strategy for victory placed them increasingly at odds with their Reconstruction past. Added to this combustible mix was the emerging conflict with the communist Soviet Union, in which race relations played a considerable part.

From its inception in the Bolshevik (the majority wing of the Communist Party led by Vladimir Lenin) Revolution of 1917, the Soviet Union's propagandists had prided themselves on only discriminating on the basis of class. The worker versus capitalist contest was the one that mattered. Everything else was supposedly a distraction created by the bourgeoisie to confuse the workers. Communists, therefore, were not racists; indeed, they opposed racism. In reality, the Soviet Union was a deeply racist society that went so far as to classify everyone according to their ethnic group and place that classification on all their identity documents, which they were to carry at all times. When Joseph Stalin became the head of the Communist Party in the Soviet Union, and as a result the de facto leader, in 1927, he began several programs of relocations, work camps that were the equivalent of slavery, and mass purges that resulted in arguably more death and human misery than that of the Nazis. These blemishes on the workers' utopia were not generally known or believed by those who had committed themselves to communist ideals, including many civil rights leaders, among them singer and civil rights activist Paul Robeson.

Regardless of the true nature of the Soviet Union, the Soviet propaganda alleging their conflict with the United States was that of the nonracist, egalitarian, worker's utopia versus the racist, unequal, capitalist-run empire gained considerable weight around the world, not the least of which was the segregation taking place in the United States' own capital. Even the conservative Republican Eisenhower administration was embarrassed by their own inability to court the leaders of the unaffiliated third world because their darker complexions excluded them from Washington, D.C.'s restaurants, hotels, and amusements. If the United States wanted to portray itself as the leader of the free world, it would help if its own citizens at least appeared to be free.

Adding to the pressure against Jim Crow was the African American community's gains over the five decades after *Plessy*. Although badly behind that of whites, with an incarceration and poverty rate appalling by any stretch of the imagination, African Americans now had a substantial middle and working class, with the all-important purchasing power that went with it. Though this made them the targets of unconscionable lending practices for all of their consumer goods, it still made the community a powerful force in American life. This increase in disposable income after World War II also gave African Americans the wherewithal to support the NAACP, their church groups, and other civil rights groups, like the Congress for Racial Equality, that would play such a significant role in the struggle they were renewing alongside the litigation of the Legal Defense Fund.

Finally, there was another obvious, significant change that affected the legal climate that was undoing *Plessy*'s Jim Crow world: the almost completely different attitudes and kind of men that were the members of the U.S. Supreme Court. The justices of the Court that would hear the cases the NAACP constructed in order to overturn *Plessy* were of a completely different generation from the *Plessy* Court. They had grown up in industrial railroad America. They did not know the Civil War firsthand. Moreover, they had become largely acclimated to the highly technical, professionalized world the *Plessy* judges had wrestled against so strenuously. Two world wars, a Great Depression, and a New Deal later, their perspective did not know a United States without the telephone, women's suffrage, or national government regulation of the economy. The idea that localities should be allowed to thwart the nation seemed as anachronistic as the horse and buggy. Though one should not exaggerate the post–New Deal jurisprudence's differences with that before it, the formalism of the nineteenth century had given way to legal realism to a great extent. Brown's opinion in *Plessy* may have been practical minded, but the legal conservatism as well as the context that undergirded it, so essential to its basic logic, was no longer ascendant.

———

The litigation that is widely cited as having overruled *Plessy* was a group of cases the Legal Defense Fund attorneys solicited in as wide an area as they could muster. Although the cases in South Carolina, Virginia, and the District of Columbia were the most troubling in terms of inequality financially, quality, and otherwise, the case that gave its name to the Court's ruling was from Topeka, Kansas. Thus, Oliver L. Brown's class-action suit on behalf of his daughter, Linda, gave its name to one of the Court's most famous pronouncements. Several details affected the specific outcome in *Brown v. Board of Education of Topeka*, including a key change in the Court's membership when California governor Earl Warren replaced Chief Justice Fred Vinson in the center chair.

Earl Warren had never held a judicial post before joining the Court in 1953. He had been a prosecutor, the attorney general of California, and a successful governor, but his commitment to civil rights had been less than stellar. Besides several questionable prosecutions of labor leaders, he had been instrumental as attorney general in convincing the Roosevelt administration to intern the Japanese American community of the West Coast for the length of World War II. This gross violation of tens of thousands of Americans' civil liberties was based on little more than prejudice and paranoia with several false statements coming before the courts, including the U.S. Supreme Court, in the litigation that resulted in the Court upholding the executive order as a matter of wartime necessity in *Korematsu v. U.S.* Although Warren later admitted to the mistake, it certainly demonstrated a passion for government action inconsistent with a truly judicial temperament. Warren's approach to *Brown* evinced this same politically minded savvy as he sought, by hook and by crook, to forge a unanimous Court on desegregating public schools.

Certainly contributing to the Warren Court's maneuvers in *Brown* was the Court's resident professor, Justice Felix Frankfurter. Frankfurter's judicial conservatism was of the New Deal and Progressivism kind. He preferred to let the so-called political branches make their choices, reserving judicial intervention only when absolutely necessary. Like others who followed the doctrine of judicial restraint, he analogized the Court's power to having a deposit in a bank. The more one drew from it, the less one had. Frankfurter, as he believed himself on other matters before the Court, also had great faith in his own experience with the South and politics in general. He counseled the newly installed, inexperienced Warren to be careful with the interference with the South's twentieth-century peculiar institution.

To gain time to convince reluctant justices Robert H. Jackson and Stanley Reed to agree to a single opinion, the Court arranged for a reargument of *Brown* in the fall of 1953 after the original argument in the spring. In an extensive foray into the origins of and the debate over the surrounding context, particularly with regards to public education, of the Fourteenth Amendment, the attorneys attempted to make their case. Thurgood Marshall was the lead attorney for Brown et al., and he reread Justice Harlan the elder's dissent for inspiration. Former Democratic presidential nominee and noted lawyer John W. Davis led the team for Kansas and segregation.

Justice Jackson was in favor of judicial deference to legislatures and was being advised by at least one of his clerks, the future chief justice William H. Rehnquist, not to overturn *Plessy*, which, according to Rehnquist's memorandum, "A Random Thought on Segregation," was correctly decided. Rehnquist reasoned: "To the argument . . . that a majority may not deprive a minority of its constitutional right, the answer must be made that while this is sound in theory, in the long run it is the majority who will determine what the constitutional rights of the minorities are." Reed was more concerned with an intrusion into a traditional concern of local government. But

Warren was not to be deterred. He circulated draft after draft until he could garner the unanimous vote he thought he needed.

To this day, there is controversy over the Warren opinion in *Brown*. At least in part, this is due to Warren's compromises in order to achieve unanimity. Besides limiting the holding to public education, there was the limited nature of the Court's action, requiring a second round of arguments that would result in a case widely labeled as *Brown* II, the implementation of the *Brown* decision. Instead of calling for the immediate desegregation of all schools with local federal judges authorized to use their equity powers—court orders—to implement the decision, the Court required litigation specific to each school district and federal judge by federal judge. Moreover, the Court gave leeway to states to resist in the form of its instructions to desegregate with "all deliberate speed." The fight to desegregate public schools lasted for another twenty years in the federal courts, with a campaign of massive resistance in many Southern states from which many of their school systems have never recovered.

Other debates over *Brown* concern aspects of Warren's opinion in which the chief justice made a spotty case for overruling *Plessy*, but only in public education. To be sure, the NAACP had arranged for a direct challenge of "equal, but separate" by including cases from Delaware and Kansas, where the facilities were found to be equal in the lower courts. Again following the practice of many a Court before him, Warren cited *Plessy*'s doctrine as being "separate but equal." He also referred to the plaintiffs as members of the "Negro race"—not assigned to be members, not recognized as members, but belonging to the Negro race.

In a similar vein to Brown in *Plessy*, Warren described the findings concerning the intent and context of the Fourteenth Amendment without reference to the actual circumstances of Reconstruction. "This discussion and our own investigation convince us that, although these sources cast some light, it is not enough to resolve the problem with which we are faced. At best, they are inconclusive." In refusing to recognize the goal of the Fourteenth Amendment to overcome racial prejudice, he trapped the Court and its successors into a more restrictive analysis—the one the *Slaughterhouse Cases*, the *Civil Rights Cases*, and the *Plessy* Courts had imposed. However, unlike those Courts, Warren did not side with the segregationists.

The chief justice's trump card was that the "status of public education at that time" differed so greatly from the present of 1954 that late 1860s America was not a good reference point. To his way of thinking, the presence of state-mandated universal schooling changed circumstances so greatly that the Court's reading of the Fourteenth Amendment had to take place with present-day considerations paramount. He used a footnote with history books to prove his point that the framers of the Fourteenth Amendment had no requisite intent for public schools. Though he was quite correct about the development of public education in the United States, as a matter of fact, segregation was present at the time in not just Southern schools, but Northern ones as well, including the District of Columbia, which the Congress had recently segregated. In footnote six regarding another matter, Warren acknowledged as much: "It is apparent that such segregation has long been a nationwide problem, not merely one of sectional concern." He ignored the relevance of this point for his contention over the original intent of the amendment.

After reciting the main cases dealing with the equal protection clause and placing heavy emphasis on the more recent cases commanding integration in graduate education, the chief justice laid out the reasons why the Court was going to vindicate the NAACP's decision to challenge *Plessy* in public education, rather than transportation. With his career as California's education-minded governor not far behind him, he declared, "Today, education is perhaps the most important function of state and local governments." And with good reason, for "it is the very foundation of good citizenship." He continued, "Today it is a principal instrument in awakening the child to cultural values, in preparing him for later professional training, and in helping him to adjust normally to his environment." Speaking for his own climb out of the lower echelons as much as the litigants before him, he intoned, "In these days, it is doubtful that any child may reasonably be expected to succeed in life if he is denied the opportunity of an education." Therefore, he concluded, "such an opportunity, where the state has undertaken to provide it, is a right which must be made available to all on equal terms." The chief justice of the United States had explained why the Court was taking such extraordinary action as to overturn one of its own precedents. However, he also was limiting this case to its facts. The case he had made for the public schools could not be easily repeated for other aspects of American life.

Warren then proceeded to provide direct evidence that segregation itself was unequal. After citing favorable language in *Sweatt* and *McLaurin*, he asserted the psychological evidence was conclusive. "To separate them [children in grade and high schools] from others of similar age and qualifications solely because of their race generates a feeling of inferiority as to their status in the community that may affect their hearts and minds in a way unlikely ever to be undone." Although the language came from the Delaware and Kansas lower courts, the studies appeared in footnote eleven in order to refute the findings in *Plessy*. "Whatever may have been the extent of psychological knowledge at the time of *Plessy v. Ferguson*, this finding is amply supported by modern authority." The studies included the doll studies of Kenneth B. Clark and a reference to Gunnar Myrdal's *An American Dilemma*.

Warren followed this with a simple statement that was to dominate citations from thereon: "Any language in *Plessy v. Ferguson* contrary to this finding is rejected." Although later cases would cite this statement as support for the idea that *Brown* had overruled *Plessy*, it did not. *Brown* was solely about public education. Warren made this clear in his conclusion: "We conclude that in the field of public education the doctrine of 'separate but equal' has no place. Separate educational facilities are inherently unequal." In some respect, therefore, the oddly coincidentally same-named ruling in *Brown* overruled Justice Brown's cast-off line about how "we consider the underlying fallacy of the plaintiff's argument to consist in the assumption that the enforced separation of the two races stamps the colored race with a badge of inferiority. If this be so, it is not by reason of anything found in the act, but solely because the colored race chooses to put that construction upon it." Warren's psychological evidence refuted this claim, but not without later controversy, considering the flawed nature of Clark's study.

The immediate reaction to *Brown* divided largely along regional lines, with the deep South expressing the greatest furor among the opponents, while the more moderate border states desegregated without much fanfare. The story of integration is too long, complicated, and entangling to cover in this volume, but the well-thought-out criticisms of *Brown* are worth considering in light of their reference to *Plessy* as precedent, jurisprudence, and larger meaning. The most common criticism comes from the right of the American political spectrum, which, in its legal form, argues that the Warren Court was exercising a kind of judicial activism or social engineering. It is a charge with some weight, considering the fact that Charles Hamilton Houston's strategy was just that.

Another long-term perspective on *Brown* was that it was its own era's *Plessy*. After all, the opinion of the Court in *Brown* reflected present-day concerns, just as Brown's opinion in *Plessy* was based on the present-day concerns of post-Reconstruction America. *Brown*, therefore, was more than just a ruling on the state-imposed segregation of schools. It was the beginning of the Warren Court's civil rights revolution. This included a series of decisions that transformed criminal justice procedures, voting rights, free speech, press, and association rights as well as involved itself deeply in the desegregation decisions that followed from *Brown*. One might also trace the conflict over abortion in America to the Warren Court's decisions regarding sex discrimination and the rights of married couples to contraceptive materials in the case of *Griswold v. Connecticut* in 1965. Alongside President Lyndon B. Johnson and the U.S. Congress' renewed commitment to civil rights in the form of the Civil Rights Act of 1964 and the Voting Rights Act of 1965 with many other measures to follow, this wave of social engineering frequently earns the label of the high tide of liberalism. This was not just a commitment to civil rights before the law, but an attempt to rework American society into a more just, egalitarian, and democratic society.

Given this surrounding environment, it is easy to understand why many authorities believe that *Plessy* died with *Brown*. In some ways "equal, but separate" did fall away from American law in 1954. Subsequent U.S. Supreme Court rulings struck down Jim Crow barriers one by one. More frequently than not, these cases cited *Brown* as having overruled *Plessy*. The actual case that overruled *Plessy* directly came in the form of the little-heralded but seminal *Browder v. Gayle* (1956), stemming from the Montgomery bus boycott. In a per curiam (unanimous and without opinion) issuance, the Court upheld the circuit court panel overturning Alabama's segregation statute. The 2-to-1 panel had held that *Brown* and other cases concerning recreational facilities had held segregation to be unconstitutional under the equal protection clause of the Fourteenth Amendment. Although the 381-day boycott had played its role, it was the Supreme Court decision that gave the district court the instructions to integrate. *Plessy* was dead.

The battles over desegregation transformed over the next two decades into conflicts over court-ordered integration, federal laws compelling equal treatment in education, lending, and the awarding of federal contracts, and finally the idea that only special programs setting aside places for minorities in employment, higher education, and voting districts, also known as affirmative action. America had begun only a new chapter in its struggle with race. Thus, to say that the central tenets of *Plessy v. Ferguson* were gone with the winds of change sweeping across late twentieth-century America would be to miss its endurance both as case law and a description of the United States' continuing struggle with race.

Epilogue
An Enduring Legacy

At the start of the presidential campaign of 2008, Senator Barack Hussein Obama of Illinois had a seemingly insurmountable set of obstacles to overcome on his way to the Democratic nomination, much less winning the presidency. Leading him in every category imaginable was the more experienced, better-funded junior senator from New York, Hillary Rodham Clinton. By the end of the nomination fight, Obama had nearly reversed his standing. Victories in primary and caucus states, both North and South, small and large, East and West, gave him a substantial lead in delegates—and, just as important, the credibility he needed to convince fund-raisers, the superdelegates, and a significant section of the electorate that he could be the next president of the United States. All this was in spite of the fact he was an African American, and like Homer Plessy, the result of an interracial union.

On his inauguration day on January 20, 2009, the nation greeted the arrival of its first African American president. Among the thousands of people who crowded the mall in front of the U.S. Capitol (not to mention the millions watching it live on television and simulcast on the Internet) to watch the president and the chief justice mangle the oath of office in an otherwise picture-perfect moment were African Americans who never thought it possible they would see such a moment in their lifetimes. On election night in Chicago the previous November, the television cameras were strategically placed both in the crowds in Chicago's Hyde Park and in historically black colleges and universities' student centers to capture the emotions of various African Americans. Most prominent among these was two-time candidate for president Jesse Jackson. He cried tears of joy at the sight of Obama making his election-night victory address. Jackson had been in Memphis on the hotel balcony with Martin Luther

King Jr. when King was assassinated in 1968. Little did he know then he would be crying tears of joy some forty years later.

Barack Obama's victory signaled to many the final chapter in the story of race relations in America—and perhaps the beginning of a new story, one in which America, like Obama himself, transcended race. However, there were several indications then and later that large portions of the United States still cared a great deal about race and were ready to raise it as an issue against Obama and his political agenda. In addition to the crude e-mails, flyers, and souvenirs at local Republican Party events during the campaign deploying the old racial stereotyping of caricatures, and watermelon, fried chicken, and pancake mix send-offs, there were the subtle attacks from Republican vice presidential nominee Sarah Palin, among others, alleging that Obama was foreign, radical, and could not be trusted. When the *New Yorker Magazine* sought to mock these attacks, its cover portrayed Obama and his wife, Michelle, as a 1960s-era Muslim and Black Panther radical, respectively. Racism was alive and well in American national politics.

Race remains a legal issue as well, garbed anew in the clothing of affirmative action and reverse discrimination. In *Parents Involved in Community Schools v. Seattle School District 1* in 2007, a High Court majority of Chief Justice John Roberts, Antonin Scalia, Samuel Alito, Clarence Thomas, and Anthony Kennedy decided that the public school districts involved could not integrate their high schools solely on the basis of the race of their students. The chief justice's majority opinion spent most of its verbiage lambasting the dissent of Justice Stephen Breyer. But the chief did offer a tautology: "The way to stop discrimination on the basis of race is to stop discriminating on the basis of race." Justice Thomas decided to emphasize this point in a lengthy concurring opinion that was not so much the reason why he agreed with the entirety of Roberts's opinion, but why Breyer's advocacy for affirmative action integration was the equivalent of the segregationists' position in *Brown*.

Breyer himself was no slouch on the use of race in American law. In a book on judging and the role of the Supreme Court in maintaining American democracy, he declared *Brown* to be a proper overturning of the precedent of *Plessy*. "On the other hand, the Court, the legal community, and much of American society had begun to see the *Plessy* decision as legally wrong and the segregated society it helped build as morally wrong." In Breyer's view, once legal and societal opinion shifted, the Court could overturn a case, and *Plessy's* time had come.

Not coincidentally, both sides of the dispute in *Seattle Schools* cited the ill-reputed *Plessy*, though neither agreed on what *Brown* and its successor cases had done to it. Again, they cited *Plessy* for the doctrine of "separate but equal." Again, John Marshall Harlan's use of Tourgée's concept of the color-blind Constitution was the ideal. Unfortunately, race was still an operative concept in American law, dividing Americans, defeating the purpose of the *gens de couleur libres*— the Creoles—who had brought the suit. All the justices used race as a category. All the opinions believed it was permissible to use race as a criteria for judgment. None of the justices had actually adopted the Harlan view. Brown's opinion, in some ways, remains good law.

Plessy was alive and well, though outwardly condemned from all sides. Oddly enough, its most strenuous legal advocate was the African American U.S. Supreme Court justice Clarence Thomas. In the very same opinion in which he condemned Breyer's dissent, Thomas questioned the benefits of integration. He cited studies that praised the historically black colleges and universities. Though he himself had gone to Holy Cross in Massachusetts and Yale Law School, both fully integrated, he doubted the merits of forced integration. In an echo of Brown's opinion in *Plessy*, Thomas concluded, "Therefore, it is not nearly as apparent as the dissent suggests that increased interracial exposure automatically leads to improved racial attitudes or race relations." His advocacy of the color-blind Constitution certainly did not extend to his own reasoning. Racial categories existed there, and even prospered. Thomas was demonstrating that *Plessy* and Jim Crow had done its work well. Even those the law classified as belonging to a group that only existed in the minds of the legislators accepted the classification.

The social statistics on the eve of the Obama presidency were equally disheartening. Black men in 1991 had a 29 percent chance of imprisonment, seven times the rate of whites. In 2004, black poverty rates were three times that of whites. In 2008, one out of six blacks were in schools that were 1 percent white or less. And in 2006, more than fifty years after *Brown* and forty years after Governor George Wallace literally blocked the door to two African Americans entering the University of Alabama, only a little over 2 percent of the entering class of the University of California, Los Angeles, was African American. Scholars like Michael Klarman, who argued that *Brown* and its successors were unsuccessful and that the *Plessy* Court was more attuned to its society, had much to support them. America was still segregated. Brown had been proved correct. One could not engineer the social equality of the two races.

However, it is difficult not to see the great changes in America since *Plessy* arrived in 1896. Current-day controversies about a publisher removing the "n" word from Mark Twain's literary classic *Huckleberry Finn* so that skittish school systems would adopt the book speak volumes about the state of race relations. Footage of whites angry about "outside agitators" stirring up trouble in the 1950s and 1960s is replete with the "n" word, and not a single use of it is positive. The pejorative was used in public, often and uncensored. Now, it elicits condemnation from all quarters, even Republican Party politicians, whose party platforms ring with the states' rights rhetoric of white supremacist Democrats from the 1860s.

The signage is also gone. Sporting events, television, movies, and the professions not only are integrated, but are replete with mixed-race couples. Tiger Woods was not threatened for marrying Elin Nordgren, despite his skin hue being darker than the blonde, light-skinned Swede. Even Clarence Thomas, who famously claimed a high-tech lynching threatened his appointment to the Supreme Court, received little to no comment for being married to a white woman. In fact, the item did not make national news. Was this also a legacy of *Plessy*? A world that could see race, but not comment on it?

What was certain was that *Plessy* had gained such an opprobrium that it was commonplace to condemn the decision as one of the worst in U.S. Supreme Court history, alongside the likes of *Dred Scott v. Sanford* and *Lochner v. New York*. But that condemnation has also come under fire. Two reasons pervade these reappraisals of "equal, but separate": that it properly reflected the society of the time, and that to do otherwise was an act of futility. That *Plessy* reflected the vast reservoir of racism in American life cannot be doubted. Both Brown and Harlan expressed not only their belief in the existence of races, but their unquestioned faith in their own supposed race's superiority. Their difference was one of constitutional interpretation. Did "equal protection of the laws" mean the same law, regardless of race, or the same treatment regardless of race? Brown believed for the sake of his opinion that Louisiana's treatment of Negroes and whites was the same, and thus equal. Harlan believed the Constitution required the same law with no recognition of race.

The justices were not typical of their society in many ways. Their commitment to conservative, formalist jurisprudence set them as far apart from the average American as their elite station in life as attorneys and justices. They also by and large shared nothing with the substantial and growing group of Americans who were immigrants or the children of immigrants. They did not come from the laboring or farming classes, but from the upper levels of American society. However, they did share one vital link with a growing phenomenon among the Civil War and postwar generations: they believed in the reconciliation between the two sections. A reunion had taken place among the large majority of whites North, South, and West. The white man's republic had been reforged.

The bloody shirt had been buried by the time of the presidential election of 1896. Even the Republicans had abandoned the South. William Jennings Bryan fought against the plutocrats not on behalf of whites and blacks, but only the whites. He was a Democrat, and Democrats did not question Jim Crow. His opponent, William McKinley, campaigned not on behalf of all Americans, but on behalf of sound money. The justices may not have been making decisions on the basis of the election returns, given that *Plessy* was decided well in advance of the election.

Tragically, none of the justices and even the lawyers on their side saw the world as Homer A. Plessy and the Comité des Citoyens saw it. It was a world of fluid racial identities where belonging or not belonging was a choice of the individual. One could walk down the street, buy a first-class ticket, and sit in a first-class accommodation if one chose. This was a true dream of liberty, of freedom, of equality. Race, a discrimination based on one's blood, did not exist here. Their challenge to the law was not even Tourgée's biracial society, but a nonracial society where their unique identities could exist, sui generis—its own kind—in isolation or not. They were not resisting solely being treated as inferiors, but as part of an identity they did not share. Their identity was as unique as their city.

As Americans have learned, New Orleans was like New York in its diversity, cultural productivity, cosmopolitanism, and range of life-styles. Unlike New York, New Orleans was part of the slave South, the Civil War, and Reconstruction. It was a city in a region that was overwhelmingly rural. It possessed a mix of peoples and cultures that the South defied. Much more so than any other urban area in the South, its citizens fought about issues of identity, belonging, and race. *Plessy* was as much about New Orleans as it was about the South. New Orleans has thus taught us much about the true nature of race in America—its permeability, its contested quality, its combustibility.

Unenforceability is the other support for the *Plessy* decision. On the one hand, to this way of thinking, even if the Court had been disposed to jettison their post-Reconstruction, reconciliation views, the justices could not have stemmed the tide of racial segregation with a decision, even if it had been unanimous. The Congress and the president were not with them. The country's armed forces were as puny as they had been during Reconstruction. The white supremacist South was as well armed and in control as it had been since before the Civil War. They would have segregated anyway, and the Court would have suffered a blow to its prestige from which it would not recover. It is tempting to claim that right makes might, but the homily is the reverse. As Thucydides' Athenians in the Peloponnesian War teach us, "The strong do what they will. The weak do what they must." The Court was powerless against the Jim Crow tide.

On the other hand, the same court had little to no difficulty with its battle against wage and workplace safety regulations. The so-called *Lochner* Court was effective at shutting down child labor laws, the minimum wage, and any prolabor legislation. They managed to frustrate the Granger laws of several Great Plains states as well as the states attempting to constrain businesses of all kinds. Judicial activism did not originate with the Warren Court. It originated under the courts of chief justices Morrison Waite and Melville Fuller. Despite this activism, the Court never did see its authority diminish or the offending legislation reach the statute book once it had struck them down. Although in the absence of any evidence one cannot know whether segregation laws would have been any different, we do know that white supremacists feared an adverse Supreme Court precedent enough to fight it, not once, but continuously. Apparently, a Supreme Court decision did matter, at least to the segregationists.

This does leave aside the question of whether *Plessy* was a poorly defended interpretation of the Fourteenth Amendment's equal protection clause. It can be argued that on its very language, "equal protection of the laws" permits states to discriminate on the basis of race, so long as it is not adverse discrimination. To this reading one could logically conclude that *Brown* was decided incorrectly when it viewed all separation on the basis of race as inherently unequal. After all, even the majority in *Seattle Schools* had to accept racial discrimination to rectify the effects of past discrimination.

Even on the grounds of original intent, the evidence is less mixed than Warren's opinion in *Brown* would have us believe. Segregation was the rule in the North as well as in congressionally governed Washington, D.C. The leadership of Congress, let alone the majorities who ratified the Fourteenth Amendment, were not the Radicals, but the moderates who sought accommodation and rejected calls for the color-blind society of Tourgée's dreams. How could a deeply racist society as well as one governed almost entirely by white men have enacted a reform to its basic law that provided for a nonracist society?

Then again, the mandates of a modification of the Constitution need not reflect the realities of life in late 1860s America. It might well have been an aspiration. Or the former Confederates might have been correct. The enactors of the Fourteenth Amendment might have had no intention of the amendment's being applicable to the North. The former Confederate South was uppermost in their minds, the likely target of their thoughts. The "equal protection of the laws" was not endangered in the North, only in the reconstructed South. Certainly, it was at least a possibility.

Regardless of these considerations, *Plessy* has much to teach us about the America that gave rise to it, the world it helped spawn, the role of law in American life, and, finally, about heroism. Homer A. Plessy and his fellow litigants defied enormous odds to challenge a violent, bigoted, ruthless regime, one cunning to the point of casting its prejudice and treason as benevolent and patriotic. They took their lives in their hands to try to swim against the tide of Jim Crow. That they failed badly helping to enact what they were trying to avoid does not make them any less valorous. *Plessy* was certainly a tragedy. A nation that prided itself on the principles of liberty, equality, and democracy via the rule of law committed itself to the opposite. However, this does not make those who stood up to fight any less heroic. They are tragic heroes whose legacy has been misunderstood for too long.

Of the principals involved in *Plessy*, all but John Marshall Harlan entered into obscurity. Thanks to the researches of Keith Weldon Medley, we know their respective fates. Plessy's attorney, James C. Walker, died two years after the Court announced its decision in the case he had done so much to shape. Albion Tourgée died in Bordeaux, France, in 1905, having been a U.S. consul there since 1897. President McKinley had paid him back to some degree for his sacrifices for the Republican Party in North Carolina. Rodolphe Desdunes died in 1928, but not before writing the history of his community in 1911. Louis Martinet had predeceased him in 1917 on the same day, June 7, that Plessy took his seat on the train two and half decades earlier. Judge Ferguson struck his head on the street and died three weeks later in 1915 at the age of seventy-seven. Justice John Marshall Harlan died on October 14, 1911, after a long, celebrated tenure on the Court. On September 4, 1914, Justice Henry Billings Brown died, childless, commemorated for his years of service, though posterity would remember him only for his opinion upholding segregation. Plessy himself died at 5:10 A.M. on Sunday, March 1, 1925, and was buried in his native New Orleans. He left behind a legacy far greater than the court case that bears his name.

The ideals of those who brought the case that became *Plessy v. Ferguson* still present us with a goal for future generations of Americans. It is not impossible to envision a society without the stigma of irrational prejudice. It is not a forlorn hope for a nation that adheres to its best principles. Education in the truth of the past is the first step in a long journey. Homer A. Plessy started this journey for us when he bought his ticket, knowing his trip would be interrupted before it even began. More recently, as reported in 2011, Phoebe Ferguson, a descendant of John H. Ferguson, the judge of *Plessy v. Ferguson*, and Keith Plessy, a descendant of Plessy's cousin, came together in New Orleans to form the Plessy and Ferguson Foundation, an organization dedicated to educating the public about *Plessy*, the struggle for civil rights, and New Orleans' central part in that history. A plaque now marks the spot where Homer A. Plessy boarded the train that led to the case that bears his name. For good or ill, *Plessy v. Ferguson* lives on in memory, law, and American life.

1841   Massachusetts passes the first law segregating railroads.

1857   In a majority opinion in the case of *Dred Scott v. Sanford*, Chief Justice Roger B. Taney denies that African Americans can ever be citizens of the United States.

1862   Homer A. Plessy is born a free person of color in New Orleans.

1865   The Thirteenth Amendment is proposed and ratified, ending slavery throughout the country. Former Confederates in Tennessee form what will become the Ku Klux Klan. Others throughout the South will either join or form their own vigilante groups.

1866   New Orleans and Memphis race riots. Congress passes the Civil Rights Act of that same year, giving the opportunity for private citizens to sue state and local authorities under §1983, among other provisions.

1865–1868   Former Confederate states enact Black Codes, reducing African Americans to semislave status.

1867   Congress passes the First, Second, and Third Reconstruction Acts.

1868   The Fourteenth Amendment is ratified. Ulysses S. Grant is elected to his first term as president.

1870   The Fifteenth Amendment is ratified. Congress passes the Enforcement Act and creates the Department of Justice.

1873   The Colfax Massacre occurs in Grant Parish, Louisiana, leading to the case of *Cruikshank v. U.S.* The U.S. Supreme Court rules in the *Slaughterhouse Cases* restricting the use of the privileges and immunities clause of the Fourteenth Amendment.

1874   On September 14, the Battle of Liberty Place leads to thirty-four dead and the temporary takeover of the Louisiana government by anti-Reconstruction forces. Federal troops eventually restore the rightful government.

1875   Congress passes the Civil Rights Act of that year, eliminating discrimination on the basis of race in public accommodations and juries.

1877   As a result of the Compromise of 1877, Rutherford B. Hayes
        becomes president and agrees to remove federal troops from
        the last of the former Confederate states, effectively ending
        Reconstruction.

1881   Tennessee enacts the first of what will be known as Jim Crow laws.

1883   In the *Civil Rights Cases*, the U.S. Supreme Court rules the public
        accommodations provisions of the Civil Rights Act of 1875
        unconstitutional.

1887   As a result of a strike by largely African American plantation
        workers, a race riot ensues in Thibodaux, Louisiana, killing thirty
        African Americans.

1890   Louisiana passes the Separate Car Act.

1891   A group of prominent African Americans in New Orleans forms
        the Comité des Citoyens to combat the Separate Car Act. Later
        that year, James C. Walker and Albion Tourgée become the
        attorneys for the effort. On March 14, an anti-Italian mob storms
        the courthouse in New Orleans and kills eleven Italians held there.

1892   On February 24, Daniel Desdunes boards an interstate train's
        whites-only car; on June 7, Homer A. Plessy does the same for
        an intrastate train. Both are arrested and charged with violating
        the Separate Car Act. Judge Ferguson dismisses the case against
        Desdunes but finds Plessy guilty; he issues an opinion upholding
        the constitutionality of the Separate Car Act on November 18.

1893   In an opinion by Justice Fenner, the Louisiana supreme court
        denies Plessy's appeal and uphold the constitutionality of the
        Separate Car Act.

1895   Booker T. Washington gives his Atlanta Exposition address, which
        contains a section acquiescing to segregation for the time being.

1896   On May 18, in an opinion by Justice Brown, the U.S. Supreme
        Court upholds a state's right to segregate under the Constitution
        using the language "equal, but separate." Justice Harlan is the sole
        dissenter. He advocates for a color-blind constitution.

1897   Plessy is charged $25 for violating the Separate Car Act.
        Segregation laws spread, and Jim Crow begins to permeate all of
        American society and culture.

1954   A unanimous U.S. Supreme Court rejects the doctrine of "separate
        but equal" with regards to public education, implicitly overruling
        Plessy, in the case of *Brown v. Board of Education*. Other decisions
        will follow, eventually overturning all segregation laws. Litigation
        concerning racial discrimination continues.

1956 In a per curiam opinion based on *Brown* in *Browder v. Gayle*, the U.S. Supreme Court ends the Montgomery bus boycott by declaring intrastate segregation unconstitutional, overruling the precedent of *Plessy v. Ferguson* directly.

1964 Congress passes the Civil Rights Act of that year outlawing racial, religious, and sex discrimination in all public accommodations under its authority to regulate interstate commerce. In *Heart of Atlanta Motel*, the U.S. Supreme Court upholds the act.

1965 Congress passes the Voting Rights Act.

2008 The United States elects its first African American president, Barack Hussein Obama.

BIBLIOGRAPHIC ESSAY

Note from the Series Editors: The following bibliographic essay contains the major primary and secondary sources the author consulted for this volume. We have asked all authors in the series to omit formal citations in order to make our volumes more readable, inexpensive, and appealing for students and general readers. In adopting this format, Landmark Law Cases and American Society follows the precedent of a number of highly regarded and widely consulted series.

The preparation, researching, and writing of this book required the extensive use of printed primary sources, a selective group of the vast secondary literature, and available reference works both in print and online, including Web pages of various kinds, including those of the landmark law cases site from the University of Kentucky, Public Broadcasting supplements to their civil rights programming, U.S. government online resources, the site of the Supreme Court Historical Society, the NAACP, and the Legal Defense Fund, as well as general information from such unreliable sources as Wikipedia. I retrieved the cases from online collections including Lexis as well as Findlaw and other such publicly available resources. When possible, I also consulted the books in the University Press of Kansas Landmark Law Cases series. The following is a summary of the primary and secondary sources I found most helpful largely in the order I used them.

For documents and newspaper accounts, I acquired R.S. 3063—Act 111, 1890 Transportation of Passengers, "An act to promote the comfort of passengers on railway trains," *Constitution and Revised Laws of Louisiana, Second, Enlarged and Revised Editions in Two Volumes, Volume 2, Compiled and Annotated by Solomon Wolff, of the New Orleans Bar* (New Orleans: F. F. Hansell & Bro., 1905), from the University of Georgia Law Library. Research librarian Kevin Baggett at the Louisiana State University Law Library kindly sent the digital copies of the relevant passages of the *Official Journal of the Proceedings of the House of Representatives of the State of Louisiana*, published by the State of Louisiana. I also consulted the *Crusader*, New Orleans, 1889–1891; the *Daily Picayune*, New Orleans; the collection of documents in Otto H. Olsen, ed., *The Thin Disguise: "Plessy v. Ferguson"* (New York: Humanities Press, 1967); and the Bedford/St. Martin's Series in History Culture volume of Brook Thomas, ed., *"Plessy v. Ferguson": A Brief History with Documents* (Boston: Bedford/St. Martin's, 1997). The U.S. Supreme Court briefs for *Plessy* are available in Philip B. Kurland and Gerhard Casper, ed., *Landmark Briefs and Arguments of the Supreme Court of the United States: Constitutional Law*, vol. 13. Tourgée's oral argument notes are available in *Undaunted Radical: The Selected*

Writings and Speeches of Albion W. Tourgée, ed. Mark Elliott and John David Smith (Baton Rouge: Louisiana State University Press, 2010).

The major cases cited in the pages of this book, in the order listed, are: *United States v. Cruikshank,* 92 US 542 (1876); *U.S. v. Reese,* 92 U.S. 214 (1876); *Hall v. DeCuir,* 95 U.S. 485 (1878), 24 L. Ed. 547, 1877 U.S. LEXIS 2197, 5 Otto 485; *Civil Rights Cases,* 109 U.S. 3 (1883), 3 S. Ct. 18, 27 L. Ed. 835, 1883 U.S. LEXIS 928; *Louisville, New Orleans, & Texas Railway Company v. Mississippi,* 133 U.S. 587 (1890), 10 S. Ct. 348, 33 L. Ed. 784, 1890 U.S. LEXIS 1935; *Bertonneau v. Board of Directors of City Schools et al.* Circuit Court, D. Louisiana 3 F. Cas. 294 (1878), 1878 U.S. App. LEXIS 1614, 3 Woods 177; *Ex Parte Homer A. Plessy* No. 11,134 Supreme Court of Louisiana 45 La. Ann. 80 (1893), 11 So. 948, 1893 La. LEXIS 345; *The Philadelphia and Westchester Railroad Company, Plaintiffs in Error vs. Mary E. Miles, Defendant in Error,* Supreme Court for the Eastern District of Pennsylvania, "Exploring Diversity in Pennsylvania History," "Public Space on the Rails," the Historical Society of Pennsylvania (http://www.hsp.org/); *The Sue* 22 F. 843 (1885), 1885 U.S. Dist. LEXIS 7; *Logwood and Wife v. Memphis & C.R. Co.,* 23 F. 318 (1885), 1885 U.S. App. LEXIS 1921; *Murphy v. Western & A.R.R. and others,* 23 F. 637 (1885), 1885 U.S. App. LEXIS 1963; *Pace v. State of Alabama,* 106 U.S. 583 (1883); *Anderson v. Louisville & N.R. Co.* 62 F. 46 (Circuit Court, D. Kentucky. June 4, 1894); *Plessy v. Ferguson,* 163 U.S. 537 (1896), 16 S. Ct. 1138, 41 L. Ed. 256, 1896 U.S. LEXIS 3390; *Cumming v. Richmond County Board of Education,* 175 U.S. 528 (1899), 20 S. Ct. 197, 44 L. Ed. 262, 1899 U.S. LEXIS 1580; *Berea College v. Commonwealth of Kentucky,* 211 U.S. 45 (1908), 29 S. Ct. 33, 53 L. Ed. 81, 1908 U.S. LEXIS 1526; *Chiles v. Chesapeake and Ohio Railway Company,* 218 U.S. 71 (1910), 30 S. Ct. 667, 54 L. Ed. 936, 1910 U.S. LEXIS 2004; *McCabe v. Atchison, Topeka & Santa Fe Railway Company,* 235 U.S. 151 (1914), 35 S. Ct. 69, 59 L. Ed. 169, 1914 U.S. LEXIS 1010; *Buchanan v. Warley,* 245 U.S. 60 (1917), 38 S. Ct. 16, 62 L. Ed. 149, 1917 U.S. LEXIS 1788; *Gong Lum et al. v. Rice et al.,* 275 U.S. 78 (1927), 48 S. Ct. 91, 72 L. Ed. 172, 1927 LEXIS 256; *Pearson v. Murray,* 169 Md. 478, 182 A. 590 (1936); *Missouri ex rel. Gaines v. Canada, Registrar of the University of Missouri, et al.,* 305 U.S. 337 (1938), 59 S. Ct. 232, 83 L. Ed. 208, 1938 U.S. LEXIS 440; *Morgan v. Virginia,* 328 U.S. 373 (1946); *Sipuel v. Board of Regents,* 332 U.S. 631 (1948); *McLaurin v. Oklahoma State Regents,* 339 U.S. 637 (1950); *Sweatt v. Painter,* 339 U.S. 629 (1950); *Brown et al. v. Board of Education Topeka et al.,* 347 U.S. 483 (1954), 74 S. Ct. 686, 98 L. Ed. 873, 1954 U.S. LEXIS 2094; *Browder v. Gayle,* 352 U.S. 903 (1956); and *Parents Involved in Community Schools v. Seattle School District No. 1,* 551 U.S. 701 (2007).

There are several books and articles on the *Plessy* case. Charles Lofgren, *The Plessy Case: A Legal–Historical Interpretation* (New York: Oxford University Press, 1987), is by far the most detailed in terms of legal precedent, the legal procedure, and the secondary literature, both at the time and afterward up until its publication. It was clearly a labor of love. Keith Weldon Medley, *We as Freemen: "Plessy v. Ferguson," the Fight against Legal Segregation* (Gretna, La.: Pelican Publishing, 2003), is the equivalent for the local history. Harvey Fireside, *Separate and Unequal: Homer Plessy and the Supreme Court Decision that Legalized Racism* (New York: Carroll & Graf, 2004), is a readable combination of the two approaches. Aimed at the youth market is Tim McNeese, *"Plessy v. Ferguson": Separate but Equal* (New York: Chelsea House Publishers, 2007; part of the Great Supreme Court Decisions series).

Several superb articles and one book chapter on *Plessy* present original arguments regarding the source, conduct, and effect of the litigation. They include James C. Cobb, "Segregating the New South: The Origins and Legacy of *Plessy v. Ferguson*," *Georgia State University Law Review* 12 (1996): 1017–1036; Michael J. Klarman, "The Plessy Era," *Supreme Court Review* 1998 (1998): 303–414; Barbara Y. Welke, "When All the Women Were White, and All the Blacks Were Men: Gender, Class, Race, and the Road to *Plessy*, 1855–1914," *Law and History Review* 13, no. 2 (Fall 1995): 261–316; Jonathan Kahn, "Controlling Identity: *Plessy*, Privacy, and Racial Defamation," *DePaul Law Review* 54 (2005): 755–782; and Cheryl I. Harris, "The Story of *Plessy v. Ferguson*: The Death and Resurrection of Racial Formalism," in *Constitutional Law Stories*, ed. Michael C. Dorf (New York: Foundation Press, 2004).

There are also several fine overall surveys of segregation in America both before and after *Plessy*. They include Richard Wormser, *The Rise and Fall of Jim Crow* (New York: St. Martin's Press, 2003); Andrew Kull, *The Color-Blind Constitution* (Cambridge: Harvard University Press, 1992); Lawrence Goldstone, *Inherently Unequal: The Betrayal of Equal Rights by the Supreme Court, 1865–1903* (New York: Walker, 2011); Paul Finkelman, "'Let justice be done, though the heavens may fall': The Law of Freedom," *Chicago-Kent Law Review* 70 (1994): 325–370; Donald G. Nieman, *Promises to Keep: African-Americans and the Constitutional Order, 1776 to the Present* (New York: Oxford University Press, 1991); Alexander Terses, *We Shall Overcome: A History of Civil Rights and the Law* (New Haven, Conn.: Yale University Press, 2008); and Michael J. Klarman, *From Jim Crow to Civil Rights: The Supreme Court and the Struggle for Racial Equality* (New York: Oxford University Press, 2004). Although I take issue with some of Klarman's conclusion, the book is a superbly researched and forcefully argued tome that will be the standard for years to come.

For Chapter One's background on New Orleans, Reconstruction, and the Redemption periods, I made extensive use of Peyton McCrary, *Lincoln and Reconstruction: The Louisiana Experiment* (Princeton, N.J.: Princeton University Press, 1978); LeeAnna Keith, *The Colfax Massacre: The Untold Story of Black Power, White Terror, and the End of Reconstruction* (New York: Oxford University Press, 2008); Charles Lane, *The Day Freedom Died: The Colfax Massacre, the Supreme Court, and the Betrayal of Reconstruction* (New York: Holt, 2008); Mark Wahlgren Summers, *A Dangerous Stir: Fear, Paranoia, and the Making of Reconstruction* (Chapel Hill: University of North Carolina Press, 2009); George C. Rable, *But There Was No Peace: The Role of Violence in the Politics of Reconstruction* (Athens: University of Georgia Press, 1984); William E. Nelson, *The Fourteenth Amendment: From Political Principle to Judicial Doctrine* (Cambridge: Harvard University Press, 1988); and Eric Foner, *Reconstruction: America's Unfinished Revolution, 1863–1877* (1988; reprint, New York: Perennial Classics Edition, 2002). Joseph G. Tregle Jr. provides a superb discussion on the Creoles of Louisiana in his book chapter, "Creoles and Americans," in *Creole New Orleans: Race and Americanization*, ed. Arnold Hirsch and Joseph Logsdon (Baton Rouge: Louisiana State University Press, 1992). For the more recent scholarship on Butler's "Woman Order," see Alecia Long, "(Mis)remembering General Order No. 28: Benjamin Butler, the Woman Order, and Historical Memory" in *Occupied Women: Gender, Military Occupation, and the American Civil War*, ed. LeeAnn Whites and Alecia P. Long (Baton Rouge: Louisiana State University Press, 2009).

For developments in New Orleans in particular during Reconstruction, I found the following helpful: U.S. Congress, House Select Committee on New Orleans Riots, "Report of the Select Committee on the New Orleans Riots," United States 39th Congress, 2nd Session, House of Representatives Report No. 16, 1867 (Freeport, N.Y.: Books for Libraries Press, 1971); James C. Hollandsworth Jr., *An Absolute Massacre: The New Orleans Race Riot of July 30, 1866* (Baton Rouge: Louisiana State University Press, 2001); Joe Gray Taylor, *Louisiana Reconstructed, 1863–1877* (Baton Rouge: Louisiana State University Press, 1974); James K. Hogue, *Uncivil War: Five New Orleans Street Battles and the Rise and Fall of Radical Reconstruction* (Baton Rouge: Louisiana State University Press, 2006); Rebecca J. Scott, *Degrees of Freedom: Louisiana and Cuba after Slavery* (Cambridge: Harvard University Press, 2005); Scott, "The Atlantic World and the Road to *Plessy v. Ferguson*," *Journal of American History* 94, no. 3 (December 2007): 726–733; Scott, "Public Rights, Social Equality, and the Conceptual Roots of the *Plessy* Challenge," *Michigan Law Review* 106 (March 2008): 777–804; and Ted Tunnell, *Crucible of Reconstruction: War, Radicalism and Race in Louisiana, 1862–1877* (Baton Rouge: Louisiana State University Press, 1984). On the *Slaughterhouse Cases*, I consulted Ronald Labbé and Jonathan Lurie, *The "Slaughterhouse Cases": Regulation, Reconstruction, and the Fourteenth Amendment*, abridged ed. (Lawrence: University Press of Kansas, 2005); Michael Ross, "Obstructing Reconstruction: John Archibald Campbell and the Legal Campaign against Louisiana's Republican Government, 1868–1873," *Civil War History* 49 (2003): 235–253;

and David Bogen, "Rebuilding the *Slaughter-House*: The Cases' Support for Civil Rights," *Akron Law Review* 42 (2009): 1129–1175. One cannot do better than to read Caryn Cossé Bell's *Revolution, Romanticism and the Afro-Creole Protest Tradition in Louisiana, 1718–1868* (Baton Rouge: Louisiana State University Press, 1997), for the singular contribution of the Afro-Creole population to the history of this period.

For Chapter Two's telling of the developments in Louisiana and around the country leading up to the passage of the Separate Car Act, I used Stanley P. Hirshson, *Farewell to the Bloody Shirt: Northern Republicans and the Southern Negro, 1877–1893* (Bloomington: Indiana University Press, 1962); *Creoles of Color of the Gulf South*, ed. James H. Dormon (Knoxville: University of Tennessee Press, 1996); Nicholas Lemann, *Redemption: The Last Battle of the Civil War* (New York: Farrar, Straus and Giroux, 2006); Labbé and Lurie, *Slaughterhouse Cases*; Joy J. Jackson, *New Orleans in the Gilded Age: Politics and Urban Progress, 1880–1896* (Baton Rouge: Louisiana State University Press, 1969); Richard Gambino, *Vendetta: The True Story of the Largest Lynching in U.S. History* (Toronto: Guernica, 1998); Mel Leavitt, *A Short History of New Orleans* (San Francisco: Lexikos, 1982); and Ted Tunnell, *Edge of the Sword: The Ordeal of Carpetbagger Marshall H. Twitchell in the Civil War and Reconstruction* (Baton Rouge: Louisiana State University Press, 2001).

For questions specifically relating to the rise of acceptance of Jim Crow, I used David W. Blight, *Race and Reunion: The Civil War in American Memory* (Cambridge: The Belknap Press of Harvard University Press, 2001); Edward J. Blum, *Reforging the White Republic: Race, Religion, and American Nationalism, 1865–1898* (Baton Rouge: Louisiana State University Press, 2005); Nina Silber, *Romance of Reunion: Northerners and the South, 1865–1900* (Chapel Hill: University of North Carolina Press, 1993); John David Smith, ed. and introduction, *Historians at Work: When Did Southern Segregation Begin?* (Boston: Bedford/St. Martin's, 2002); Roger Fischer, "The Post–Civil War Segregation Struggle," in *The Past as Prelude: New Orleans, 1718–1968*, ed. Hodding Carter, William Ransom Hogan, John W. Lawrence, and Betty Werlein Carter (New Orleans: Tulane University, 1968); C. Vann Woodward, *The Strange Career of Jim Crow*, commemorative edition with afterword by William S. McFeely (New York: Oxford University Press, 2002); and Edward L. Ayers, *The Promise of the New South: Life after Reconstruction*, 15th anniversary edition (New York: Oxford University Press, 2007). Pamela Brandwein has provided a thought-provoking reappraisal of the U.S. Supreme Court's Reconstruction decisions in *Rethinking the Judicial Settlement of Reconstruction* (New York: Cambridge University Press, 2011). Although I do not believe her conclusions unassailable, they are impossible to ignore.

In addition to Medley and Lofgren, I consulted the following for Chapter Three's discussion of the litigation before the Supreme Court's decision:

Rodolphe Lucien Desdunes, *Our People and Our History: Fifty Creole Portraits*, trans. and ed. Sister Dorothea Olga McCants (1911; reprint, Baton Rouge: Louisiana State University Press, 1973); the documents in *The Thin Disguise: Turning Point in Negro History; "Plessy v. Ferguson," a Documentary Presentation (1864–1896)*, ed. and with an introduction by Otto H. Olsen (New York: Humanities Press, 1967); Kenneth W. Mack, "Law, Society, Identity and the Making of the Jim Crow South: Travel and Segregation on Tennessee Railroads, 1875–1905," *Law and Social Inquiry* 24, no. 2 (July 1999): 377–409. Harvard University, Digital Access to Scholarship at Harvard (http://nrs.hard.edu/urn-3:HUL.InstRepos:2790089); Stanley J. Folmsbee, "The Origin of the First 'Jim Crow' Law," *Journal of Southern History* 15, no. 2 (May 1949): 235–247, for the Tennessee law; Mark Elliott, *Color-Blind Justice: Albion Tourgée and the Quest for Racial Equality, from the Civil War to "Plessy v. Ferguson"* (New York: Oxford University Press, 2006); Stephen J. Riegel, "The Persistent Career of Jim Crow: Lower Federal Courts and the 'Separate but Equal' Doctrine, 1865–1896," *American Journal of Legal History* 28 (1984): 17–40; the aforementioned Scott pieces; and *Undaunted Radical: The Selected Writings and Speeches of Albion W. Tourgée*, ed. Mark Elliot and John David Smith (Baton Rouge: Louisiana State University Press, 2010), for Tourgée's oral argument notes.

I made extensive use of the following for Chapter Four's examination of the opinions and the biographies of the justices: James W. Ely Jr., *The Fuller Court: Justices, Rulings, and Legacy*, ABC-CLIO Supreme Court Handbooks (Santa Barbara: ABC-CLIO, 2003); Peter Charles Hoffer, N. E. H. Hull, and Williamjames Hull Hoffer, *The Supreme Court: An Essential History* (Lawrence: University Press of Kansas, 2006); Carl Brent Swisher, *Stephen J. Field: Craftsman of the Law* (Hamden, Conn.: Archon Books, 1963); Willard L. King, *Melville Weston Fuller: Chief Justice of the United States, 1888–1910* (Chicago: University of Chicago Press, 1967); Robert B. Highsaw, *Edward Douglass White: Defender of the Conservative Faith* (Baton Rouge: Louisiana State University Press, 1981); Marouf Hasian Jr., "Revisiting the Case of *Plessy v. Ferguson*," Daniel Mangis, "Dissent as Prophecy: Justice John Marshall Harlan's Dissent in *Plessy v. Ferguson* as the Religious Rhetoric of Law," and Clarke Rountree, "Setting the Stage for *Brown v. Board of Education*: The NAACP's Litigation Campaign against the 'Separate but Equal' Doctrine," in *Brown v. Board of Education at Fifty: A Rhetorical Perspective*, ed. Clarke Rountree (Lanham, Md.: Lexington Books, 2004); Trevor Broad, "What Was Really at Stake in *Plessy v. Fergusson*," in Historical Society for the United States District Court for the Eastern District of Michigan, special annual meeting issue, *Court Legacy* 16, no. 4 (November 2009): 1–11; Ross Parker, "Henry B. Brown—First Assistant United States Attorney in the Eastern District of Michigan," in special annual meeting issue, *Court Legacy* 16, no. 4

(November 2009): 11; Robert J. Glennon Jr., "Justice Henry Billings Brown: Values in Tension," *University of Colorado Law Review* 44 (1973): 553–604; Tinsley E. Yarbrough, *Judicial Enigma: The First Justice Harlan* (New York: Oxford University Press, 1995); Linda Przybyszewski, *The Republic According to John Marshall Harlan* (Chapel Hill: University of North Carolina Press, 1999); Malvina Shanklin Harlan, *Some Memories of a Long Life, 1854–1911* (New York: Modern Library, 2002); Loren P. Beth, *John Marshall Harlan: The Last Whig Justice* (Lexington: University Press of Kentucky, 1992).

I also made use of Richard Kluger, *Simple Justice: The History of "Brown v. Board of Education" and Black America's Struggle for Equality* (New York: Vintage Books, Random House, 1975, 1977); Mark Golub, "*Plessy* as 'Passing': Judicial Responses to Ambiguously Raced Bodies in *Plessy v. Ferguson*," *Law and Society Review* 39 (September 2005): 563–600; Ariela Gross, *What Blood Won't Tell: A History of Race on Trial in America* (Cambridge: Harvard University Press, 2008); and Gabriel J. Chin, "The *Plessy* Myth: Justice Harlan and the Chinese Cases," *Iowa Law Review* 82 (1996): 151–182.

For Chapter Five's study of the aftermath of *Plessy*, I consulted the various essays and documents in *Racism and the Law: The Legacy and Lessons of "Plessy*," ed. Gerald J. Postema (Norwell, Mass.: Kluwer Academic, 1997); *The Age of Segregation: Race Relations in the South, 1890–1945*, ed. Robert Haws (Jackson: University Press of Mississippi, 1978), in particular Derrick A. Bell Jr., "The Racial Imperative in American Law," and Mary Frances Berry, "Repression of Blacks in the South 1890–1945: Enforcing the System of Segregation"; Stephen Duncombe, ed., *Cultural Resistance Reader* (London: Verso, 2002), for an account of lynching; Leon F. Litwack, *How Free Is Free? The Long Death of Jim Crow* (Cambridge: Harvard University Press, 2009); *Remembering Jim Crow: African Americans Tell about Life in the Segregated South*, ed. William H. Chafe, Raymond Gavins, and Robert Korstad (New York: New Press, 2001); and Catherine M. Lewis and J. Richard Lewis, eds., *Jim Crow America: A Documentary History* (Fayetteville: University of Arkansas Press, 2009).

Other scholars have done pathbreaking work on the relatively unnoticed civil rights movement during this early period of Jim Crow, including Blair L. M. Kelley, *Right to Ride: Streetcar Boycotts and African American Citizenship in the Era of "Plessy v. Ferguson"* (Chapel Hill: University of North Carolina Press, 2010); and R. Volney Riser, *Defying Disfranchisement: Black Voting Rights Activism in the Jim Crow South, 1890–1908* (Baton Rouge: Louisiana State University Press, 2010). Some of the mandates segregating America can be found at "Jim Crow Laws," Martin Luther King Jr., National Historic Site, National Park Service, U.S. Department of the Interior (http://www.nps.gove/malu/forteachers/jim_crow_laws.htm); and the comprehensive *States' Laws on Race and Color and Appendices, Containing International*

Documents, Federal Laws and Regulations, Local Ordinances and Charts, ed. Pauli Murray, Woman's Division of Christian Service, 1950.

There are several works on Jim Crow and American movies, including Donald Bogle, *Toms, Coons, Mulattoes, Mammies, and Bucks: An Interpretive History of Blacks in American Films* (New York: Viking, 1973); Thomas Cripps, *Slow Fade to Black: The Negro in American Film, 1900–1942* (New York: Oxford University Press, 1977); Thomas E. Wartenberg, "Humanizing the Beast: *King Kong* and the Representation of Black Male Sexuality," in *Classic Hollywood, Classic Whiteness,* ed. Daniel Bernardi (Minneapolis: University of Minnesota Press, 2001); Harry M. Benshoff and Sean Griffin, *America on Film: Representing Race, Class, Gender, and Sexuality at the Movies* (Malden, Mass.: Blackwell, 2004); and Charlene Regester, "The Cinematic Representation of Race in *The Birth of a Nation*: A Black Horror Film," in *Thomas Dixon Jr. and the Birth of Modern America,* ed. Michele K. Gillespie and Randal L. Hall (Baton Rouge: Louisiana State University Press, 2006).

For the controversy surrounding whether Justice Brown regretted *Plessy,* see Mark A. Graber, "Judicial Recantation," *Syracuse Law Review* 45 (1994): 807–814; Henry Billings Brown, "The Dissenting Opinions of Mr. Justice Harlan," *American Law Review* 46 (May–June 1912): 321–352; and Trevor Broad, "Forgotten Man in a Tumultuous Time: The Gilded Age as Seen by United States Supreme Court Associate Justice Henry Billings Brown" (senior honors thesis, University of Michigan, 2005). But also note Henry Billings Brown, with Charles Artemis Kent, *Memoir of Henry Billings Brown: Late Justice of the Supreme Court of the United States: Consisting of an Autobiographical Sketch with Additions to His Life* (New York: Duffield, 1915).

The work to undo *Plessy* has been documented and analyzed extensively. I used only the following: Mark V. Tushnet, *The NAACP's Legal Strategy against Segregated Education, 1925–1950* (Chapel Hill: University of North Carolina Press, 1987); Douglas O. Linder, "Before *Brown*: Charles H. Houston and the *Gaines* Case," A Profile of Charles Hamilton Houston, Famous Trials, University of Kentucky (http://law2.umkc.edu/faculty/projects/ftrials/trial-heroes/charleshoustonessayF.html); Rawn James Jr., *Root and Branch: Charles Hamilton Houston, Thurgood Marshall, and the Struggle to End Segregation* (New York: Bloomsbury Press, 2010); Genna Rae McNeil, *Groundwork: Charles Hamilton Houston and the Struggle for Civil Rights* (Philadelphia: University of Pennsylvania Press, 1983); and Catherine A. Barnes, *Journey from Jim Crow: The Desegregation of Southern Transit* (New York: Columbia University Press, 1983).

For the Epilogue, besides the common knowledge of Barack Obama's campaign for the presidency and the *Seattle Schools* opinions themselves, I found Destiny Peery, "The Colorblind Ideal in a Race-Conscious Reality: The Case for a New Legal Ideal for Race Relations," *Northwestern Journal of Law and Social Policy* 6 (Spring 2011): 473–495, quite stimulating. David R. Roediger, *How Race Survived U.S. History: From Settlement and Slavery to the Obama Phenomenon* (London: Verso, 2008), provided the illuminating statistics about the persistence of racism. Justice Stephen Breyer's book on judging and precedent is *America's Supreme Court: Making Democracy Work* (New York: Oxford University Press, 2010).

Cain, Christopher C., 67
Campbell, George, 53
Campbell, John Archibald, 32
Carolene Products, 135–136
Carter, Robert L., 167
caste systems, 9, 89
Catholic Church, 45, 83, 154
Central Law Journal, 141–142
Chae Chan Ping v. U.S., 111
Charles, Robert, 157
Chesapeake, Ohio, and Southwestern Railroad Co. v. Wells, 51
Chesapeake and Ohio Railway Company v. Kentucky, 147
Chiles v. Chesapeake and Ohio Railway Company, 148–149
Chinese Exclusion Act, 43–44, 111, 115
Chinese immigrants, 43–44, 57, 128–129, 138, 150
Christian fundamentalism, 47–48
Christophe, Firmin, 60
Citizens Committee. *See* Comité des Citoyens
citizenship
    birthright, 112
    Dred Scott case, 25, 137, 182
    equal rights, 133–134, 138
    Morse's treatise on, 99
    race-blind, 55, 106–107
    rights, 33, 90
    See also Fourteenth Amendment
Civil Rights Act of 1866, 23
Civil Rights Act of 1875, 34, 50, 51, 77, 81, 91, 93
Civil Rights Act of 1964, 177
Civil Rights Cases
    cited in *Plessy*, 77, 91, 93, 100, 103, 122, 126–127
    dissent, 61, 119
    Phillips as solicitor general, 81

civil rights groups, 51, 52, 177–178, 179–180. *See also* NAACP
civil society groups, 62, 159
Civil War
    Afro-Creoles in, 13, 17
    Lincoln's policies in South, 13–19
    New Orleans occupation, 13, 17–18
    reconciliation, 117, 121, 183
    runaway slaves, 13, 16, 17, 120
    stages of grief following, 143–144
    Tourgée's service, 63–64
    veterans' groups, 143
    See also Reconstruction
Clark, Kenneth B., 176
Cleveland, Grover, 84, 112, 114
Clinton, Hillary Rodham, 179
Cobb, Thomas R., 126
Colfax Massacre, 33, 35
Comité des Citoyens
    attorneys selected, 63
    courage, 185–186
    formation, 60
    funding, 61–62
    goals, 108, 183
    members, 60, 83
    opposition to Separate Car Act, 60–62, 89
    reaction to antimiscegenation law, 82
    selection of defendant, 65–66
    test case, 3, 62, 63, 69–70
common carriers, railroads as, 50, 54, 78, 133
Communism, 170–171
Comstock, Anthony, 48
Congress
    African American members, 28–29, 162
    Force Bill, 83, 84

race
  color-blind Constitution, 1,
    106–107, 136, 140, 181
  definition, 101–102
  Harlan on, 133, 136, 138
  theories, 159–160
  Tourgée on, 64–65, 95, 96, 106–107
  vision of nonracial society, 183
race riots, 24–25, 33, 157–158
racial groups
  acceptance of categories, 85–86,
    106, 107–108, 118–119, 181
  arbitrary categorizations, 68,
    101–102, 107, 130
  hierarchy, 86, 106, 125
  identification, 71, 89, 95, 96–97,
    98, 101–102, 105–106, 123
  legal definitions, 68, 82, 83, 95,
    107, 130
  reputations associated with skin
    color, 128
  stereotypes, 2, 11–12, 154, 155,
    180
  See also African Americans;
    Afro-Creoles; mixed-race
    individuals; segregation; white
    supremacists
racism
  black separatism, 163
  in everyday life, 150–155
  in integrated schools, 150–151
  in military, 164
  of Nazis, 169
  persistence, 180
  pervasiveness, 1, 5, 118–119, 136,
    159–160
  in Plessy arguments, 86, 93, 95,
    106, 107–108
  in Plessy dissent, 136, 182
  in Plessy majority opinion, 122–
    123, 128, 129–130, 131–132,
    182

in popular culture, 153–154
of scientists, 118–119
in South, 11–12, 31, 57, 148
in Soviet Union, 170–171
See also Jim Crow system; white
  supremacists
Railroad Company v. Brown, 87, 103
railroads
  as common carriers, 50, 54, 78,
    133
  construction, 42
  integrated cars, 45–46, 53
  shipping, 43
  strikes, 44
railroad segregation
  first-class compartments, 50–51,
    101
  on interstate railways, 52–53,
    70–71, 147
  justifications, 124–125, 148–149
  laws, 45, 50–51, 52–53, 55–56, 94
  legal challenges, 50, 51, 52–53,
    67, 70–71, 77–78, 94, 127
  as legal distinction, 122–123
  in South Africa, 51–52
  unequal facilities, 58, 130, 162
  See also Louisiana Separate Car
    Act
reasonableness test, 33, 72–73, 97,
  128–129, 135, 148–149
Reconstruction
  African American tactics, 33–34
  Congressional, 23–24, 25–27,
    28–29, 30, 64, 127, 131, 139
  corruption, 31
  critics of, 76
  economic, 42
  end of, 35–36
  in history textbooks, 154–155
  in New Orleans, 17–18, 21–22, 31
  Presidential, 13–14, 19–22,
    23–24, 25, 92–93

violence, 33, 36, 46, 137–138, 140, 152–153, 159

See also Jim Crow system; racism

white supremacists in Louisiana

Bourbons, 40

paramilitaries, 44

violence, 21–22, 24, 25, 31, 33, 34–35, 60

voter intimidation, 29

white women

Confederates, 17–18

nurses, 146

protection from black men, 45, 146, 152, 164

Whitney, Eli, 10

Wilson, Woodrow, 160

women

segregated transportation, 45, 66

Victorian attitudes toward, 66

voting rights, 63, 156

working hours, 161

See also African American women; marriage; white women

Wong Kim Ark, United States v., 112

Wong Wing v. United States, 115

Woods, Tiger, 182

Woods, William B., 39–40

World War I, 164

World War II, 169–170, 172–173

Yick Wo v. Hopkins, 128–129, 138